Living & Working in

FRANCE

Living & Working in

FRANCE

Chez vous en France

4TH EDITION

Geneviève Brame

KOGAN
PAGE

London and Philadelphia

First published in France as *Chez Vous en France* by Editions Dunod in 1993
First published in Great Britain as *Chez Vous en France – Living & Working in France*
by Kogan Page Limited in 1999
Second edition 2001
Third edition 2004
Reprinted 2007
Fourth edition 2008

Kogan Page Limited
120 Pentonville Road
London N1 9JN
United Kingdom
www.koganpage.com

Kogan Page US
525 South 4th Street, #241
Philadelphia PA 19147
USA

© Geneviève Brame, 1993, 1999, 2001, 2004, 2008
Translated by Linda Koike
Illustrations by Béatrice Tollu

ISBN   978 0 7494 5409 8

British Library Cataloguing in Publication Data

A CIP record for this book is available from the British Library.

Library of Congress Cataloging-in-Publication Data
Brame, Genevieve.
   [Chez vous en France. English]
   Living and working in France: chez vous en France/Genevieve Brame. — 4th ed.
      p. cm.
   ISBN 978-0-7494-5409-8
1. France—Social life and customs—Handbooks, manuals, etc. 2. Visitors, Foreign—France—Handbooks, manuals, etc. 3. France—Guidebooks. 4. France—Description and travel. 5. Employment in foreign countries—Handbooks, manuals, etc. I. Title.
   DC33.7.B7513 2008
   944.084—dc22

                                                          2008022628

Typeset by Saxon Graphics Ltd, Derby
Printed and bound in India by Replika Press Pvt Ltd

Contents

Contents

Contents

About the author

'UNE FRANÇAISE'

Geneviève Brame was born in Normandy. At the University of Caen, she took a degree in Humanities and then a Master's in International Human Resources Management. Since 1996, Geneviève has worked as a consultant in the International Mobility Department of Ernst & Young, Société d'Avocats in Paris. Inspired by her intercultural communications work with multinational companies, business schools and universities, she has written for French and foreign expatriates, both adults and children.

Geneviève Brame received a medal in the form of a star on a blue ribbon emblazoned with *République Française* at the Senat on 3 December 2002. She is a Knight of the National Order of Merit.

Her publications (books, articles and studies) include *Chez Vous en France* (Co-edition), *Lamy Mobilitié Internationale* (Editions Lamy, 2002) and *Chez Vous en France Le Documentation Française – France info*. She is creative director and author of the Editions Hachette collection *Pays d'enfance: Chez Toi en France*, 2006 (English summary), *A chacun sa route des épices* (Les cahiers Ernst & Young editions Autrement), the website *asapfrance.info* (English/French), with the French Embassy in London, and in Brussels.

I do not flatter myself that I can make you understand France. I do not know if I understand her myself. I do not try to understand her, because she does not leave me the time, she carries me along with her on her great adventure.

Georges Bernanos, in a Letter to the English

Je ne me flatte pas de vous faire comprendre la France. J'ignore si je la comprends moi-même. Je n'essaie pas de la comprendre, parce qu'elle ne m'en laisse pas le loisir, elle m'emporte avec elle dans sa grande aventure.

Foreword

Each year, a great number of people come to spend some time or even permanently settle in France. They include foreign visitors, tourists, investors, students, people in love with its landscapes and history and those attracted to its quality of life. France's culture, rich history and robust technology are among some of the factors contributing to France's status as the most visited country: 80 million chose it as a destination in 2007. However, the cultural mores of our country can lead to some confusing situations for our guests – this book attempts to guide you through the maze.

An author and consultant in international mobility, Geneviève Brame identifies and explains the many areas of French daily life with sharp insight and humour (covering social legislation, professional conduct and codes, etiquette, etc), in order to assist visitors or expatriates living in France.

Where do I get legal advice? How do I enrol my children in school? When can I use 'tu' without making a *faux pas*? *Chez vous en France* draws on the rich and varied experience of people and companies from all over the world who have chosen to come to France. Their accounts will help other residents come to terms with France's social and economic make-up.

Readers will be deeply grateful to the author for having offered such a clear and unequivocal guide, without compromising any of the pleasures of new discovery. We wish them luck on their journey with *Chez vous en France*.

Ministry of Foreign Affairs
Communication and Information Directorate

Preface

France has a big place in my heart and always will. It has been home to the start of many adventures for me... Preparing my boat for my first solo transatlantic race, the Mini Transat, in 1997, working for nearly six months in a French boat yard. I became immersed in the French way of life and culture, working alongside people from the boat-building industry, that have such expertise... I learnt to speak French in this period and it was where the expression 'a donf!' originated as it captured my philosophy to 'just go for it'. I will never forget my first Route du Rhum in 1998 departing from Saint Malo lined up against the very best French solo sailors and for the first time experiencing the awesome enthusiasm the French hold for this sport. I was a newcomer, inexperienced and totally unknown but all the French who had come to see the skippers depart wanted to wish me well – it was very humbling for me. And, of course, the Vendée Globe, an event that captures the imagination of so many and that the French hold close to their heart. It seems France will always have a role to play in my life – even my sponsors are both French and English!

I have been very fortunate to live and work in France for periods of time over the last few years. I feel at home there as much as I do in England and I know this will always be the case.

I will certainly recommend Geneviève Brame's book to fellow sailors and team members that often go to France – I am sure they will find it useful to quickly feel 'Chez vous en France!'

Dame Ellen MacArthur

What a wonderful experience as a chef, than to convert so many products full of rich history, into such a tremendous culinary joy! In a convivial and peaceful atmosphere around the table guests savour French cuisine.

Together, chefs and guests are the best ambassadors of the 'Joie de vivre' on this planet. Welcome to France, where the 'art de la table' forms part of our culture. It is even our signature tune!

Guy Savoy
Chef – Three Michelin stars

It is not that easy to grasp the subtle paradox of France. Elias Canetti stated that France, as well as its entire history, represent the Revolution, just as the forest represents a true image of Germany. What could give a more enchanting picture of France, before experiencing it for oneself on a daily basis, than Geneviève Brame's book, by its colourful palette painting successive images of this revolutionary country?

Gerard Mortier
Directeur de l'Opéra national de Paris

In ten chapters Geneviève Brame sets out more details about life in France than I learned in my first ten years living here. The new edition of this handy and well-written survival guide is packed with facts and information, items not always in oversupply. Whether you are just visiting France or planning a life-changing move, you can start off no better than reading this lively and authoritative handbook to French life.

Jim Bittermann
CNN Senior Correspondent, and resident of France since 1980

For my part, I include France in my world not just because I admire the French countryside or its monuments, wonderful though they are, but rather because French people have been willing to share their experiences with me, which are even more wonderfully varied, warm and cold, enriching, touching and ridiculous, an inexhaustible commentary on wisdom and folly. A shared experience is more than a bond; it is a joint discovery of unexpected possibilities. That is why no life can be full until it has at least a small French element in it. And no French life is in fact totally closed to foreigners or foreign ways.

Professor Theodore Zeldin
St Anthony's College, Oxford, UK

Everywhere I travel around the world, people talk about the French 35-hour week and how the French live from holiday to holiday. On the contrary, I see lights in offices and people working much later in the evenings than in most parts of the world and the level of productivity is second to none. This is part of the paradox of France.

I am always fascinated by the attention to details, which for me is a major success factor for France in the luxury sector. Whether it be the tassel around a niche perfume bottle or the way a shop-window is decorated, every detail is clearly thought through and lends to the overall effect.

Geneviève Brame's book will teach many French what they do not know about their own country. From the rich historical and cultural heritage to the intricacies of the administration, it is a must read for anybody who wants to better understand the French way of life.

Michaël Carlos
President, Givaudan France Fragrances

As Europe becomes border free, and with the euro, united as one continental culture, its people are clinging on to what differentiates them from their neighbours, namely their social customs. The French, long known for their strict character and their sophisticated *savoir faire*, are particularly rejecting the temptation to erase cultural differences in favour of homogenization of Europe, as has happened in the last decade in the United States. As a result, their Frenchness is becoming even more acute, and the secret to decoding it is to first understand the history and second know the rules.

Geneviève Brame's book *Chez Vous en France* cracks the code and explains step-by-step how to integrate in French society, from how to cut through government red tape to how to behave at a formal dinner party, and puts it all in perspective historically. As Geneviève Brame points out, France is more than 'culture, cuisine and couture'. And it's becoming more so everyday.

Dana Thomas
Author of *Deluxe: How luxury lost its lustre*

The day I officially arrived in France, in the fog-bound Norman port of Ouistreham, I had to find a customs official to stamp my long-stay visa. When a laid-back *douanier* eventually emerged from the port terminal and inspected my passport, his eyebrows shot up. 'You're from New Zealand? Why do you want to live here?' he asked, grinning. 'The taxes are far too high.'

A few months later, I was having my hair cut in Caen. 'Perhaps if I cut your hair just like mine, we could swap passports', the hairdresser said. We looked at each other in the mirror and laughed. He was only half joking.

France is at a turning point. It retains a great deal of justified pride in its values and achievements, but it is only just beginning to realize the depth of the problems it faces. At the same time, it seems to me, the French people in general remain remarkably open to others, curious about others' lives and willing to stick together to ride out the rough patches. Why do I love living in France? I think it is partly because of this intriguing mixture of self-confidence, self-doubt and solidarity.

Andrew Johnston
New Zealand poet & journalist, *International Herald Tribune*

I love China, I also love France. They are two countries who have a long history and brilliant civilization. I studied in France for four years, and with my colleagues we have developed a good Sino-French cooperation between Nanchang University and Poitiers University. The fruit of which is the creation of the first Confucius Institute in France in 2005.

When we started to work for our cooperation, I told my French friends: comme le disait le philosophe Laozi 'il faut trouver la voie'. I think that the Sino-French cooperation in education has found a road to understand each other for us, and Geneviève Brame's book *Chez Vous en France* has found another road, which will help more Chinese to know France. I hope that our two countries can amicably develop what Confucius calls 'harmonie mais différence'.

Dr Gan Xiaoqing
Président of Jiujlang University
Directeur de l'Institut Confucius à Poitiers

My love of France stems from my childhood. At the age of six, I left Spain with my parents and brother for new horizons in France. Indelibly marked in my memory is my father's great admiration for the social advancement of this country which welcomed us. He told us that in France, health care and state-education were available for all. Even for me as a young child, it was clearly obvious that France has so much to offer. A country that allows the same right for everyone to learn, to create, to progress, to succeed. This has always seemed to me to truly define the country.

It is also so endearing, with a melodic and sophisticated language, never satisfied with just being itself, but playing an international role with such pride. It is for these very reasons, that today, even many years later, I am so attached to France! A 'Republic' as well as a host, a generous and somewhat demanding country, with a desire to be on the world stage. At the same time both small and large, a little grumpy sometimes, but nonetheless, so touching.

I feel one should fight unceasingly each day to ensure that this 'certaine idée de la France' continues to exist, so that she remains the welcoming, diverse country that she is, that she maintains her specific and fascinating model of integration, with her belief in shared knowledge and that she never doubts for one moment that a 'small' country can be politically, economically and culturally rich. This perception of France has always inspired me and has enabled me to forge ahead day after day.

Merci la France!

Mercedes Erra
Executive President, EURO RSCG Worldwide

Acknowledgements

My warmest thanks to Mary Louise Stott and Denise Starrett, for their support of *Chez vous en France* from the start. Thanks Béatrice Tollu, illustrator.

I would like to give my special thanks to Le Ministère des Affaires étrangères et européennes, Greater Paris Agency and Ernst & Young. I am honoured by their sponsorship.

I have had the pleasure of meeting literally hundreds of other people, both in France and abroad, during my interviews and research to update the book, and I thank each and everyone.

The French Embassies and Consulates, and the Alliances Françaises have always kindly welcomed me. Greetings to Yann Battefort who is a BA, not a Business Angel but he has been my real 'Book Angel' since I first met him at *le Quai d'Orsay* in 2001.

The Paris Capitale Economique 'Welcome to France' lobbying group and especially Chiara Corazza, Managing Director for her enthusiastic encouragement.

The numerous Préfectures and the Direction Départementale du Travail, de l'Emploi et de la Formation Professionnelle who showed interest in my works and gave me advice.

Thanks also to the editorial and marketing team at Kogan Page for their hard work and very warm thanks to Ian Hallsworth, Publisher, and Helen Savill, Project Editor, without forgetting Jon Finch, Publishing Director. Many thanks to Martha Fumagalli, Publicity Manager, who knows how to promote France so well.

Furthermore, I am really delighted that my book can be read twice, once in English (Kogan Page publisher) and again in French (Edition La Documentation française et France info, 2007).

All my gratitude goes to you, Madame, Monsieur, for so generously taking the time to read, reread and enrich the manuscript of my books *Chez Vous en France* and *Living & working in France*.

Sebastian Barnes	Paris – Londres
Elza Chambel	Lisbonne
Valérie Cordier	Business immigration consultant – Australia
Xavier Denecker	Directeur Général, Coface United Kingdom and Ireland
Marie Desjardins	Ecrivaine – Montréal
Hélène Duval	Harvard Business School, Boston
Jean-Pierre Evain	Consultant UFE – Paris
Philippe Guiraud	Délégation à l'information et à la communication Ministère de l'Intérieur
Môn Jugie	VO International – Lille
Kyoko Koma	Université de Lituanie – Vilnius
Joanna Lanman	Hub Manager, Acted, Paris
Jason Levin	Washington
Setsuko Murakami	Présidente de l'Association des Boursiers de la Fondation du Rotary international
Bo Lim	UN New York
Greg Long	Melbourne – Australia
Vincent Merk	Université de Technologie – Eindhoven
Martine Pergent	Communication, Astrolabe
Joe Ray	Journaliste
Renée Roth-Hano	Ecrivain, New York
Marie Claire Trespuech	Always my welcome home in London

Special thanks to the Communication Department of Ernst & Young for their continued help to promote the book, in particular Agnès Caradec, Sylvie Kermoal, Mélissa Lévine, Claire de Loynes, Isabelle Masson, Nadège Montant, Fabrice Beaudoin, Sylvie Ferrier and

Anne-Claude Villemin. Credit to Jean-Pierre Llopis for the charming photos. Last but not least, *un grand merci* to Julia Powley, Business Immigration Consultant, the most English Francofile lady living in France missing her unforgettable Marmite!

Introduction

Destination France

'What would a universal society be which had no separate countries, which was neither French, nor English, nor German, nor Spanish, nor Portuguese, not Italian, nor Russian, nor Tartar, nor Turkish, nor Persian, nor Indian, nor Chinese, nor American, or which was, rather, made up of all those societies together? What would be its customs, its sciences, its arts and its poetry?'

'Quelle serait une société universelle qui n'aurait point de pays particulier, qui ne serait ni française, ni anglaise, ni allemande, ni espagnole, ni portugaise, ni italienne, ni russe, ni tartare, ni turque, ni persane, ni indienne, ni chinoise, ni américaine, ou plutôt qui serait à la fois toutes ces sociétés? Qu'en résulterait-il pour ses moeurs, ses sciences, ses arts, sa poésie?'

Chateaubriand, 1850

Beyond the hackneyed clichés of the Frenchman with his beret and baguette, the Eiffel Tower, and the *'culture, cuisine, couture'*, which adorn the postcards, France is a modern country blessed with strong economic potential. Its people are talented and enterprising, if slightly undisciplined, and they will be delighted to welcome you.

If you are planning to visit, to work, to study or live in France, either alone or with your family, this book is aimed at you. This country – the 'Hexagon' – is an undiscovered territory to which you must find the keys.

Idiosyncracies that might be charming to the casual visitor or tourist can cause serious problems for the new resident who is keen to settle in. What you need is a French friend to welcome you from the very start, to show you the ropes and make you feel safe; a friend who understands your mixed feelings of anticipation and apprehension. *Living and Working in France*, which aims to introduce you to France and its culture, can be that friend. And, since all aspects of life are important, it also deals with the subjects that will preoccupy you on a daily basis – administrative formalities, home, health, work, school, leisure time, customs and ways, and resources and opportunities.

A practical guide and a cheerful book, it gives you much more than the essential information. You will save time and worry by knowing what to expect, and knowing a little about France and its people will help to enlarge your opinion about their personality and identity.

Living and Working in France was written with the help of people of different nationalities and cultures who have chosen to make France their home for various periods of time, from 2 months to 20 years. Their experiences, advice and secrets make this a little bit their book, and a better book for you. Over a hundred private and public multinational companies and organizations also willingly expressed their point of view and added their expert advice.

Intended primarily for foreigners, this book is also for French people who, although they may know France well, perhaps need to rediscover its charms.

Even though professional and geographic mobility is now commonplace, for the person involved it is always an event that is out of the ordinary. So, browse at your leisure, and welcome to *Chez Vous en France!*

1 The French way

– les Français:
usages et humeurs

*'France always welcomes new ideas as well as
new technologies. It is the country of transient
fashions and eternal classics. It is quite
impossible to live fully the modern world
without breathing the scent of France.'*

'La France est ouverte aux nouvelles idées autant
qu'aux nouvelles techniques. C'est le pays des
modes passagères et des classiques éternels.
Impossible de vivre le monde moderne sans
respirer le parfum de la France.'

Shimon Peres

Who are the French?

France has a tricolour flag for a multicoloured community: over the centuries, through its ability to adapt to other civilizations – Roman, Celt, Germanic, Slavic, Nordic, Occitan – France, and its people, have become an astonishingly complex blend of cultures and contrasts.

Impressions

'When you ask for the time in France, they will teach you how to make a watch.'

Certain clichés reinforce or oversimplify the reality. What do foreign students say about the French? 'The French are chameleons, spoilt children who are simultaneously querulous, conformist, conquering, disorganized and brilliant; they are extremely resourceful, creative, talkative and erudite; they are strongly attached to their freedom of thought and action; they have the advantage of being independent and the disadvantage of being individualists; they seem deeply rooted in their native land. In Paris they ignore you, in the countryside they take the time to explain their country to you.'

'Is it the Frenchness? The French oscillate between individuality and altruism, equality and hierarchy, fantasy and reality, reason and emotions, *tu* and *vous*, *croissant au beurre* or *croissant ordinaire*, tranquillizers and champagne!'

Seen and heard, here and there

'The French wit is as complicated as French spelling, there are always exceptions.'

'If they grumble, it's a sign of good health; they are distinguished pessimists and they criticize their country, but do not like others to do so.'

'They are too hot today and they will be too cold tomorrow.'

'They like novelty, but they do not like change.'

'Men and women share household chores more often here than elsewhere without making it a feminist issue.'

'The French know how to live, and they live well.'

'The French are wary. They see danger where there is only risk.'

'Here, the past is always present. The French are a backward-looking people.'

'France is eternal, the French are mortal.'

'A marvellous country, a bizarre people.'

'France: extra, French: terrestrial.'

'In France, they foresee everything and it is often the opposite which happens. . . they are unbeatable these French.'

'France has kept a tradition now lost in the USA: a healthy critical sense.' (Robert Bell)

'What is irreplaceable in France is the French.' (Lutz Krusche)

'The French are wiser than they seem.' (Francis Bacon, 1625)

'France is a country of contrasts and contradictions, the fruit of an extraordinary juxtaposition, that is reflected in the faces of her people.' (Terence Conran)

'France is a theatre in which one tries to blend the ancient pleasures with modern ideas.' (Theodore Zeldin)

What is your idea of France? Do you see it as a country as enigmatic as the *Mona Lisa's* smile?

Are the French mutants, mutins ou moutons?

The sociologist Gérard Mermet identified three types of French: 'the "mutants" follow the path of technological progress and are open to the world. The "mutineers" represent the principle of precaution and resist change. Whereas the "sheep" are the more classic followers when... proof of progress has been made.'

*S*ocial contacts and relationships

Social conventions in France adhere to principles that are firmly rooted in family life.

■■■ *The hierarchy of French relationships*

Caution and respect for others prevail in all encounters. Friendship is earned and therefore takes time to mature.

First, there are *connaissances*, people briefly encountered, with whom you might establish closer contact, or whom you might meet again only at the same dinner next year.

In a train or on an aeroplane, it is normal to exchange a few words with your fellow travellers, about the weather, the countryside or the newspaper your neighbour is reading. Two hours later, you might exchange addresses with a view to meeting up again, or, alternatively, part without ever knowing with whom you have spoken.

Then there are *relations*, those who are not yet friends, but who have a secure place in your address book. The French like to have a *réseau de relations* – a network of people who are always ready to help each other in personal or professional affairs. However, each member is expected to maintain this network by making regular calls, and by keeping the others up to date with their news – if they plan to count on them, that is.

Some people are quick to say that 'friends of our friends are our friends', but the French take their time to get to know each other well in order to establish long-lasting friendships. Good friends often share their worries and their pleasures, ask each other for advice, and help each other out in time of need. Some people are proud to have childhood friends, whom they have known for 20 or 30 years. Family and close friends form a group of *proches*, who meet regularly to share a meal or a drink, at the weekend or during the holidays. Any pretext will do. As Rudyard Kipling said, *'There is no pleasure like meeting an old friend, except perhaps making a new one.'*

'Britain and France are friends, partners and allies. Sometimes we are rivals too. But we should never lose sight of how much we have in common, and of how many interests we share.'
Tony Blair

Neighbours

When you arrive in a new neighbourhood, or in a block of flats, certain faces will start to become familiar, and these will no doubt be those of your neighbours. Introduce yourself to those who seem to be the most friendly. The French have a tendency to be rather distant, so do not be surprised if you are not invited in the first time you exchange a few words with a neighbour. Above all, do not hesitate to ask for help, because they will often not make the first move for fear of being indiscreet. If you fall upon people who are less than gracious, try another door; you will find others who are more helpful and friendly.

In the big cities, Paris in particular, the rhythm of life (family, work, commuting, shopping) is not conducive to making acquaintances, and people may often seem to be in a hurry and, therefore, unwelcoming. It is a question of patience; in time, they will certainly want to say a few words to you.

'In Paris no one interferes. The neighbours couldn't care less who you have at home (provided that you don't make any noise).'
Zoe Valdes

Courtesy and conformity

Each country has its own rules and rituals regarding courtesy or politeness, and these differ from one culture to another. In France, *savoir-vivre* is not a list of obligations or principles to follow, but, rather, a form of kindness and attentiveness, which oils the social wheels and becomes less formal from one generation to another. Decoding the manners and customs will allow you to feel at ease in any situation and, should you wish to break the rules, you will then be able to do it intentionally!

At what time?

• Lunch is served between noon and 2 pm. In the provinces, shops often close and many people go home to eat.

• Dinner is served after 7 pm, but the time varies according to family habits and the age of the children. An invitation to dinner is usually for about 8.30 pm. When invited to dinner, your *cordon bleu* host will appreciate your thoughtfulness when you arrive 15 minutes late, allowing him or her to put the finishing touches to his or her masterpiece.

• The correct time to arrive for drinks or at a reception varies. Do not arrive too early, as you will be the first, or too late, as there will be no more *petits fours* left for you.

• Telephoning between 8 am and 9.30 pm is considered reasonable; you should only ring later than that if you know the person's habits well.

HAVE YOU EVER RECEIVED A BRISTOL?

The word *Bristol* is included in the French dictionary, meaning 'invitation'. The British town of Bristol was famous for the production of the high-quality paper traditionally used for invitations.

You will need to learn to tell the difference between an invitation and a suggestion. For example, if someone asks you '*Voulez-vous venir au théâtre avec nous?*' ('Would you like to come to the theatre with us?'), it does not necessarily imply that they are offering to pay for your ticket. It is also increasingly common for friends to eat together in a restaurant, and for each to pay for their own meal. At other times, a suggestion will be a genuine invitation, which you will have the pleasure of accepting.

The art of receiving

Introductions are made spontaneously, either directly by the person newly arrived – 'I am John Smith' – or by the host or friend present. Shaking hands briefly, while maintaining eye contact, is the ritual greeting. First names and the *tu* form are not used automatically, even between people of the same generation. It is often necessary to suggest it: 'On se tutoie?'

Social relations between men and women have been simplified and French women are sufficiently independent to be comfortable in all private or professional encounters. Courtesy will, however, always make life more pleasant.

B… comme Bise

Hugs and kisses are reserved for close friends and relations. There are no rules as such, instead, it is a question of regional and family custom. Kissing comes easily between women who are friends or colleagues, and between men and women who are close friends. Men, if they are father and son, brothers, or old friends, often kiss each other on meeting. Little children will usually offer their cheek for a kiss, even if it is the first time they have met someone. According to Brillat Savarin, '*Un baiser complet est un baiser donné et un baiser rendu.*' ('A real kiss is a kiss given and a kiss received.') 'Une bise, ce n'est pas du vent, c'est plus doux.' 'A little kiss is not like the freezing wind, it is softer.' 'Bisou' is the diminutive of 'bise'. It is a more loving way of saying 'kiss'.

You will sometimes be told, *'Faites comme chez vous'*, or 'Make yourself at home', when you are invited to dinner, but do not take the offer too literally. Do not wander around the house unless accompanied by your hostess, or turn on the television, sit down and pick up the newspaper as soon as you arrive, or use the telephone without asking.

Bouquet or chocolates?

A gift to a host or hostess is never an obligation, but a kind thought, which shows your awareness of social niceties. A bouquet of flowers will always be appreciated. Either present them when you arrive for dinner, or, if the invitation seems at all formal, have them delivered before, or send them the next day with a thank-you note. Your neighbourhood florist will make up a very pretty bouquet, always of an uneven number of flowers. The meaning of flowers is changing but avoid marigolds (*soucis,* also the word for 'worry') and chrysanthemums, which are considered to be funeral flowers in France and Southern Europe. A special regional treat, such as chocolates, will also be appreciated. The gift of a bottle of wine or a book will indicate a closeness between host and guest. You know your friends' tastes and preferences: red or white wine, poetry or a thriller.

'C'est pour offrir?' The vendor will spend time wrapping it up perfectly, including a ribbon and bow – even for a little pastry! The gift is usually opened at once in front of all the guests, and given a place of honour: flowers are arranged in a vase, a box of chocolates is set out to be tasted, a pretty ornament is displayed on the mantelpiece.

Between friends who see each other often there is less formality. For example, it is very common to have a 'potluck supper'. It is usually a simple meal, but a pleasant evening. It is, however, always considered courteous to *rendre une invitation* – that is, to return the invitation and ask your friends to dinner. As Sonia Rykiel said, *'Ce qui est beau en gourmandise, c'est de partager.'* ('The best thing about treats is sharing them.')

The cocktail hour

'The aperitif is the evening prayer of the French.'
'L'apéritif c'est la prière du soir des Français.'
Paul Morand

L'heure de l'apéritif is a ritual and a pleasure – the French often gather for a drink, accompanied by a few *amuse-gueules*, or cocktail snacks. Cocktails, sweet wine, fruit juice or stronger drinks with ice, whet the appetite for dinner, and provide the opportunity for a pleasant moment of relaxation. The traditional expression *'A votre santé'* ('Your good health') is the signal to raise your glass, and, if there are only a few people present, to clink glasses and toast a person, a happy event, or simply to welcome one and all.

A sit-down dinner or a buffet

Tablecloth, candelabra, 6 to 10 places set – these are the ingredients for a sit-down dinner. It is customary for the guests of honour to be placed to the right of the hosts, who sit at the centre of the table, and then to seat the other guests, alternately men and women, in the way that will be most likely to please them. The signal to start comes when the hostess lifts her fork to start eating. *Bon appétit!*

On the table there will be at least two glasses: the biggest is for water and the other for wine. The host makes sure that your glass is always half-full. 'A good meal encourages conversation. A good wine makes it spirited.'

Dinner-table conversation begins with generalities: the weather, holidays, sport, and finally, if you are among friends, the latest political news. The French are reserved regarding questions of religion, 'a private luxury', and money. Most people are raised to believe that *'l'argent ne fait pas le bonheur'* ('money does not bring happiness') and feign little interest in it. It is quite common for a French person not to know how much his or her brothers and sisters earn. The discussion can be controversial but intelligent disagreements will remain friendly.

> ### CONVERSATION
>
> Pleasant conversation might make a dinner last several hours:
> '*Les deux principes du dîner en ville sont qu'il faut traiter
> superficiellement des sujets importants et qu'une soirée est
> réussie quand tout le monde parle à la fois.*' 'The two prin-
> ciples of dining out are to treat serious subjects lightly, and
> that an evening is successful when everyone speaks at once.'
>
> Jean François Revel

Culinary trends are changing, but a traditional dinner consists of
an *entrée*, *plat principal* or *plat de résistance*, *salade*, *fromage* and
dessert – a starter, a main dish, salad, cheese and dessert with
assorted wines. Help yourself to bread and place it on the napkin
beside your plate. Each dish in turn is brought to the table and guests
serve themselves, except at formal dinners, where they will be
served. If you have dietary problems, which may be physical, philosophical or religious, then say so simply, in order to avoid misunderstandings; alternatively, explain them to your hostess when you are
invited.

If you are a smoker the best place for you is outside! At the end
of the meal, when you leave the table to take your coffee and after-
dinner drinks in the drawing room, it is time to change neighbours
and conversation, and to comfortably prolong the evening.
However, do not forget to leave the moment your hosts seem tired!

A home-cooked dinner is nice, but if you do not like to cook, you
could always serve a dinner prepared by a caterer, or invite your
friends to a good small, or 'grand', restaurant.

A buffet is less formal and allows guests to mingle and take the
time to sample all the dishes at their leisure.

PETIT DÉJ or BRUNCH

> *'On Sunday mornings in France, it smells of baguette and warm croissants.'*
> Léo

The *baguette,* a thin loaf about 70–80 cm long, was created in Paris in the 1950s in order to help people forget the black bread of wartime. The French have been seduced by the pleasure of sharing *le brunch* on Saturday or Sunday with close friends – a late breakfast with savoury and sweet dishes, without the worry of cooking.

Delicious, crusty *baguette*. Foreigners find it funny to see the French tuck into the crust at one end of the baguette and immediately eat the other end as soon as they have left the bakery.

The *croissant* was apparently invented in Austria, but the French have certainly adopted it. Fancy bread rolls of all kinds are called *viennoiseries*. This word comes from Vienna, where Louis XVI's wife, Marie-Antoinette, was born.

*T*he art of living... and living well
– art de vivre... et bon vivant

> *'I realized that eating is a ritual, a civilized act, almost like stating a philosophical position.'*
> Cioran

▬▬ *Cooking – pleasures and flavours*

Cooking in France is more than the simple provision of food – it is culinary art, and great chefs are seen as genuine artists. A national council of the culinary arts has been created, with the aim of identifying and preserving regional cuisine. The variety and quality of agricultural products all over France has created a tradition – passed on from generation to generation – of amazing gastronomy. A dish will often have a name that recalls its history, referring to a special place or person: *escalope normande, boeuf bourguignon, ficelle picarde, bouchée à la reine, Paris-Brest*.

France, a country where you can buy 400 different cheeses, cannot be represented by just one national dish; there are simply too many good regional dishes. However, a recent survey has identified *quiche lorraine* as the favourite.

In the debate over modern and traditional cuisine, the *cuisine nouvelle* blend of savoury and sweet flavours has been judged a little too sophisticated and not sufficiently filling. Everyone is agreed on one point: the essential ingredient at the dinner table is shared pleasure.

> *'In France, recipes and meals are made to be shared and enjoyed.'*
> Patricia Wells, food critic for the *International Herald Tribune*

Of course, the professional lifestyle of most Frenchwomen today has now led to some significant changes in *l'esprit cuisine*. During the week, meals are usually light and simple, using fresh or frozen ingredients, designed to fulfil dietary needs and quick to prepare.

Most French people think that having three meals a day is good for their health. Lunch and dinner are usually well balanced and comprise various types of food – meat or fish, vegetables, cheese or fruit. Even a rapid meal is taken sitting down at the table, either in the kitchen or the dining room. The hurried cooking of weekdays becomes a pleasant pastime at the weekend. Men enjoy showing off their *cordon bleu* talents to family and friends. *Gourmandise* (greediness) is a word that tastes wonderful.

'*At my French friend's place, the whole family eat together at the same time, eat at the same place around the table and talk as they eat.*'
Jonathan

Over the year, the seasons dictate the dishes. Springtime brings fresh young vegetables; summer is the time for mixed salads, grilled meats and a hint of the spicy and exotic; in autumn, *gratins* are enjoyed hot from the oven; and in winter, soups and slowly simmering casseroles warm the heart.

CORDON BLEU, BLANC, ROUGE

Most magazines have a cooking section with recipes and restaurant reviews, and there is also a specialized press written by professional food critics for the true gourmet.

Awards to restaurants and chefs are hard-earned. In the 1930s, the *Guide Rouge Michelin* was the first to award stars to restaurants. Published each year and alphabetically classified by town, the 'red bible' is the reference book for gourmets and food lovers.

The *Pudlo France* selects 5,000 reputable places: famous chefs and new talents welcome tourists and gourmets.

At any time

At a cafeteria, a standard, speedy service is offered; most have the same décor and menu – it's best to have a quick meal on the spot.

Some favourite hot dishes are *crêpes* (wafer-thin pancakes), *quiche lorraine* (cheese and ham tart), or *croque-monsieur* and *croque-madame* (both toasted cheese sandwiches, with a fried egg on top for *madame*, which were first served in Paris in 1910).

Casse croûte: if you ask for a '*Paris-Beurre*' in a traditional café, you will be served a ham sandwich. In the 18th century, the Earl of Sandwich, John Montagu, preferred to stay at his gaming table and

LIVING AND WORKING IN FRANCE

eat a slice of meat between two slices of bread than interrupt the game to go to dinner. Since then, sandwiches have been the most popular fast food of France, eaten on trains, at the office or on picnics. Out of 10 quick meals, French people would eat nine sandwiches and one hamburger.

Restaurants

There are countless restaurants in France, of all styles, and for all budgets. If you would like to eat quickly, at a reasonable price, there are many small French and foreign restaurants and bistros, which offer a *plat du jour* or a *menu fixe* (the specials of the day), and give rapid service. They can be found by asking friends or colleagues, or simply by wandering around a neighbourhood and browsing through menus, which are always posted outside the restaurants. Some companies issue *tickets restaurant* (luncheon vouchers), with a face value that are accepted in many restaurants for lunch (see a ticket sticker on the door).

FOREIGN FOOD

The French also love foreign food and they consume more Dutch cheese and Norwegian or Scottish salmon, and drink more Port, than any other Europeans. Pizza, chilli con carne, naan bread, paella, sushi, and hamburgers all bring variety and colour to daily menus in France.

Bread and tap water are free of charge, but you must pay for bottled mineral water, which can be *plate ou gazeuse* (plain or sparkling). Unless otherwise indicated on the menu, drinks are not included in the price of the meal. Service is included in the price, but waiters are always grateful for a few euros left on the table as an extra tip; this is not an obligation, and is usually given when the service has been especially friendly or attentive. Restaurants generally serve lunch between noon and 2 pm, and dinner between 8 pm and 10 pm. Most close for one day a week. All restaurants and cafés are non-smoking areas.

The *grands restaurants* have a menu comprising regional specialities and gourmet fare. They also offer a special atmosphere and a more refined service, which add to their reputation. A flower vendor is sometimes allowed to sell roses in the restaurant. Feel free to buy or refuse as you prefer. It is always a good idea to reserve your table in advance, giving the number of guests and the time of arrival. NB: Frogs' legs, that national cliché, are nowadays more common on tourist menus than in conventional French meals. Most frogs' legs are frozen and imported from Eastern Europe or Asia because frogs are a protected species in France.

▬ *Great wines and modest wines* – grands crus et petits vins

'Behind each wine, there is a countryside, the men who made it, a whole culture and symbolic meaning.'

'Derriere le vin, il y a les paysages, les hommes qui le font, toute une culture et une symbolique.'
Jean-Paul Kauffman

International investors have shown a growing interest in the prestigious French vineyards and, through some spectacular acquisitions, have transformed what were once traditional family-run properties.

Blanc, rosé, rouge – white wine, rosé wine, red wine – you may drink whichever wine you want with any dish. Enlightened wine lovers drink dry white wine or a chilled red first, before moving on to a red wine served at room temperature (*chambré*); a young wine is drunk before an older one. An old bottle will often be served still covered with the dust collected from its years in the cellar – it seems more authentic; alternatively, the wine may be decanted into a *carafe* to allow its aroma to develop.

It is traditional to offer everyone a glass of wine, or a *vin d'honneur*, at inaugurations or to celebrate a marriage, as a sign of friendship.

■ *Champagne*

Before it got its present name, this pale golden wine with delicate bubbles was known as *'saulte bouchon'*, which refers to the unforgettable sound of a champagne cork popping. Champagne symbolizes festivity and is associated with the great moments of life. When the bubbles tickle the palette, it is said that the champagne has a *belle expression*. When the big champagne producers announce their *cuvée speciale* (special vintage), which they do regularly, they always emphasize the elegance of the bottle. The law says that the word *champagne* must be printed on the cork. *Brut* or *demi-sec* (dry or semi-dry) champagne is served chilled, but not ice-cold, as an aperitif, or, as a great luxury, to accompany a festive meal. Everywhere in the world champagne is served either in a *coupe*, a wide bowl-shaped glass, or a *flûte*, a tall, narrow glass. There are about six *coupes* or nine *flûtes* to a bottle. The *flûte* retains the aroma, the bubbles and the chill longer.

WINE WORDS

'One looks at wine, one smells it, and only then does one put down the glass and talk about it.'

'Le vin, on le regarde, on le hume, après seulement on pose son verre et on en parle.'
Talleyrand

- *à l'œil* (to the eye) *sa robe* (its appearance… is brilliantly beautiful, it sparkles ruby red… it has) *jambage* (legs);

- *au nez* (to the nose, it is) *fruité, fleuri, légèrement boisé* (fruity, flowery, slightly woody; this is its) *bouquet* (aroma);

- *en bouche* (to the palette, it may be) *gouleyant* (with a delicate flavour, its taste lingers on the palette. In other words, it is a gentle wine, well made and flattering to the palette, and will please many tastes.

Knowing how to drink wine also involves knowing how to describe it and enjoy it! The study of wine (*oenologie*) is recommended to all wine lovers. There are close to 2,000 words used to talk about wine and almost 500 for cheese.

■ *Bordeaux*

Bordeaux, or claret wine, is known by its *château*, which indicates its *domaine*, the property where the grapes were grown. This is an officially attributed name. On the label the words *mis en bouteille au château* (bottled at the château) guarantee its origin and its authenticity. The Bordeaux region is the biggest vineyard in the world, with over 247,000 acres of vineyards and more than 4,000 châteaux!

LES GRANDES REGIONS VINICOLES FRANCAISES
(THE GREAT WINE REGIONS OF FRANCE)

■ *Bourgogne*

Wines from the Bourgogne, or Burgundy wines, are generally great wines that must be aged for several years at the vineyard before they are ready to be drunk. Connoisseurs will tell you that the wine needs to *prendre de la bouteille* (take to the bottle). It was in Burgundy that the famous Canon Kir invented the most popular cocktail in France – a drop of *crème de cassis* in a glass of Burgundy white wine makes a Kir. It becomes a Kir Royal when the white wine is replaced by champagne.

■ *Beaujolais*

Le Beaujolais nouveau est arrivé! The arrival of the new crop of Beaujolais wine is an annual event celebrated at midnight on the third Thursday of November from Paris to Tokyo and from New York to London. It is said that three rivers water Lyon: the Rhône, the Saône, and the *Beaujolais*.

■ *Alsace, the Loire Valley, the Côte du Rhône, Provence, Roussillon*

… there are so many different wines to discover.

COMPAGNONS DU BEAUJOLAIS

Since medieval times, there have been brotherhoods of wine and food lovers in France. Each has its own arms, garb, motto and initiation rites.

The *Compagnons du Beaujolais* wear green aprons with black jackets and hats; they look like very proud and jolly wine growers. The *compagnons*, both men and women, swear to honour and promote Beaujolais wines at all times. There are 10 kinds of light, fruity, flowery, irresistible Beaujolais wines to try. How could anyone resist the sparkling brilliance of a wine called *Saint Amour*?

■ *Labelling*

The great wines are available at all prices. *Appellation d'origine contrôlée* (AOC) guarantees that the label accurately describes the product's origin; it is found on a number of food products: cheeses, wines or other alcohols. In the case of wine, this indicates a specific vineyard, vintage and growing method. From now on, products will receive a special European stamp, *Appellation d'origine protégée* (AOP), which guarantees the method and the geographic area of production.

Since 1919, every bottle of wine has a label stating its name, category, year of production, the name of the producer, where it was bottled, and the percentage of alcohol. A *Marianne* and the words *République française* must also be stamped on the foil that covers the cork, to prove that all taxes have been paid.

THE HIERARCHY OF WINES: A VOCABULARY

- *vins de table* – a blend of wines
- *vin de pays* – wine from a specific region of France
- *AO VDQS* – *Appellation d'Origine, Vin de Qualité Supérieure* (a high-quality wine from a specific vineyard)
- AOC – *Appellation d'Origine Contrôlée* (a wine from a specific area, including *vin griffé, cru classé, cru bourgeois*)
- VDL – *Vin de Liqueur* (such as *Pineau des Charents*)
- VDN – *Vin Doux Naturel* (a sweet wine, such as *Muscat*)

■ Wine and cheese

Red wine and cheese are natural companions. You will find special breads at your local bakery, such as a nut bread eaten with goat's cheese, cumin bread with Munster cheese, or raisin bread with blue cheese; they will add considerably to your pleasure. French cheeses vary by region. Cheese made with goat's and sheep's milk is common where these animals are plentiful, in the arid regions; cheese made from cow's milk comes from the areas where there are lush pastures.

According to statistics, the average French person eats 25 kilos of cheese washed down, of course, with wine, and also consumes 149 litres of mineral water and 2 litres of champagne per year.

REGIONAL HIGH SPIRITS

France is also known for spirits, distilled alcohol or brandies. Age is the great virtue of these often subtly blended *alcools*. These after-dinner drinks are served, following coffee, in a warmed tulip-shaped glass:

- Calvados – apple brandy from Normandy;
- Kirsch – cherry brandy from Alsace;
- Cognac – grape brandy from Charentes;
- Marc – grape brandy from Burgundy.

On the bottle, the age of the contents is indicated as follows:

- *Vieux or Réserve* – three years old;
- *Vieille Réserve* – four years old;
- *VSOP* ('very special old pale') – five years old. This is an English classification, but the French have made up their own definition just for fun: *'Verser sans oublier personne!'* ('Pour it, without forgetting anyone!').
- *Hors d'âge* – over six years old.

■ *Even in Paris*

In the 14th century, the monks of the Passy Abbey in Paris grew their own grapes and made wine. In the Rue des Eaux in Passy, three vaulted cellars remain, now used as a wine museum with a wine-tasting bar.

New vines have been planted in the parks and gardens of Paris, giving new life to wine from the capital.

*B*istros and café terraces

'The café is an institution which defies definition... it is a lawyer's office, a stock exchange, the back stage of the theatre, a club, a reading room...'

'Le café est une institution indéfinissable... un cabinet d'avocat, une bourse, une coulisse de théâtre, un club, une salle de lecture...'
Honoré de Balzac

Whether it is traditional, popular or the 'in place', the French café is eternal. Café names recall their history – *Le Café d'Epoque, Le Bar de l'Eglise, Le Bistrot Gaulois, La Brasserie de France, Chez nous.*

▬▬ *The neighbourhood café* – bistrot de quartier

The *bistrot* is a part of French social life; *bistrot* means both the place and a drink. It is a popular place to pass a little time, or to spend long evenings. It is a place where friends can put the world to rights over a cup of coffee, or a *noisette* (black coffee with a dash of milk), and a hard-boiled egg at the bar. Some come to lean on the *zinc* (the bar), to drink an expresso (a tiny cup of strong coffee), or a glass of red wine (*un ballon*). Others come to read, to work, to daydream, or to meet friends for endless discussions, or for a confidential *tête à tête*.

▬▬ Bar-tabac

The *bar-tabac* is a multi-purpose café. As its name indicates, it sells cigarettes and tobacco; often you can also play the lottery, or bet on horses (if the PMU sign is shown). Clients stop by, to win or to lose, and regulars stay on. The *tabac* is licensed to sell *timbres fiscaux* (Inland Revenue stamps).

Le bistrot à vins

The French are passionate about the art of wine. The owner of a wine bar is at heart a wine grower; building the reputation of their cellar by selecting a few good wines, and thus winning the loyalty of the clients.

A bistro will reflect the character of its owner who is warm-hearted and authentic. Wine is served by the glass, in a pitcher, or by the bottle. It is usually served with *un plat du chef* (cheese or cold meat from the same region as the wine).

Brasseries

The *brasseries* are dedicated to beer, whether draught (*pression*), bottled, pale ale or brown ale. *Un demi* is a standard measure for draught beer (25 cl); a *panache* is a shandy, a mixture of beer and lemonade. At busy times, the waiter may seem impatient if you hesitate over an order; his first concern is to serve everyone as quickly as possible. The tables with cloths are reserved for quick meals, usually served between noon and 2 pm, to neighbourhood clients who are often in a hurry.

On the terrace

With just a tiny ray of sunshine and a speck of blue sky, the terrace of a café becomes an outdoor theatre. Umbrellas take over the pavement, and the customer has a front row seat for the street scene. This pleasure is something that other countries envy. At the first sign of a chill in the air, the terrace is enclosed by plastic windows, so that customers can watch the street without catching cold.

Some tall buildings with terraces in Paris such as the Institut du Monde Arabe, Centre Beaubourg, Musée d'Orsay, Tour Montparnasse and Tour d'Argent offer spectacular views of the city and are worth a detour.

In recent years, there has been an increasing number of *café-terrasses* in the tourist neighbourhoods – sometimes so exclusively 'tourist', that you may not hear French spoken. Food and drinks are often very expensive, and the owners seem to prefer clients who are just passing through.

FAMOUS PARISIAN CAFÉS

French writers, politicians and artists have always gathered in cafés, forming groups of *habitués* (regulars); some cafés have kept that literary, political or artistic tradition, and even cultivated the reputation. The atmosphere of such cafés is refined; people go there to see and to be seen.

Le Procope, on the rue de l'Ancienne Comédie, was the first real café in Paris. Procopio came from Sicily in 1686 to open a boutique for the sale of the 'new' beverage, coffee; he also made ice cream and sherbet. His success was immediate. His shop became *the* place for literary Parisians, and history was made by Voltaire, Diderot, Victor Hugo. Three centuries later, Procope still serves coffee, and many other drinks; at mealtimes, the café becomes a fine restaurant.

Le Fumoir, situated on the Right Bank, conveniently close to the Louvre, is quite simply a chic and cosy bar and restaurant. The lovely leather chairs, parquet flooring and candles provide a pleasant atmosphere in which to unwind. There is also a selection of international newspapers for the fashionable regulars to peruse. The library corner is a unique haven of peace, especially for the literary-minded.

Cafés philo, cybercafés, sports cafés

Theme cafés flourish in the big cities in France, for example:

- café philo, where you may hear philosophical debates that are a little more abstract than those at the Café du Commerce. It is a rendezvous for budding intellectuals who debate in a friendly atmosphere;

- cybercafé customers search the web, while having a snack or a cup of coffee; and

- sports cafés are equipped with giant screens for watching sport; customers share the excitement of the big games.

The British and the Irish

PUBS

The British and the Irish have brought the special atmosphere of the pub to France. Pubs are increasingly popular meeting places, both for the English-speaking community, and for French people who wish to speak English.

OR... TEA ROOMS – SALONS DE THÉ

English teatime has its admirers in France, and teashops are usually found in the chic neighbourhoods. As well as tea, the shops serve other hot or cold non-alcoholic drinks, and an assortment of goodies to eat. The atmosphere is comfortable and calm, offering an ideal place for the discreet conversation of ladies. Some bookshops also serve tea; a friendly welcome gives the reader an appetite both for books and for *petits fours*.

▬*Practical details*

Cafés and restaurants offer various services to their patrons, including telephones and toilets. Opening hours for cafés vary according to the region, climate, neighbourhood, clientele and the whim of the owner. The prices must be clearly posted, or written on the menu and are higher in the evening, on the terrace or at a table in the café rather than standing at the bar. You pay the price marked on *l'addition* (the bill – service is included), either when you leave the café, or when the waiter asks.

*M*ode et couture

'Fashion is a woman's literature, the outfit is her personal style.'

'La mode est la littérature de la femme, la toilette est son style personnel.'
Octave Uzanne

To dress in a classic style, to be casually dressed or dressed up, takes imagination and style in all countries, regardless of climate or season. For spring fashion or winter wear, the French are increasingly looking for natural, comfortable clothes that are easy and pleasant to wear.

How can you reconcile your desires and needs with the constraints of your purse? Whether you just want to dream, or to spend a little or a lot, you will find hundreds of boutiques in France offering the traditional or the modern, designer fashions or cut-price wear. If good value and quality are your priorities, the *lignes bis* are the less expensive non-couture collections offered by the fashion houses. In addition, discontinued lines of designer clothes are always on sale (*en solde*).

Collections and brand names

Fashion houses present their collections twice a year – spring/summer and autumn/winter – at shows that bring designers and the well-dressed of the world to Paris (by invitation only). The international press promotes and reports on the events – according to *Newsweek*, 'It's chic, it's French.'

The big fashion houses also market leather goods, jewellery and sunglasses, perfume and scarves – all those little luxuries that are such a pleasure to give and to receive.

A WORK OF ART

65 grams of silk, 90 centimetres square, chic and always à la mode? Of course, it must be *un carré* – a square silk Hermès scarf of the type known and loved the world over. Since 1937, the House of Hermès has created 1,500 different original versions, in all colours and styles; each has a name, such as *Brides de Gala, Ex-libris, Emblèmes d'Europe.* Hermès makes a scarf for every occasion, and brings out two new collections each year.

Style and styles

Each activity has its own dress code. For the business world, it is the 'business suit and fountain pen' for men, or an elegant tailored

suit for women – simple but classic, with matching seasonal accessories, and always in fashion. People in the art or advertising worlds
tend to wear more colourful, original clothes.

If an invitation specifies *tenue de soirée* or *tenue de ville*, you are
expected to dress in evening clothes (dinner suit, or black tie), or
in smart 'town clothes', respectively.

In 1920, Coco Chanel launched the famous *petite robe noire*. A
little black dress is elegant in all circumstances especially for an
evening event. On stage, the singer Edith Piaf always wore a little
black dress with a heart-shaped neckline.

'Fashion, an essential frivolity'
'La mode, une frivolité essentielle'

PETITE ROBE NOIRE ET VIE EN ROSE

'I'm totally overwhelmed with joy and sparkles and fireworks
and everything that goes "boom boom boom"' declared
Marion Cotillard, who won an Oscar for Best actress and
Golden Globe award for her portrayal of the legendary Edith
Piaf in *La Vie en Rose*. In 2008, she also picked up a BAFTA in
London and a Cesar in Paris for her role in *La Môme*, the
French title of the film and the nickname of Piaf.

Designer uniforms

In France, even uniforms have designer labels. It improves the
public image of French institutions and makes the function easy to
recognize.

'*La mode habille les musées*' is the chic slogan of the Musées
de France for which the great fashion designers created the
uniforms: Yves Saint-Laurent for the Louvre, Lanvin for the men at
the Musée d'Orsay and Sonia Rykiel for the women. Balenciaga
designed the clothes for the personnel at the Château de
Versailles.

Christian Lacroix created the uniforms for Air France. Pierre Balmain was chosen to design the blue and yellow uniforms of the Post Office hostesses, as well as the uniforms for the Eurostar staff.

Pierre Cardin was received as a member of the Académie Française des Beaux Arts – a great honour – and was the first member ever to make his own gown for the occasion. It was made of black cloth and embroidered with sumptuous green olive leaves. Special feminine garb had to be made in 1980 for the reception of Marguerite Yourcenar, the first woman elected to the Académie Française. Born in Belgium, she grew up in France and lived in America. She loved to say, 'Construire c'est collaborer avec la terre: c'est mettre une marque humaine sur un paysage qui en sera modifié à jamais' (*'To build is to collaborate with the world... to put a human print on a landscape that will be modified by it forever'*).

LAPEL DECORATIONS

'The desire for privilege and a taste for equality have always been the dominant and contradictory passions of the French.'

'Le désir du privilège et le goût de l'égalité sont les passions dominantes et contradictoires des Français de toute époque.'
Charles de Gaulle

'At the bottom of his heart, the Frenchman is convinced that all men are equal...' (Somerset Maugham), but he still attaches importance to decorations and awards.

The Legion of Honour, created by Napoleon in 1802, recognizes eminent people while the National Order of Merit, established in 1963 by General de Gaulle, rewards distinguished people. These prestigious decorations honour those who have served France in military or civilian life, in the arts, business, sciences and sports. Proposed by an authority to the appropriate ministers, (it can never be requested), the chosen few are awarded one of five grades *'au nom de la République française'*.

What gift from France?

What gift would you like to receive from France? France could be the country or a person's name!

'To be invited to dinner with a French family who would tell me all their family stories while showing me their photograph album.'
Sara Williams

'To have her apartment's keys – as long as it faces the Eiffel Tower.'
Alain Machu

■■■ A gift from France to America: the Statue of Liberty

The original Statue of Liberty, properly known as 'Liberty enlightening the World', is an emblem of French-American friendship, given by France to commemorate the centenary of the American War of Independence. (Inscribed on the tablet in Liberty's left hand is *July iv MDCCLXXVI*: 4 July 1776.) Sculpted by the Alsatian Auguste Bartholdi, the work was inspired by his memory during the 1848 French Revolution of a young woman, torch in hand, throwing herself upon barricades. Gustave Eiffel built the structure in metal.

Located on Liberty Island in New York Harbor, the Statue of Liberty stands on a pedestal 93 metres high. 354 steps lead up to her crown with its seven rays representing the seven seas and continents. On 30 November 1884 Victor Hugo said that the Statue of Liberty was the emblem of friendship between France and America: *'La mer, cette grande agitée, constate l'union de deux grandes terres apaisées.'* ('The sea, this great agitated mass, confirms the union of two great peaceful lands.')

From Paris, standing on the smallest island in the Seine (l'Ile aux Cygnes near the Eiffel Tower), Lady Liberty's little sister looks out towards America. The statue, a gift from America to the French in 1885, is an exact replica of the original Statue of Liberty on Liberty Island in New York.

Just a stone's throw from the French statue, near the Pont de l'Alma, there is a full-sized copy of the flame from Liberty's torch. This was given to Paris in 1987 by the *International Herald Tribune* to celebrate its hundredth anniversary; however, since Princess Diana was killed in a car crash at this very place in 1997, many visitors now assume that the flame is a memorial to her.

*F*or further information

Do as the French Do, Ross Steele (McGraw-Hill, 2002)
Witty and wise; what the French think about being French
Terence Conran's France (Conran Octopus Books, 1997)
Rural life, the French home, food of France, design
Cultural Misunderstandings: The French-American experience,
 Raymonde Carroll (University of Chicago Press, 1988)
De Bonheur d'être Français, Ulrich Wickert (Félin, 2001)
Mastering the Art of French Cooking, Simone Beck and Julia Child, 2 vols
Cuisine des Régions de France (Ouest-France, 1998)
French Vineyards: Complete guide and companion, Michael Busselle
 (Pavilion Books, 1998)
Eating out en Français, Simon Collins (Bloomsbury, 2003)
www.insee.fr, www.ined.fr – National Institutes for demographic studies
www.bestgourmet.fr – French restaurants and hotel bookings
www.ifrac.org – IFRAC (Institut français de formation et de recherche sur
 les arts culinaires)
www.museeduvinparis.com/english
Patriciawells.com/books/about_books.htm
Msglaze.typepad.com – Blog/Culinary adventures in Paris: chef stories and
 tasty recipes
The French, Theodore Zeldin (Pantheon, 1986)
Sixty Million Frenchmen Can't be Wrong, Jean-Benoît Nadeau et Julie
 Barlow (Sourcebooks, 2003)

French Ways and their Meaning, Edith Wharton (Berkshire House, Massachusetts 1997: 1st edn 1919)

France – A quick guide to customs and etiquette, Barry Tomalin (Kuperard, 2003)

French Vertigo, Peter Gumbel (Grasset, 2006)

From Here, you Can't See Paris: Seasons of a French village and its restaurant, Michael S. Sanders (Bantam Press, 2003)

Français et Américains : L'autre rive, Pascal Baudry (Village mondial, 2004)

Francoscopie, Gérard Mermet (Larousse, 2007)

A Little Bit of France, Jean-Jacques Sempé, (Random House, 2008)

Chez Vous en France, Geneviève Brame (Co-édition La Documentation française et France info, 2007)

2 *France*

'France is far more than just a next-door nation: it represents a natural link, a spontaneous affinity. France is a place of great contrasts. These contrasts gave birth to an idea and an understanding and philosophy of the principles of liberty which are now the grounding of modern Europe...'

'La France est beaucoup plus qu'une nation aux portes de la maison: c'est un lieu naturel, c'est une affinité spontanée. La France est une terre de grands contrastes. De ces contrastes sont nées une idée et une pratique de la liberté qui constituent les fondements de l'Europe moderne...'

Giovanni Agnelli

*O*verview

France is a very cosmopolitan country... used to dealing with varied cultures. It's got a rich history.... It welcomes diversity. It welcomes challenge.'

J T Battenberg

With 550,000 square kilometres (212,300 square miles) for 63.8 million inhabitants, metropolitan France has industrial centres and agricultural land, fishing and sailing ports, commercial towns and tourist sites. Blessed by nature, France has oaks and olive trees, apple and orange trees, and, in the course of the year, sun, rain, wind and snow. The landscape, the faces, and the accents vary from north to south, and from east to west, and these variations give the country its natural charm and personality.

Today, France is a place where innovation goes with tradition. Both the economy and cultural life are facing the future, with cultural references being paired with industry or technology. For an example, see the delivery of beaujolais wine by TGV.

According to Paul Morand, 'our Hexagon is only understood when seen in context', as it is surrounded by six countries – Belgium, Germany, Italy, Luxembourg, Spain and Switzerland – and by the principalities of Andorra and Monaco. France is linked with Great Britain by the Channel Tunnel.

French territory extends beyond the Hexagon and a little of France can be found in all four corners of the world – Guadeloupe, Martinique, the Reunion Islands, French Guyana have the status of both *départements* and *régions*. (Kourou, in French Guyana, has been the space station for the Ariane space programme since 1979.) New Caledonia, St Pierre-et-Miquelon, sui generis collectivity, French Polynesia, Wallis and Futuna, and Mayotte, are the *Collectivités d'Outre-mer* (the overseas territories), while the Kerguelen Archipelago and the Terre Adélie in Antarctica are French research bases where a handful of researchers and military personnel live. Overseas territories are part of the French Republic but not of the EU.

'France is like a stamp; it is all torn around the edges on the seaside.' (Edouard, age nine.) There are 3,200 kilometres (2,000 miles) of coastline dotted with islands sheltering commercial, fishing and recreational ports. Swimmers may bathe in the North Sea and the English Channel, known for their big tides; in the Atlantic Ocean with its huge waves; or in the deliciously warm Mediterranean, which also embraces the island of Corsica. For those who love the mountains, enjoying both summer and winter sports, there are the Alps, with the highest peak in Europe (Mont Blanc at 4,810 metres), the Jura, the Vosges, the Massif Central and the Pyrénées. All offer many opportunities for hiking and skiing. Most of the big cities are less than two hours from the sea or from the mountains... or both. There are 960,000 kilometres of roads, of which 11,000 kilometres are motorways.

In the 1960s, the need for development often took precedence over any concern for the environment. Power lines, railways, motorways, gigantic *HLM* (*habitation à loyer modéré*) low-cost housing projects and numerous commercial centres sprang up – heedless of the urban planning or architectural standards that are common today.

Since then, the French have become more aware of the need to protect their country's natural resources. The fight against pollution, the preservation of areas of natural beauty and the improvement of the urban environment are now important priorities. Long-term development is not only a trend, it should influence the actions to take in all aspects of daily life. Consumer habits, health and security make new regulations necessary in industry, energy, transportation, agriculture and tourism. The 'Greens' and the ecologists are watching.

*F*rench institutions

Presidential power and the parliamentary regime

French political institutions are governed by the Constitution of the Fifth Republic, drafted by General de Gaulle and ratified by the citizens of France on 28 September 1958. The Constitution states that 'France is a democratic and social Republic, indivisible and secular, and that national sovereignty belongs to the people who exercise it through their elected representatives and by referendum.' Over the last 50 years it has been revised 24 times in keeping with the evolution of the country.

Secularity: laïcité

Freedom of religion is a constitutional right according to the Declaration of the Rights of Man and of the Citizen, and the French Republic is a secular state. It ensures the equality of all citizens before the law without distinction of origin or religion, and respects all beliefs.

Since Clovis (465–511), France has had a strong Roman Catholic religion and tradition. There is at least one church per commune, and there are 95 cathedrals. According to a study (*La Vie* magazine, 2007) Catholics make up about 64 per cent of the population, while 3 per cent follow Islam, 2 per cent are Protestant and 1 per cent Jewish, with small numbers of other faiths. Of the French citizens who responded, 27 per cent said they were atheists. The harmonious integration of all religions in France has been based on what the French call 'laïcité'. The 1905 law imposes separation between state and church, considering religion as a private domain. However Alsace and Moselle, which were part of Germany from 1871 until 1919, have kept a religious regime. Public education throughout France is free and secular. A new law in 2004 confirms this principle. The banning of religious apparel helps to preserve equality between children of all cultures.

The three elements of the state are independent

- legislative power – Parliament legislates;

- executive power – the President of the Republic and the government apply the law;

- judicial power – magistrates sanction violations of the law. There are three types of court: civil, criminal and specialized.

The President of the Republic, as head of state, is the centre of the political system and governs the country. He appoints the Prime Minister, who in turn names his government's ministers.

Parliament is made up of the *Assemblée Nationale* (577 deputies at the Palais Bourbon), and the *Sénat* (321 senators at the Luxembourg Palace). The principle is the separation of powers between the executive and legislative branches. The head of state may dissolve the *Assemblée Nationale* if it goes against the policy of the government, and return the deputies to their electors. The *Assemblée Nationale* may censure the government.

Presided over by the head of state, the Conseil des Ministres meets every Wednesday in the Murat Salon at the Elysée, 55 rue du Faubourg St Honoré, 75008 Paris. This has been the President's residence since 1873. Nicolas Sarkozy was elected the sixth President of the Fifth French Republic in May 2007 for five years.

▬ *Vive la République, Vive la France*

Traditionally, the President of the Republic addresses the French on 31 December at 8 pm in order to wish them a happy new year. On 14 July for Bastille Day after the traditional military parade on the Champs Elysées he gives a Garden Party at the Elysée Palace and receives elected guests. His speech starts with 'My dear compatriots' and ends with 'Long live the Republic, long live France'.

▬ *The 'watchdogs'* – des institutions de contrôle

- The *Conseil Constitutionnel* judges the constitutionality of the laws and may suggest legislative or administrative reforms of general interest. It also monitors the elections. Its lofty responsibilities confer the title of *Sage* on the nine members. All former presidents of the Republic automatically become members.

- The *Conseil d'Etat* supreme administrative court resolves conflicts between individuals and the state services. It is the court of final recourse.

- The *Cour des Comptes* monitors, and exposes, irregularities in public spending.

- Protocol establishes the following hierarchy among state officials: President of the Republic, the President of the Sénat, the President of the Assemblée Nationale, the Prime Minister.

▬ *The advisers* – institutions consultatives

The *Conseil Economique et Social* (CES) is consulted on important economic and social questions. It reports to the government the various positions taken by its component socio-professional groups (unions, industry, associations and other qualified groups).

The Haute Autorité de lutte contre la discrimination et pour l'egalité (HALDE) is dedicated to fighting for equality and against discrimination. This organization has an investigative power and an informative role in the seizure of justice.

▬ *From the Assemblée Nationale*

Since 1995, Parliament has met for a single annual session. It opens on the first working day of October and closes on the last day of June. The number of session days is limited to 120; however, the President of the Republic may call for an extraordinary session.

Assemblée Nationale sessions are open to the public and there are seats reserved for the first 10 people to arrive at the Palais Bourbon. Places may also be reserved by post.

The daily *Journal Officiel* ('JO'), www.journal.officiel.gouv.fr, publishes the laws and decrees and the full text of parliamentary debates.

There are live television broadcasts of the questions put to the government by members of parliament during the Wednesday session. The debates are passionate and the atmosphere in the *hémicycle* (the semi-circular hall in which the debates are held) is often boisterous when sensitive subjects, such as the budget (or the finance law) are broached; on the other hand, the hall becomes a little sleepy, even deserted, when the topics discussed are mundane. The deputies perhaps prefer to return to their constituencies and

---

THE SYMBOLS OF THE RÉPUBLIQUE FRANÇAISE

- The blue, white and red flag (three vertical stripes): in 1789, Lafayette had white (the colour of the royal flag) added to the blue and red rosette of the Garde Nationale of Paris, thereby creating the tricolour flag inspired by the three colours of freedom chosen by the young states of America. The 'tricolor' flies at official ceremonies.

- The letters 'RF' for the République Française.

- The motto 'Liberté, Egalité, Fraternité', which reflects the Republican philosophy of the Age of Enlightenment. These three words are engraved on the front of public buildings. 'Liberty' is written in the Constitution, 'Equality' in the Civil Code, while 'Fraternity' brings to these legal notions the idea of solidarity.

- The *Marseillaise* has been the national anthem since 14 July 1795. In 1792, Rouget de Lisle called it the 'Battle hymn of the Army of the Rhine'.

- The *Quatorze Juillet* is the national holiday that commemorates the taking of the Bastille (14 July 1789) and the celebration of the Fédération (14 July 1790).

- *Marianne* is the source of inspiration of the République; there is a bust of her in all town halls. Her image also appears on postage stamps and euro coins.

other functions. A law reducing the number of elected offices held by one person is currently under consideration.

The official logo

The country's symbolic colours of red, white and blue; the symbol of the Republic, Marianne and the national motto Liberty, Equality, Fraternity have been combined to create a logo for the French government and its various ministries and services.

The practice of naming an 'unofficial Marianne' is contested by most mayors in France, who refuse to acknowledge stars as Marianne, arguing that they don't represent the country's civic values.

THE COQ

- The 'coq' is part of the insignia of the French people – it was a nickname given by the Romans, *gallus* meaning both *gaulois* (France was formally Gaul) and 'cock'. It appears on the Seal of the République. The *Grille du Coq* is the gate that opens on to the Elysée Palace. The cock, a symbol of vigilance, is also the official emblem of the French sports teams in international competition. It is also on the weather vanes of all the steeples of France, watching for the sunrise to herald the country's liberty.

The political parties

The idea of political parties being on the 'Left' or the 'Right' came about at the time of the French Revolution. The Monarchy's defenders sat to the right of the President of the Assemblée Constituante (1789), while the opponents sat on the left and, in time, Left and Right assumed their current political symbolism. The Constitution recognizes a multi-party system.

The French citizen and elections

'Elire c'est choisir' ('to elect is to choose') – the revolutionaries of 1789 celebrated 'the universality of the Rights of Man and of the citizen', but universal suffrage was not established until much later, when the political rights of every man were recognized in a free and equal manner.

French women did not have the vote until 1945, and are still too rare on the political stage in France. In 1996, Laurent Fabius said, 'It is easier to give your place to a woman on the bus than at the Assemblée Nationale.' During the legislative elections of 16 June 2007, only 107 of the 577 deputies elected were women (18.5 per cent), yet 53 per cent of the French electorate are women and the words for the symbols that define France are feminine (*la République*: republic; *Marianne; la liberté*; *la fraternité*; and *la solidarité*)!

Every French citizen, aged 18 and over, who is a registered voter in his or her community, has the right, the liberty and the duty to vote. Automatic registration is forbidden because voting is a free civil act.

In cities with more than 3,500 inhabitants, the law of 6 June 2000 institutes the equality principle (parité). This means that women have an equal access to the elections. In 2008, 48.53 per cent of women were elected in local elections, including mayors.

THE MAIN PARTIES

- La Droite (The Right)
  UMP (Union pour un Mouvement Populaire)
  MoDEM (Mouvement Démocrate) Nouveau Centre
- La Gauche (The Left)
  PS (Parti Socialiste)
  PRG (Parti Radical de Gauche)
  PC (Parti Communiste)
  Les Verts (The Greens)

Both left and right extremists also have their own political parties.

FRENCH ELECTIONS

- Elections take place by direct universal suffrage: the elector votes him- or herself (or by proxy) for the candidate of his or her choice.

- Only senators are elected indirectly: the voters are representatives, who are themselves elected; these are the 'big voters'.

- Voting day is always a Sunday. The length of the mandate varies:

	ELECTIONS	length mandate	2007	2008	2009	2010
Commune	**Municipal elections** Conseil Municipal and Maire	5 ans		X		
Départements	**District election– Cantonales** Conseiller Général	6 ans	Renewable by third			
Régions	**Regional elections** Conseiller Général	6 ans				X
	Senatorial elections Sénateur	6 ans	Indirect election ('big voters')			
Etat	**Legislative elections** Député	5 ans	X			
	Presidential elections Président de la République	5 ans 'Quinquennat'	X			
Union Européenne	**European elections** Député Européen	5 ans			X	

The French may also be consulted by referendum: the first took place in 1791. There have been 10 referendums since the beginning of the Fifth Republic in 1958. The most recent ones date back to 2000 (regarding the reduction of the presidential mandate, which resulted in its reduction from seven years to five) and 2005 (refusing the ratification of the European Constitution).

In some French towns, representatives of foreign nationals have been permitted to sit on the town council and to be consulted on certain questions, without having the right to vote. The right to vote and the eligibility of foreigners at local and European elections are in effect in France but only for European Union (EU) members living in France. They were able to vote in the elections of the European parliament. In the municipal elections in March 2008, 244 Europeans were elected.

*D*iplomatic relations

Embassies were created to establish dialogue and develop relations between nations. Until 1914, French was the diplomatic language of Europe. The French Ministry of Foreign Affairs currently has 160 embassies, 21 diplomatic missions and 97 consulates throughout the world. In return, 160 foreign countries are represented in France by an embassy (192 countries are represented in ONU in 2008).

The ambassador is the representative of the President of the Republic, the government and all the ministries, attached to a foreign head of state, and charged with coordinating French activities in the country of residence. His or her administration is responsible for sending political, economic and social information to the French Ministry of Foreign Affairs, so that it may effectively pursue international policies.

An embassy may have cultural (services of cooperation and cultural actions) and scientific services; a service that deals with military affairs, under the authority of the Minister of Defence; and a post for economic expansion responsible for promoting French exports, which is under the direction of the Ministry of Economy and Finance.

The consulate, or the consular service of the embassy, is responsible for the French community residing in the host country. The consul keeps records on the population under his or her protection, and functions as the registrar for official documents (birth, marriage, divorce, and death certificates, and so on). He or she also monitors requests from foreigners wishing to enter France and delivers the necessary visas after they have been processed in France.

In addition to the diplomatic services, '*Cultures France*' is the agency responsible for international cultural exchanges. The French Institutes, the Cultural Centres and the *Alliance Française* form a unique network which diffuses and circulates French language and culture. They are meeting places for all those who wish to learn about France prior to their arrival, or who wish to keep in touch with France after they leave.

More than 400 French schools and lycees are managed by L'AEFE (Agence de l'enseigement Français à l'étranger) and the MLF (Mission Laïque Française).

JOURNALISTS' JARGON

When you hear, or read in the press, that diplomats go to the 'Quai d'Orsay', they are referring to the Ministry of Foreign Affairs; 'Hexagone' means France; 'Elysée' refers to the President's residence, 'Matignon' is the Prime Minister's residence, where by tradition he plants a tree when he takes office; 'Quai des Orfèvres' is the police headquarters; 'Bercy' is the Ministry of Economy and Finance; 'Place Vendôme' is the Ministry of Justice; 'Place Beauvau' is the Ministry of the Interior; 'Palais Brongniart' is the Bourse, or Stock Exchange; 'la dame de fer' ('the iron lady') is the Eiffel Tower; 'la ville lumière' is Paris; 'la ville rose' is Toulouse and 'la grande bleu' is the Mediterranean (la Méditerranée).

---

*F*rance's population in numbers

INSEE (the National Institute for Statistical and Economic Studies) has regularly conducted a population census since 1946. The French population is estimated to be 63.8 million inhabitants for 200,000 square kilometres (77,200 square miles) of inhabitable

POPULATION: 63.8 MILLION FRENCH PEOPLE

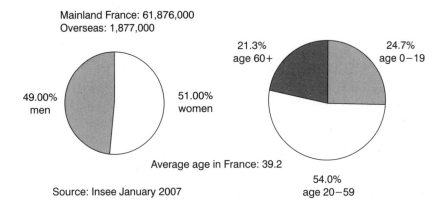

Mainland France: 61,876,000
Overseas: 1,877,000

49.00% men

51.00% women

21.3% age 60+

24.7% age 0−19

54.0% age 20−59

Average age in France: 39.2

Source: Insee January 2007

area (the total area is 550,000 square kilometres, or 212,300 square miles). Over half of these live in cities.

The French abroad

There are almost 2 million French citizens living abroad (60 per cent in Europe, 19 per cent in America and 5.3% in Asia and Oceania). Most of them are temporary expatriates for international companies. They are represented by the *Conseil Supérieur des Français de l'étranger* who elect 12 Senators sitting at the *Sénat* in Paris.

> 'The French myth has not only served to enchant man's imagination, it has defended, protected, and sometimes saved him.'
> Bernanos

The French at home

A diverse mixture of people is part of the history of France. The country of the Declaration of the Rights of Man of 1789 (inspired by the United States) has welcomed many foreigners.

At the beginning of the 20th century, immigration was a political factor: the Russians fled the 1917 Revolution; the Central European Jewish and Italians fled Mussolini's dictatorship and the Spanish fled the Civil War.

Southern Europeans, Nordics and Slavs have been absorbed into the French population over the generations. After the two world wars, the need for manpower led to increased immigration. In the 1960s, workers from the Maghreb (Algeria, Morocco, Tunisia) came in response to the needs of the industrialized regions. Despite a tumultuous history, links with North Africa and other African countries instigated the arrival of French speakers within the Hexagon. More recently, there has been increased economic immigration from Asia. The immigrants have mostly settled in the region of Ile-de-France.

About 130 different nationalities live in France; since the economic oil crisis of 1974 immigration has been tightly controlled. French Republican values have always eased the integration of foreigners. However, unemployment and housing remain a major problem for the second and third generation of French young people born of foreign parents.

'France could play a unique intermediary role in avoiding a clash between the West and Islam, which is the great challenge of the next 30 years.'
Theodore Zeldin (quoted by Thomas Sancton in *Time*, Dec 1995)

CITÉ NATIONALE DE L'HISTOIRE DE L'IMMIGRATION (CNHI)

The National Centre of the History of Immigration in Paris is a multi-purpose centre dedicated to the culture of immigrants. 'They made France' and 'Their history is our history' are the leitmotifs of the place which recognizes and spreads knowledge of the contribution of immigration to French society.

'France shows its true tricolour nature thought its multi-colour make up. With its Zidane, and before then Offenbach, Picasso, Kopa or Mimoun, Marie Curie or Félix Eboué.'
Jean-François Kahn

THE BIGGEST CITIES AND URBAN AREAS

Dépt	Ville	Population Ville	Aire Urbaine
75	Paris	2,153,600	11,174,800
13	Marseille	820,900	1,516,340
69	Lyon	466,400	1,648,200
32	Toulouse	435,000	964,800
6	Nice	347,900	933,100
44	Nantes	281,800	711,120
67	Strasbourg	272,700	612,100
34	Montpellier	244,300	460,000
59	Lille	225,100	1,143,125
33	Bordeaux	230,600	925,300
35	Rennes	209,900	521,200
76	Le Havre	184,000	296,800
51	Reims	184,800	291,740
42	Saint Etienne	175,700	321,700
83	Toulon	166,800	564,830
49	Angers	152,700	332,625
29	Brest	145,200	303,500
38	Grenoble	156,800	514,600
21	Dijon	150,800	326,630
72	Le Mans	144,500	293,200
63	Clermont Ferrand	140,700	410,000
37	Tours	136,600	376,400
76	Rouen	109,600	520,000
57	Metz	124,500	429,600
45	Orleans	113,500	355,810
54	Nancy	105,400	410,500
14	Caen	109,200	370,900

In 36,780 communes France has 37 cities of over 100,000 inhabitants. There are fewer than 1,000 inhabitants in 31,678 of French villages.

'The invention of France is a process of making a nation from varied and contradictory elements' and 'as long as there is diversity, France will be condemned to tolerance.'
H Le Bras and E Todd

'France is the most "Latin" of the countries of the north, the most "Nordic" of the countries of the south.'
Claude Legros

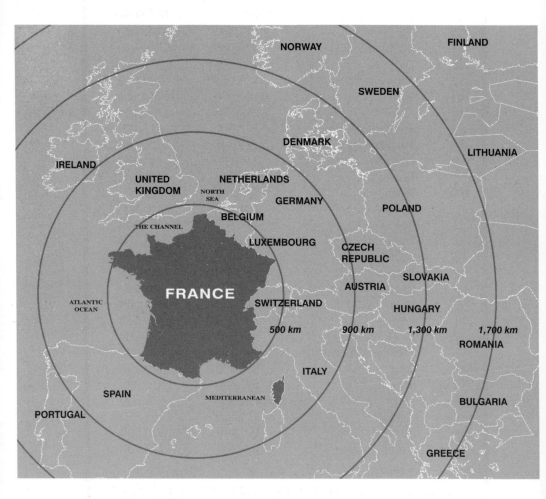

Source: Invest in France

It is not enough to arm oneself with a compass or a GPS to find a commune in France among the total of 36,780. It's also important to be aware of similar and identical names. For example, *Aube* is my village in the department of *Orne* in *Normandy*, and *Aube* is also a village in Moselle and a department in *Champagne*. There are 240 villages called Saint Martin. It is therefore wise to ask for the exact address, including the name of the department and the region.

French and also European

> *'For peace to really have a chance, there must first be a Europe.'*
> Jean Monnet

Creation of a united Europe

As a result of Jean Monnet's initiative, the idea of a united Europe was conceived in France on 9 May 1950, and confirmed in Rome on 25 March 1957.

The countries of the EU are creating a fellowship of European interests in response to worldwide political, social and economic challenges. They have transferred specific powers to the European level. The search for unity in diversity is also a real challenge.

Norway and Switzerland have refused the offer to enter the EU for the moment. Other East European countries are knocking at the door, and cultural, economic and political rapprochements are under way, gradually reconstructing the geographical area of Europe.

> *'Europe will not be made in a day... It will be made by concrete accomplishments, by first forming a fellowship...'*
> Robert Schuman

EUROPEAN UNION MEMBER STATES: STEP BY STEP

25.03. 1957	6	Germany (D) €	Belgium (B) €
		France (F) €	Italy (I) €
		Luxembourg (L) €	Netherlands (NL) €
1.01. 1973	9	Denmark (D)	Ireland (IRL) €
		United Kingdom (GB)	
01.01. 1981	10	Greece (GR) €	
01.01. 1986	12	Portugal (P) €	Spain (E) €
1990	12	Reunification of Germany	
01.01. 1995	15	Austria (A) €	Finland (FIN), €
		Sweden (S)	
01.05. 2004	25	Cyprus (CY) €	Estonia (EST)
		Hungary (H)	Latvia (LV)
		Lithuania (LT)	Malta (M) €
		Poland (PL)	Czech Republic (CZ)
		Slovakia (SK)	Slovenia (SLO) €
01.01. 2007	27	Bulgaria (BG)	Romania (RO)

Schengen area underlined + EEA + Swiss

(D) International registration plates

€   15 Euro countries

1950: 6 pm on 9 May, in the Salon de l'Horloge, Quai d'Orsay, Paris, the Minister of Foreign Affairs, Robert Schuman, announces that together France and Germany wish to create a peaceful Europe.

1957: The six founders (Belgium, France, Germany, Holland, Italy, Luxembourg) sign the Treaty of Rome, the birth certificate of the EEC (European Economic Community). The first industrial co-operation agreement and the unification of agricultural prices agreement are concluded. It is the only international treaty in which the word 'ideal' is written.

1968: The Customs Union is decided between these six.

1974: The decision to elect a European Assembly by universal suffrage is taken, and the first election is held in June 1979. Simone Veil is the first President.

1986: The 12 sign the Single European Act of political, economic and monetary union. They agree to create a Single European Market in 1993.

1992: The Treaty of Maastricht creates a political entity and the European Community (EC) becomes the European Union (EU). The creation of a single currency is decided.

1993: 1 January of this year signals the opening of a market without borders within the Union.

1998: Birth of the single European currency, the 'euro', and the naming of the 'Euroland' countries.

The euro is used in public accounting and in business in 1999 and for citizens in 2000.

2004, June: election of the European Parliament (732 deputies, 78 for France).

2007, 13 December: The Treaty of Lisbon, effective on 1 January, is ratified (instead of the EU Constitution).

'Come on, buck up, Europe's springtime is still before us.'

'Allons, courage, le printemps de l'Europe est toujours devant nous.'
Jacques Delors

Benefits and challenges

'Old Europe happens to have new ideas: the euro currency.'

The major European event of the third millennium is the passage from national currencies to a single currency: the euro. In 2008, 15 of the 27 countries are boarding the euro train. Denmark, Sweden and Great Britain have decided to 'wait and see'.

Since 4 January 1999, the euro has been used in public accounting and in business, and since January 2002 we have had the coins and the banknotes in our pockets. Europe, with 494 million inhabitants, is no doubt becoming a dynamic region in the world.

'A priori, the Euro should not have worked... but so much effort was made that it can no longer fail.'
Henry Kissinger

A European citizen may retain his or her own nationality. Citizens of the Member States are free to work, settle, study, and move between the countries of the EU. Nationals from Bulgaria and Romania will remain liable to hold a resident's permit during a transition period, should they wish to exercise an economic activity in France. The free movement of capital, products and services still needs a legal structure to harmonize the European social and fiscal laws. There is so much wealth and so many ideas, but there are also problems to share if the Union is to succeed. Although each country is distinct from the others, the 27 countries are sufficiently alike to be complementary.

EUROPEAN UNION COUNTRIES

Countries	Code ISO	Area 1000 km²	Population million
Austria – Österreich	AT	84	8.2
Belgium – Belgïe Belgique	BE	31	10.6
Bulgaria – Balgarija	BG	111	7.7
Cyprus – Kunpoç-Kibris	CY	9	0.8
Czech Republic – Ceska Republik	CZ	79	10.3
Denmark – Dammark	DK	43	5.4
Estonia – Eesti	EE	45	1.3
Finland – Suomi	FI	337	5.3
France – France	FR	544	63.8
Germany – Deutschland	DE	357	82.4
Greece	GR	132	11.2
Hungary – Magyarorszag	HU	93	10.1
Ireland – Eire	IE	70	4.3
Italy – Italia	IT	301	59.0
Latvia – Latvija	LV	65	2.2
Lithuania – Lietuva	LT	65	3.4
Luxembourg – Luxembourg	LU	3	0.5
Malta	MT	0.3	0.4
Poland – Polska	PL	313	38.1
Portugal – Portugal	PT	92	10.3
Romania – România	RO	238	21.5
Slovakia – Slovensko	SK	40	5.4
Slovenia – Slovenia	SI	20	2.0
Spain – Espana	ES	505	44.5
Sweden – Sverige	SE	411	9.1
The Netherlands – Nederland	NL	41	16.3
United Kingdom	GB	244	60.1
27 European Union countries	EU	**4,189**	**485.9**
Russia	RU	17,075	142.0
China	CN	9,597	1,320.0
India	IN	3,287	1,110.0
Japan	JP	378	127.0
United States	US	9,373	302.0

The Schengen Agreement

Signed in Luxembourg in 1985, the Schengen Agreement brought about the gradual abolition of border checks at the common frontiers of European Member States. The Schengen Information System (SIS), based in Strasbourg, is a secured database system used by European countries for maintaining and distributing information related to border security and law enforcement.

'Europe is too big to be united. But too small to be divided. Her double destiny lies there.'
Daniel Faucher

'Europe is like a multinational country.'
Jean-Noël, age 13

'Europe is a family. As with all families… we embrace, we argue, we turn our backs but we always speak the same language.'
Marc Fumaroli

The European Economic Area (EEA)

The EEA was established between the EU and the European Free Trade Association member countries (EFTA) – composed of Iceland, Liechtenstein, Norway and Switzerland – in order to preserve economic and commercial relations under conditions of equal competition.

The Council of Europe

The EU is not to be confused with the Council of Europe, created in 1949. That international organization, with headquarters in Strasbourg, numbers 47 Member States, and defends democracy and the Rights of Man; their actions contribute to the cooperation between all the nations on the European continent.

EUROPEAN SYMBOLS

- The *flag of Europe*, chosen by the Council of Europe in 1955, shows a circle of 12 golden stars on an azure background (the number 12 represents harmony). It was adopted by the EEC in 1986 and now flies alongside the national flags of the EU countries.

- The EU passport is a *bordeaux* colour and bears the name of the country of origin. At airports, there is a queue reserved for EU travellers. •

- The European *anthem* is an adaptation of the prelude to Beethoven's Ninth Symphony, the 'Ode to Joy'.

- From 2002, the euro will be issued in eight special coins for each country and seven banknotes, which will be used by the 'Euroland' countries plus their overseas territories and Andorra, Monaco, San Marino and the Vatican City. The euro logo '€' is inspired both by the Greek letter ipsilon and the letter 'E' from Europe.

- The *motto* chosen from the 80,000 suggestions submitted by young Europeans is: 'Unity in diversity' (adopted on 4 May 2000 at the European Parliament in Strasbourg).

- *Brussels, Luxembourg* and *Strasbourg* are the three capitals of the EU. The Palace of Europe at Strasbourg is the seat of the Council of Europe and the site of the European Parliament; the seat of the European Commission is in Brussels. *Frankfurt* houses the European Central Bank.

- The *Official Journal of the European Communities* (*OJEC*) is the organ of the European Union. It is published in the 11 official languages of the Union.

- *Europe Day* is 9 May, commemorating 9 May 1950, the day when Robert Schuman, French Minister of Foreign Affairs, announced the agreement with Germany, thereby making official the creation of Europe.

International organizations

OECD and UNESCO have their headquarters in Paris:

● OECD (Organization for Economic Cooperation and Development), created in 1960, coordinates the economic and social policies of its 30 Member States in order to help developing countries.

● UNESCO (United Nations Organization for Education, Science and Culture), created in 1946, unites 188 countries in their efforts to maintain peace among nations through education, science and culture.

● UNO – France and the UK are the only EU permanent members of the Security Council (with the right of veto). France participates in many peacekeeping operations under the UN flag with the 'casques bleus' and supports development actions such as child protection initiated by UNICEF.

G8

The most powerful industrial nations of the world belong to this club, created in 1975 by Valéry Giscard d'Estaing (former President of France) and Helmut Schmidt (former Chancellor of Germany). At first five countries made up the group, then it grew to seven: Canada, France, Germany, Great Britain, Italy, Japan and the United States, and with Russia there are now eight. They meet once a year to debate economic and political world questions. The President of the European Commission is an observer. In 2008 the G8 took place in Hokkaido, Japan.

*A*n economic point of view

'Your outstanding technology, your industrial advances, your scientists are overshadowed by your foie gras *complex.'*
Richard Bernstein

It is common knowledge that France, the world's fifth largest economy and the most popular tourist destination, has an enviable reputation for the three Cs: *culture, couture* and *cuisine*, which can be found among French noblesse and French postcards. Today, due to economic competition, we have to 'dot our "I"' with innovation, invention and imagination. As a result, the French and Europeans have a proven record in the fields of aerospace, aeronautics, car manufacture, robotics and electronics. The following are some of their prominent achievements:

- The chip card (memory card) invented by Roland Moreno has become an international visiting card.

- The 343 metre-high Millau viaduct, in the area of Roquefort, is the highest in the world.

- The Airbus A380, assembled in Toulouse, is a rare European bird.

- The *Queen Mary II*, a 345 metre-long cruise liner built at the Chantiers de l'Atlantique shipyard, is a true floating island.

- Ariane 5, the biggest communication satellite in the world, went into orbit launched off French Guyana.

- GALILEO, the European system capable of localizing to a distance of 1 m, enables civilian and military control of road, rail, maritime and air traffic.

- ITER is a European scientific research project on energy for the future.

- The TGV (high-speed train) launched in 1981 is a phenomenal success. France holds the world speed record (574.8 km/h achieved in June 2007).

- The Thalys train has linked Paris, Brussels, Amsterdam and Cologne since 1994.

- The Eurostar travels between Paris and London, via the Channel Tunnel, in two and a quarter hours.

- The Channel Tunnel is 49.31 km long, of which 38 km is under the sea.

▬▬Awards

France has always had strong links with the sciences, physics, chemistry, mathematics and information technology. Twelve French people have received the Nobel Prize for physics. Albert Fert shared his prize with Peter Gründberg, a German scientist, in 2007.

The Fields medal is the Nobel prize for discipline, awarded every four years to brilliant mathematicians under 40 years old. Since its creation by the Canadian John Charles Fields, 44 prizes have been awarded, 9 of which were given to French nationals, notably to Laurent Lafforgue in 2002 and to Wendelin Werner in 2006.

Alexis Lemaire, who is 27 years old and from Champagne, became the world mental arithmetic champion in New York on 11 December 2007. Like a sportsman in training, he exercises his fantastic memory for several hours every day.

The Nobel prize for chemistry was awarded to Yves Chauvin who shared the honour with two Americans, Robert Grubbs and Richard Schrock, who further pioneered his discovery in the area of medicines and plastics. Joseph Sifakis, the French computer scientist, was laureat of the 2007 Turing Award (the Nobel prize for computer science).

In 2008, Leopold Eyharts, who was born in Biarritz, completed his second space shuttle mission aboard the Atlantis where he joined the International Space Station (ISS) to carry out research for the European Space Agency (ESA).

THE STORY OF THE METRIC SYSTEM

The search for a common metric system is the story of an amazing scientific collaboration. This adventure began in France during the Enlightenment, following the French Revolution.

Over the years, physicists, mathematicians and astronomers searched intensely for the formula which would 'bring back all measures to one taken from nature'. Such a system would not belong to any one nation, but would be adopted by all – or almost all. The earth would be the ideal reference and would represent the universal dimension hoped for.

Competitive advantages of the Hexagon

The largest EU country, France is well located, enjoys wide open spaces and has a necessarily vast communications infrastructure. Its rail and road network is the most extensive in Europe; its telecommunications system is highly efficient and the cost of energy affordable.

For centuries, France has enlarged its presence abroad developing new markets. One job in four is related to export. At the same time, the country is the third most popular place for foreign investment (according to OECD), and promotes this fact to welcome international companies and their expatriates. Foreign investors appreciate the skills of French workers, the level of research and the high technology. The hourly productivity in France is one of the highest in the world. Could this be a French paradox?

Innovation, research, training are the key words of competitiveness. These goals have driven different regions to create 'technopoles' and 'clusters' (*pôles de compétitivité*) bringing together academic, industrial and business expertise.

Working closely together with public and private organizations and all economic partners, the Invest in France Agency (Afii), the CIDAT (Regional Planning Committee), Chambers of Commerce and Industry, and economic expansion committees, these high-tech centres are at the heart of a dynamic local appeal.

The projects granted the 'competitive cluster' label cover technological fields such as nanotechnologies, microelectronics and aeronautics. Certain areas of France are world leaders in particular fields, notably Toulouse and Bordeaux in aeronautics, Lyon in healthcare, Grenoble in communications. Paris is a leader in visual and multimedia fields, and numeric systems or complex computer programs.

SOPHIA ANTIPOLIS: THE PIONEER

Silicon Valley in California was the first area to develop the concept of high-tech centres. Based on this model, in the middle of Mediterranean pines, Sophia Antipolis has brought high-tech to the Riviera-Côte d'Azur. It is the biggest such centre in Europe. Industrialists, researchers and students of almost 70 different nationalities have been busily inventing the future there for the last 30 years.

'The 5,700 acre Sophia Antipolis Park is home to 1,200 companies employing 23,000 people. Who would have thought? The Riviera: no glitz, just serious technology.'
Christopher Dickey, *Newsweek*, 2001

━━━ *The heart of France*

The IGN (the French National Geographic Institute), after careful calculation, has placed the centre of France; its location is claimed by several villages. For the IGN, the heart of France (not counting Corsica) is at Vesdun, in the department of Cher (18). Calculating the centre with Corsica included would mean that Nassigny, in the department of Allier (03), is the winner.

In 1891, France ran according to Paris Mean Time. It was by measuring the distance of the Paris Meridian (Dunkirk to Barcelona) that French cartographers created the metre, 'a measure for all men and for all times' (Condorcet). In 1911, universal mean time was fixed to Greenwich Mean Time. As one of the proposals to celebrate the year 2000, Paul Chemetov imagined an extraordinary natural monument: a 'green meridian' of trees, in a line from Dunkirk in the north, to Prats de Mollo in the south. With oak trees in the north and olive trees in the south, this 1,200 km long natural wonder would pass through 336 communes – that is to say, 20 *départements* and eight *régions*. The new trees are growing and, because the French are fond of food, they organize a 'Republic picnic' on 14 July which runs along the green meridian.

22 metropolitan regions

France has almost forgotten the names of its old provinces and now refers to 'territorial collectivities'. The country is made up of 22 regions composed of two to eight departments (see the maps on page 65). The French use the term *province* to describe any place that is not in Paris or its suburbs. (Parisians often say that they are spending the weekend '*en province*', regardless of their actual regional destination.)

In the 1800s, Napoléon created a highly centralized administrative structure. Since 1982, the catchword has been 'decentralization'. Each region promotes its own economic, social, sanitary and cultural activities, in conjunction with its departments and communes.

Part of the regional affairs are conducted by an elected *Council Regional* and its president. The regional Prefect, named by the council of ministers, represents the state and implements the government's economic and social policies. The partnership between state and region reinforces decentralization, while maintaining the equity and unity of the territory.

Unequal in size and resources, the regions include areas that are rich in manpower, industrial or agricultural resources, as well as areas that are arid and uninhabited, or are the location for traditional manufacturing sectors that are in transition to alternate uses. Their resources come in part from local taxes (property taxes, professional taxes and house taxes).

'France, thy name is Diversity.'
'La France se nomme diversité.'
Fernand Braudel

■ *A quick look at the French regions*

Each region is different, but, stimulated by European competition, all are showing genuine political and economic vigour. Each has had to learn to capitalize on its experience and to develop and market its special resources – quality of life and friendliness, unique geographic location, access to transportation networks, a qualified workforce, educational and research capabilities, national monuments, culture and tourist sites and so on.

French people have a real attachment to their region. When two people from Normandy meet, they tell stories about Normandy.

Regional councils and inhabitants were asked to describe their region in a few words, including economic or technological characteristics, geographic or tourist sites, historical events, famous literary, artistic or political personalities, gourmet specialities and professional or traditional crafts museums. The results are on pages 67–70.

22 METROPOLITAN REGIONS

96 DEPARTMENTS OF THE HEXAGON

100 departments: *96 in the* Hexagon

*'The paradox is that this mosaic gave birth to Europe's most centralized state. The state affirms the unity of the Republic through its representatives (*préfets*) at department and commune level, through the public service and particularly the education system.'*
Armand Fremont

Over the centuries, France has indulged in a strange carving up of its land, and the country's departmental system now resembles no other territorial structure in Europe. The system of the *départements* was conceived after the Revolution; a department will often bear the name of the river or mountain range that crosses it.

The *Conseil Général* (general council) and its president govern the affairs of a department in an administrative *circonscription* – an intermediary between the region and the commune. Its powers are much the same as those of the *Conseil Régional* (regional council), mostly in the area of education, social services, tourism, environment, culture, youth and sports. The department is also the privileged financial partner in the commune's larger projects, including land development, building of amenities and so on.

Departmental revenues come from local taxes, state funding, and even the licences paid annually by car owners.

The state is represented in each department by a *Préfet* (Prefect), nominated by the Council of Ministers. The Prefect's mission is to apply the laws, to maintain public order, and to manage the public services that deal with administrative affairs (identity cards, passports, driving licences, temporary residence cards). The Prefect is the only civilian to wear a uniform during official ceremonies.

ALSACE

Bas-Rhin (67)   Haut-Rhin (68)
8,300 sq km   1,817,000 inhabitants

STRASBOURG

- capital of European Institutions
- the smallest region of France, but the third economically
- the Rhine is the link with Germany
- bilingual region
- land of the storks
- *choucroute* and beer
- Albert Schweitzer Frediric Bartholdi
- national automobile museum at Mulhouse

AQUITANE

Dordogne (24)   Gironde (33)
Landes (40)   Lot et Garonne (47)
Pyrénées-Atlantique (64)
41,300 sq km   3,100,000 inhabitants

BORDEAUX

- the wine capital, world heritage city, UNESCO
- the longest beach in France (the Atlantic)
- tourism and vineyards
- agribusiness
- the biggest coniferous forest in Europe
- Basque country and its beret
- wine, *foie gras*, truffles
- Montaigne, Montesquieu and Mauriac
- Aquitaine Museum

AUVERGNE

Allier (03)   Cantal (15)
Haute-Loire (43)   Puy de Dôme (63)
26,000 sq km   1,333,500 inhabitants

CLERMONT-FERRAND

- capital of rubber and plastic
- lakes and volcanoes (Massif Central)
- thermal springs
- agriculture
- *cantal* and *bleu d'Auvergne*
- gentian and chestnuts
- Vercingétorix, Lafayette, Pascal
- cutlery museum at Thiers

BOURGOGNE

Côte d'Or (21)   Nièvre (58)
Saône et Loire (71)   Yonne (89)
31,600 sq km   1,624,000 inhabitants

DIJON

- the mustard capital
- agriculture and prestigious vineyards
- iron and steel
- Lamartine
- Nicéphore-Niepce Museum (the inventor of photography – Chalon-sur-Saône)
- Roman buildings
- *cassis*, Bourgogne snails

BRETAGNE

Côtes-d'Armor (22)   Finistère (29)
Ille-et-Vilaine (35)   Morbihan (56)
27,200 sq km   3,100,000 inhabitants

RENNES

- telecoms capital
- sea and earth: two sources of wealth
- marine construction
- agriculture-food products
- birthplace of the Celts
- *crêpes* and cider
- Chateaubriand, Jacques Cartier
- Océanopolis (Brest)
- pleasure and fishing ports

CENTRE

Cher (18)   Eure-et-Loire (28)
Indre (36)   Indre-et-Loire (37)
Loir-et-Cher (41)   Loiret (45)
39,000 sq km   2,510,000 inhabitants

ORLEANS

- heart of France and Europe
- 'Cosmetic Valley'
- cereals: 'the bread basket of France'
- *tarte tatin*
- Rabelais, Georges Sand, Descartes
- nuclear energy museum (Chinon)
- ancient forest, hunting

CHAMPAGNE-ARDENNE

Ardennes (08)	Aube (10)
Marne (51)	Haute-Marne (52)
25,500 sq km	1,340,000 inhabitants

CHALONS-SUR-MARNE

- champagne (*Dom Pérignon* and *Veuve Cliquot*)
- forests, hunting, and wild boar
- textiles
- foundries
- Arthur Rimbaud, Général de Gaulle
- historical automobile centre (Reims)

CORSE

Corse-du-Sud (20A)	Haute-Corse (20B)
8,500 sq km	279,000 inhabitants

AJACCIO

- *Ile de Beauté*
- tourism
- between sea and *maquis*
- citrus fruits and chestnuts
- Napoléon Bonaparte
- sheep cheese (*brocciu*)
- Etnography museum (Bastia)

FRANCHE-COMTÉ

Doubs (25)	Haute-Saône (70)
Territoire de Belfort (90)	Jura (39)
16,200 sq km	1,146,000 inhabitants

BESANCON

- industrial identity: automobile, clocks, spectacles, toys
- mountains, forests and water
- the Jura mountain range
- cross-country skiing, ATV
- *vin jaune, vin de paille*
- Victor Hugo, Pasteur
- clock museum (Besançon)

ILE-DE-FRANCE

Paris (75)	Essone (91)
Hauts-de-Seine (92)	Seine-et-Marne (77)
Seine St. Denis (93)	Val d'Oise (95)
Val-de-Marne (94)	Yvelines (78)
12,000 sq km	11,492,000 inhabitants

PARIS

- the capital of France
- many company headquarters
- cultural and business tourism
- nature region: 20 per cent urban!
- birthplace of Gothic art
- *Paris-beurre!*
- Louis XIV, Gustave Eiffel, Edith Piaf
- air and space museum (le Bourget)

LANGUEDOC-ROUSSILLON

Aude (11)	Gard (30)
Hérault (34)	Lozère (48)
Pyrénnées-Orientales (66)	
27,000 sq km	2,252,000 inhabitants

MONTPELLIER

- oldest medical school
- today: Euro-medicine
- France's biggest vineyard
- salt, *le bœuf gardiane*
- *Occitanie* and *Catalogne*
- region of migration
- Pont du Gard (Roman ruin)
- Georges Brassens
- pharmacy museum (Montpellier)

LIMOUSIN

Corrèze (19)	Creuse (23)
Haute-Vienne (87)	
17,000 sq km	725,300 inhabitants

LIMOGES

- capital of porcelain, tableware and slippers
- rural economy: Limousine cows
- forestry
- Festival des Francophonies
- paper industry
- Aubusson tapestry
- *crêpes*, chestnuts
- Renoir
- Musée National de la Porcelaine

LORRAINE

Meurthe-et-Moselle (54) Meuse (55)
Moselle (57) Vosges (88)
23,500 sq km 2,339,000 inhabitants

METZ

- borders with Belgium, Germany, Luxembourg
- industry: metalwork, wood, glass, smart
- Verdun: WWI battlefields
- the Vosges mountains
- Epinal
- mineral water: *Vittel, Contrexeville, quiche lorraine*
- crystal museum (Baccarat)
- Jules Ferry

MIDI-PYRÉNÉES

Ariège (09) Aveyron (12)
Lot (46) Gers (31)
Haute-Garonne (32) Tarn (81)
Tarn-Garonne (82) Hautes-Pyrénées (65)
45,300 sq km 2,755,400 inhabitants

TOULOUSE

- *ville rose,* second university town
- aerospace industry (Concorde, Airbus)
- the Pyrénées
- rugby
- *cassoulet* and *roquefort*
- Toulouse-Lautrec
- Armagnac museum (Condom)

NORD-PAS-DE-CALAIS

Nord (59) Pas-de-Calais (62)
12,400 sq km 4,043,000 inhabitants

LILLE

- the flat lands (*plat pays*)
- Eurotunnel: France/Great Britain
- *'Furet du Nord'*, Europe's biggest bookshop
- textiles, mail order
- metal industry
- *beffrois* and *pavés du nord*
- mussels and chips and beer
- birthplace of Robespierre and Matisse
- mining museum and pubs
- Nœx-les-mines

BASSE-NORMANDIE

Calvados (14) Manche (50)
Orne (61)
17,600 sq km 1,449,000 inhabitants

CAEN

- historical sites: Mont-St Michel WWII beaches
- household appliances
- nuclear energy
- stud farms
- camembert and calvados
- Comtesse de Ségur, Marcel Proust (room 414, Grand Hôtel at Cabourg)
- Norman architecture museum, Schumberger Foundation (Crèvecœur en Auge)

HAUTE-NORMANDIE

Eure (27) Seine-Maritime (76)
12,300 sq km 1,811,300 inhabitants

ROUEN

- city of 100 steeples
- industrial Seine Valley oil refineries, chemistry
- Le Havre, connected to 500 ports worldwide
- Cliffs of Etretat
- birthplace of the Impressionists: Claude Monet at Giverny
- Guy de Maupassant, Pierre Corneille
- *musée des terres-neuves* and fishing (Fécamp)

PAYS DE LA LOIRE

Loire Atlantique (44) Maine et Loire (49)
Mayenne (53) Sarthe (72)
Vendée (85)
32,100 sq km 3,426,400 inhabitants

NANTES

- gateway of the Atlantic Ocean and the Loire
- produce from land and sea
- 500 km coast, countryside
- the market garden of France
- Muscadet and Saumur wines
- Saumur cavalry school
- Jules Verne, le douanier Rousseau
- automobile museum, Le Mans 24-hour race track

PICARDIE

Aisne (02)   Oise (60)
Somme (62)
19,400 sq km   1,886,500 inhabitants

AMIENS

- food-processing (biotechnology)
- sugar production
- prehistoric sites and archaeology
- Gothic cathedrals (Beauvais, tallest cathedral in the world)
- national forests, hunting
- Jean de la Fontaine
- Jules Verne museum (Amiens)

POITOU-CHARENTE

Charentes (16)   Charentes-Maritime (17)
Deux-Sèvres (79)   Vienne (86)
25,800 sq km   1,712,700 inhabitants

POITIERS

- *Futuroscope*: park of the future
- comic-strip festival (Angoulême)
- agriculture and fishing
- old port of La Rochelle
- Roman art
- marshlands
- oysters, *cognac*
- Pierre Loti
- paper workshop/museum (Angoulême)

PROVENCE-ALPES-CÔTE D'AZUR

Alpes-de-Haute-Provence (04) Drôme (26)
Alpes-Maritimes (05)   Hautes Alpes (06)
Rhône (69)   Bouches-du-Rhône (13)
Var (83)   Haute-Savoie (740)
Vancluse (84)
31,500 sq km   4,781,000 inhabitants

MARSEILLE

- Mediterranean basin
- formerly Roman Gaul
- Côte d'Azur-Riviera
- the first French microelectronics hub
- mimosa, herbes de provence, bouillabaisse
- Marcel Pagnol, Cézanne
- international perfume museum at Grasse

RHÔNE-ALPES

Ain (01)   Ardèche (07)
Isère (38)   Loire (42)
Savoie (73)
43,700 sq km   6,005,000 inhabitants

LYON

- gastronomy capital: only Lyon
- second economic region of France
- first ski station in the world: the Alps
- first in electricity production
- chemicals, pharmaceuticals
- border with Italy and Switzerland
- gratin dauphinois
- the brothers Lumière (cinema)
- Jean Jacques Rousseau
- Ampère electricity museum (Neuville-sur-Saône)

LES ANTILLES

GUADELOUPE
971
1,780 sq km   447,000 inhabitants

Basse-Terre

MARTINIQUE
972
1,100 sq km   399,000 inhabitants

Fort-de-France

REUNION
974
2,500 sq km   784,000 inhabitants

Indian Ocean   Saint Denis

GUYANE
973
90,000 sq km   202,000 inhabitants

Cayenne
European
Spatial Kourou

ADMINISTRATIVE AND POLITICAL ORGANIZATION IN FRANCE

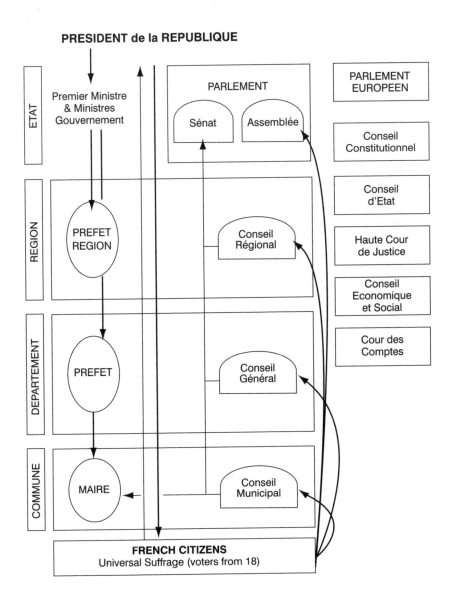

City folk and country folk

The 36,780 communes

After the 1789 Revolution, the 40,000 parishes in France were transformed into cities and villages. The people were to have a common house – the city hall (*hôtel de ville* or *mairie*).

There are 36,780 towns and villages in France with the status of *commune*, also known as *municipalités*. It is the smallest administrative unit and governed by a mayor and town council. The number of councillors depends on the number of inhabitants (from 9 town councillors for villages of less than 100 inhabitants, to 69 for a town with over 300,000 inhabitants). Several towns united around a city are part of the 'community district' (*communauté de communes*).

BONJOUR MONSIEUR LE MAIRE

Ken Tatham is the first and only British citizen to be elected Mayor in France. Born near Leeds, he became French to fully take part in the political life of Saint-Céneri-le-Gérei, one of France's most picturesque villages located in Normandy. Monsieur le Maire was re-elected in 2008 for a third term. With the *Conseil municipal*, he manages the affairs of the commune of 140 inhabitants. 'I am French but will always still feel English at heart. One of my most memorable experiences was being introduced to Queen Elizabeth in a capacity of being a French mayor!'

The mayor (*maire*) is the favourite elected official of the French – a neighbour known to everyone. Elected by the town council, the mayor represents the state at the local level, and has many and varied duties – acting as registrar and chief of police, publishing and enforcing the law, issuing building permits and so on. The tricolour blue, white and red scarf is the symbol of office, worn during official functions, for example, when performing a marriage at the local town hall.

The *Mairie*, the church, the school and *le Monument aux morts* (the war memorial) are the main symbols of a commune. The memories of the First and Second World Wars have become part of French families' histories. In each commune, in the main square or in the cemetery, there is a war memorial engraved with the names of the soldiers who died for France (*Morts pour la France*). French people pay their respect on 8 May and 11 November to those killed in action.

Municipal finances are mostly funded at the local level via local taxes, which vary annually according to the public services and amenities offered by the *commune*. Some are richer than others, depending on the degree of economic activity.

According to the size of the *commune*, the *mairie* (town hall) offers various services. It is open to the public, and performs the following official functions:

- information for visitors and residents;
- *état civil* (birth, marriage and death certificates);
- social services;
- school authority; and
- culture and sports, including libraries, workshops, sports equipment, swimming pools.

The PLM (Paris, Lyon, Marseille) law divides these, the three biggest cities in France, into *arrondissements* – respectively 20, 16 and 9. Each *arrondissement* has its own mayor and *arrondissement* council. The council in turn elects representatives to the municipal council.

THE TOWN HALL – MAIRIE OU HÔTEL DE VILLE

The word *hôtel* does not always mean a place to sleep. In the past, it referred to a mansion, or grand town house, and these buildings have often been transformed into *hôtels du département*, *hôtels de la région*, *hôtels des impôts*, *hôtels de police*, *Hôtel de la monnaie*, in other words, they now house the administrative offices of the department, the region, the tax office, the police headquarters and the finance office, respectively. Of course, none of them has any *étoiles*, or a *maître d'hôtel*!

Learning about democracy

Children and adolescents also have a place at the *mairie*. Elected by their peers, these junior town councillors have seats in the council chamber of their town. They seriously examine the daily problems of youth, development, environment and so on. Elected officials have learned to listen to their young advisers, who offer innovative ideas and demonstrate a good sense of civic duty.

The first children's town council (*Conseil Municipal d'enfants*) was conceived at Schittigheim, Alsace, in 1979. The idea has since been adopted by many French towns.

In 1989, a 'regional youth council' (*Conseil régionale des jeunes*) was created in Picardy. It is composed of 130 young people, elected from public and private schools. Divided into committees, the young people work on social, economic or cultural projects, which they then present three times a year to the president of the regional council. The same format is used at a departmental level with the *conseil général de jeunes*, or 'general youth council'.

'Villages are extended families.'
Charles Ceyrac

> ### TWIN TOWNS
>
> What do Rome and Paris have in common? Liège, Lille and Leeds? They are twin towns. Since 1956, a number of French *communes* have made twinning agreements with other communities in Europe, or elsewhere in the world, to forge and develop friendly relations, and to encourage cultural and economic exchanges between their communities.
>
> Paris is united with Rome, while the region of Ile-de-France is linked with both Madrid and Mexico City. The State of Georgia in the United States is linked with La Lorraine, and the Department of Calvados with Devon (Great Britain) and Franconie (Germany). *Poisson d'Avril* means 'April Fool', and two villages in France (Lorraine) called *Poisson* and *Avril* thought it would be fun to be twinned.

A focus on Paris and Ile-de-France

Historic Paris

'To M. Eiffel, the Engineer, the brave builder of so gigantic and original specimen of modern engineering from one who has the greatest respect and admiration for all....'
Thomas Edison: Eiffel Tower Guestbook, 10 September 1889

Paris enjoys the prestige and influence of a city rich in history, art and culture. For more than 10 centuries, the history of France has been made in this city on the banks of the Seine. The Paris of kings, and then of the *République*, has long exerted its power over the provinces, and cultivated cultural and historical centralization.

Paris has always been the capital of France. Decisions are made there, and important national and international events are held there. Its role is intrinsic to France.

There are several towns in the world called Paris – 12 in Canada, 12 in America, one in Denmark, one in Russia. However, there is only one true 'City of Light'.

Paris – political capital

Parliament, ministers, embassies and consulates are neighbours in Paris, for the most part gathered in the 7th, 8th and 16th *arrondissements*. Paris is the centre of government. However, the policy of decentralization has led to the *délocalisation* of the large state bureaucracies to various places around the country (eg ENA Ecole Nationale d'Administration is now located in Strasbourg).

The 20 arrondissements of the city of Paris have the pattern of a snail shell spiral

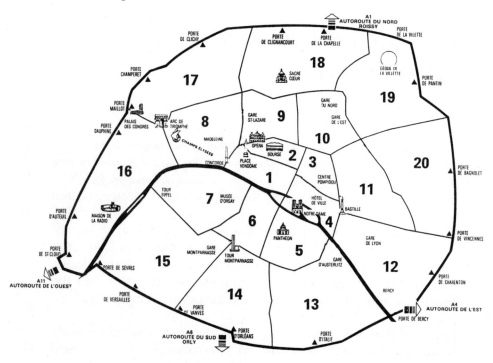

▬ *Paris – economic capital*

International banks, corporate headquarters and other businesses create a financial centre. Paris has long been a business city. Since the 14th century, it has promoted international commerce through universal *expositions*; the Gare d'Orsay, for example, was originally constructed for the 1900 Exposition, and has since been used as a railway station serving the suburbs, a theatre and now as a major museum. Paris is considered the premier city in the world for international congresses, *salons* (trade fairs) and *expositions*. Its communication networks and convention facilities offer excellent services to business tourism.

▬ *Paris – a trade mark*

'With three more letters, Paris would have been "paradis" (paradise).'

Jules Renard

Paris is a city of universities and intellectual exchange, and a city of information, and the national media and publishing houses have, naturally, set up shop there. The city offers the attractive cultural and tourist benefits of a world-renowned metropolis. All architectural styles and periods are represented there, from romantic to futuristic.

Proud of its past, yet forward-looking, Paris offers an enthusiastic welcome to foreign visitors and residents. The Parisian ambiance – shops, and cafés with their terraces – is unique. There are 5,300 streets, avenues and boulevards, covering a total of 1,700 kilometres (1,050 miles), 426 gardens, and a tree for every five inhabitants! You can also find vineyards in Paris!

Paris is sometimes disparaged for its problems (traffic jams, the high cost of housing, noise, pollution), but such difficulties are confronted in all the world's urban centres. Public action is of course required, but sensible and careful behaviour on behalf of the city's inhabitants can also play an important part.

'I dream of making a map of Paris for people with time to spare, that is to say, for ramblers who have time to waste and who love Paris.'

Léon-Paul Fargue

Paris and Ile-de-France

Paris is the capital of the Seine 'departement' which, in 1968, was divided into four: Les Hauts de Seine (92), La Seine-Saint-Denis (93), Le Val de Marne (94) form a ring around Paris. Today Paris has the status of both city and department.

Paris	105 km²	2,184,000
Inner ring	657 km²	4,255,000
Outer ring	11,250 km²	4,991,000
	12,012	11,430,000

ILE-DE-FRANCE: EIGHT DEPARTMENTS, FIVE NEW TOWNS

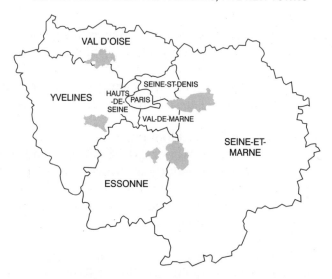

The Parisian region is surrounded by four rivers (the Seine, the Oise, the Marne and the Aisne), hence its name 'Ile-de-France' ('Island of France'). Its inhabitants are known as the 'Franciliens'.

Confident of its economic potential, the diversity of its employment market and its qualified workforce, Ile-de-France has the standing and the will to rank at the top of any list of European regions. Ile-de-France plays a crucial role at the national economic level.

Greater Paris is the first location in Europe for the top 500 world-wide companies: 172 headquarters are located in Ile-de-France, that is to say, one third of the world's biggest companies according to Fortune 500.

▬▬ *Ile-de-France in figures*

- 12,000 square kilometres (4,600 square miles); 1281 communes and almost 11,430,000 people (20 per cent of the population of France) live on 2 per cent of the land. L'Ile-de-France has a higher population than Sweden, Belgium or Portugal.

- 320,000 companies, representing one-third of the gross domestic product, and the largest employment market (one *cadre,* managerial or executive level, in two works in Ile-de-France). There is some social and economic disparity between the eight *départements.*

- Ile-de-France is (with the region of Provence-Alpes-Côtes d'Azur) the nation's largest producer of flowers and plants. The agricultural industry is important.

- On the outskirts of the big towns, some neighbourhoods consist of housing projects, home to an underprivileged population and young people confronted with unemployment and boredom. Various initiatives are in place to try to improve their situation. Saint-Denis (93) is a good example with the Stade de France, which hosts concerts and famous sporting events such as the rugby World Cup.

- France has over a million students, of whom one in three is enrolled in one of the 13 universities in Ile-de-France. There are also many business schools (HEC, INSEAD, ESSEC, ESCP, for example).

- Two hundred museums and 2,000 officially designated historical monuments.

● Two international airports: Orly (12 km) and Roissy-Charles de Gaulle (25 km), the second largest airport in Europe after London Heathrow. Roissy is also a central station for the TGV network. Le Bourget is the first European business airport.

La Défense

La Défense is the leading European business district managed by EPAD (Etablissement Public pour l'Aménagement de la region de la Défense). The 3,600 companies of all sizes generate a total revenue equivalent to the budget of the French state.

La Défense reflects the 21st century. Architects, urban planners and landscape gardeners have made it a modern and dynamic place to work, and one of the most visited places. In the international business quarter, office workers and residents coexist – computers challenge contemporary art, commercial centres and meeting halls are filled daily. From its open-air observation deck, the Grande Arche offers an extraordinary view of Paris. The longest perspective in the world allows the observer to see as far as the Louvre, via the Arc de Triomphe, the Place de la Concorde and the Jardin des Tuileries. The name 'la Défense' is connected not with the defence forces but with a statue, 'La Défense de Paris'.

Tour signal

EPAD has launched an ambitious development programme for La Défense with twelve new skyscrapers to be built. The famous French architect Jean Nouvel, the 2008 Pritzker prizewinner, has designed the Signal Tower building to be inhabited (offices and apartments). It will reach a height of 301 metres – the Eiffel Tower is 320 metres high.

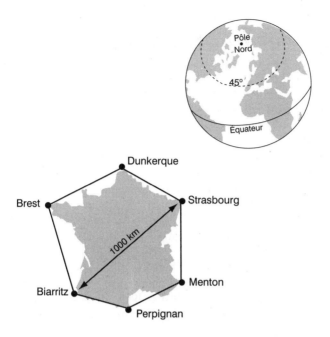

'France is neither round nor square – "The Hexagone" is its nickname.'
Edouard, aged 12

'I see France as a modern democractic power, essential to building the Europe of tomorrow… Its recent history proves its technical prowess with Airbus and Ariane, the TGV and Eurotunnel… To me, France has always been a second home, with its own unique personality, culture and vision.'

'Je vois la France comme une puissante démocratie moderne, essentielle à la construction de l'Europe de demain… Son histoire récente ce sont aussi des prouesses techniques, comme Airbus et Ariane, le TGV et l'Eurotunnel… Pour moi, la France a été et sera toujours une seconde patrie, avec une personnalité, une culture et une vision uniques.'
Felix G Rohatyn, former US Ambassador in France

*F*or further information

Principals of French Law, John Bell, Sophie Boyron and Simon Whittaker (Oxford University Press, 1998)

France, Clin Jones (Cambridge University Press)

Francoscopie, Gérard Mermet (Larousse, 2003)

L'Etat de la France, Le Crédoc et la Découverte, 2004

La Documentation Française, 29 quai Voltaire, 75007 Paris;

www.ladocumentationfrançaise.fr

www.fr/canalipsos (market research)

www.premier-ministre.gouv.fr/en – French government

www.diplomatie.gouv.fr/en/ – Ministry for Foreign Affairs

www.parlement.fr, www.assemblee-nationale.fr/english, www.senat.fr/lng/en

www.europa.eu/index_en.htm – Gateway to the European Union

www.invest-in-france.org/international/en

www.europinvest-paris.com – Great Paris – Paris Ile-de-France Capitale Economique

www.ile-de-france.fr

www.paris.fr

www.ladefense.fr

www.ladocumentationfrancaise.fr

www.ign.fr (géoportail)

www.asapfrance.info – France for youngsters

The Discovery of France: A historical geography from the Revolution to the First World War, Graham Robb (1st American edn (Picador, 2007)

Dangerous De-liaisons – What's really behind the war between France and the US, Jean-Marie Colombani et Walter Wells (Melville House, 2004)

France on the Brink, Jonathan Fenby (Arcade New York, 2000)

3 Living, working, studying, in France

– résider, travailler, étudier en France

'As big business takes over the world, life becomes more mobile and State government more complicated.'

'A mesure que la grande industrie s'empare du monde, la vie devient plus mobile et le gouvernement de l'Etat plus compliqué.'
Guglielmo Ferrero

*I*nternational mobility: an old story

'You have never been abroad, have you, Mrs McGregor?
– No, I have not. From all I hear, it is not a very nice place.'
Punch, **30** (iii) 32

Since the beginning of time, history has told of explorers and tireless travellers who speculated on the vastness of the world, and went out to discover it. Along the way, they sold their wares and brought back products, ideas and customs which, with time, enriched their lives and those of their fellow countrymen.

At present the world economy is moving and creating movement. Moving, creating, starting a business in a foreign land, this is the modern-day version of venturing out on to the old 'spice route'. The challenge of internationalism is opening up the world. Businesses now think in international terms and cultivate a mobile workforce. Today's candidate needs not only the expertise but motivation to work in a multicultural environment and the ability to live far from home.

To prepare for this, under the auspices of international cooperation programmes, France welcomes foreign students and trainees. These young people come to study in France, and when they return to their own countries they reinvest the knowledge they have acquired, and become ambassadors of France.

'Our fathers were sedentary, our sons will be even more so, since they
will only have the Earth on which to move.'
Paul Morand

*F*rench law

France is a country with a written legal code. It is often believed to be bureaucratic and its procedures are frequently criticized. It sometimes seems that there are endless forms to fill in, and stamps of authorization to be acquired, and the different processes can be mystifying. However, all you really need to do is to have the right papers ready, at the right place and at the right time – elementary! The French administration is on the web and every ministry has a site with very useful and accurate information, also given in English.

▬▬ *A few ground rules: legal and cultural aspects*

The administrative formalities that will be necessary prior to your departure will depend on your project (work, study, travel) and your resources. As a general rule, a foreigner must have a valid passport to enter France; and some nationalities will also need a visa. An identity card is all that is necessary for EU citizens, the European Economic Space (EEA) and Switzerland.

'Every foreign national wishing to come to France must have ready for presentation at the border documentary evidence of the purpose of the visit, means of support for the duration of the stay, and accommodation arrangements. In some cases a visa is required. It must be requested from the French consulate before departure.'
Ministère des Affaires étrangères

WELCOME TO FRANCE

According to statistics kept by the French customs service, France welcomes more than 80 million foreigners per year (tourists, visitors, workers, students, trainees). This far exceeds the approximately 64 million people who reside in France.

▬▬ *Immigration: a brief insight*

For 20 centuries France has had a turbulent history and different cultures have intermingled to form the mixed-race French nation of today. In the 1950s immigration became an economic factor with

France seeking to re-establish a much needed workforce. A decrease in the population resulted after the two World Wars. Gradually, foreigners arrived in France: Belgians, Italians, then Spanish and Polish followed by Portuguese. From further afield, Chinese, North Africans and Africans started to arrive, providing cheap labour and contributing to the development of industrial sectors of the country.

The historical links between France and French-speaking Africa and Asia have made it easier for young people to come and work in France. Since 1974 and the first oil and economic crisis, immigration of workers and their families has been strictly regulated due to unemployment in France. A new Law in July 2006 added new conditions and limits on immigration.

Like other Europeans countries, France wants to attract particularly foreigners who come to participate in the economy and development of the country. Immigration is therefore more selective than previously and immigrants are 'chosen'. This policy comes under the authority of the new Minister of Immigration, Integration, National Identity and Co-development.

Citizens of the EU and the EEA, and the Swiss

Europeans of the EU the EEA, and the Swiss, are free to travel, live and work in any of the EU countries. They do not need a work permit in France, and are not required to have a carte de séjour, although their professional or personal situation could justify their requesting one. However, the new members (Bulgaria and Romania since 1 January 2007) are subject to a maximum 'transition period' of seven years before fully benefiting from this freedom.

The Schengen Agreement

Signed in Luxembourg in 1985, the Schengen Agreement brought about the gradual abolition of border checks at the common frontiers of EU member states. Systematic controls are carried out by the

24 EU countries that have signed the Schengen Agreement. The 'unique' Schengen visa enables non-European tourists to travel to any member countries (except Ireland and the UK) using one single visa. However, each EU state remains free to apply individual border controls, if this is felt necessary to control security risks.

*I*mmigration regulations

The ANAEM (the Office of International Migrations called Agence Nationale de l'Accueil des Etrangers et des Migrations), a public institution attached to the Ministère de l'immigration, de l'intégration, de l'identité nationale et du co-développement implements the government's policy regarding the entry and employment of foreigners in France, and also assists French people who go abroad. To this end, the ANAEM administers an introduction procedure for non-EU, non-EEA and non-Swiss foreign workers. This is carried out in conjunction with the French Consulate nearest to the applicant's home, and the DDTEFP (Direction Départementale du Travail, de l'Emploi et de la Formation Professionnelle) nearest to the corporate headquarters, or to the job site, if it is different.

CONTRAT D'ACCUEIL ET D'INTÉGRATION (CAI)

Immigration offices, ANAEM, are in charge of foreigners authorized to reside in France and implement a compulsory welcome and integration contract. The CAI is an undertaking that ties the signatories to follow a civic training and, if necessary, language tuition.

ANAEM has set up a compulsory health test to be taken by every adult member of a family upon their arrival in France. The medical certificate gained from this will be required to obtain the *carte de séjour temporaire* (CST) in France.

The ANAEM has a fixed charge for these procedures. It may be paid either by the applicant's company, or, for a personal project, by the applicant.

A change of residence certificate, approved by the Consulate, will be required for the move to France.

Working in France

To work in France, every foreigner (apart from EU, EEA and Swiss citizens) must meet certain requirements laid down by the French authorities. French Immigration and Labour Laws define different statuses depending on each individual's situation.

There are various categories of foreign workers in France.

• *Salarié en mission* (intra-company transfer): the employee possesses a specialized knowledge or holds a particular position in an international company and is sent to France on an intra-company transfer. He or she must have a minimum length of service of three months with the foreign employer in order to benefit from the *salarié en mission* permit, valid for three years. The status to be applied to the employee in France depends on the description and term of the assignment. The minimum monthly gross salary must be 1,900 euros but commensurate with the position held. According to the nature of the professional activity to be undertaken in France, the assignee is either:
   – a '*salarié détaché*' remains on home country payroll and pro-vides technical assistance, a reporting role or transfer of expertise, on a temporary basis;
   – a '*salarié permanent*' is hired locally in France under a 'French contract' and is paid via the payroll of the French entity.

• Special conditions exist for '*cadre de haut niveau*' (a highly qualified executive) earning a minimum of 5,000 euros gross per month. Accompanying spouses of these assignees are issued with a resident's permit entitled '*vie privée et familiale*' which gives them access to the employment market. It is the host company's responsibility to initiate the process for work authorization and to ensure that the collective bargaining agreement conditions are applied to the foreign employee.

● *Salarie* (direct local hire): an executive may be hired locally in France and will be paid via the French payroll and affiliated to the French Social Security scheme. The employee must receive a minimum gross monthly salary of 4,000 euros. A simplified procedure exists for the hire of workers for sectors of activity in short supply, such as information technology, construction, agriculture, retail, catering (according to a list published by the State).

● Employed and a national of an EU member state. Nationals of the new member states of the EU (since 1 January 2007) and all non-EU

THE WORK AND RESIDENCE PERMIT PROCESS
INTRA-COMPANY TRANSFER «SALARIÉ EN MISSION»

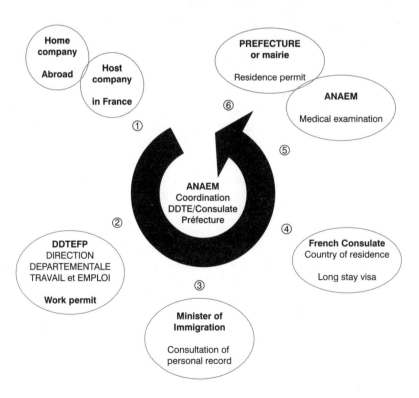

nationals who are employed in an EU member state, and are holders of valid work and residency permits and social security cover in that state, may 'export' their rights to work on a 'temporary' basis in France. A French work permit is not required. The foreign employer who sends employees, irrespective of their nationality, to France, must complete a pre-printed 'prior secondment' form (in French), which outlines the conditions of the assignment. Failure to do so will result in a fine.

● European spouses: the spouse of an EU national has the right to work in France, providing that the couple both live together in France. They may both apply for a resident's permit entitled '*member de famille UE*' from the Prefecture of their place of residence.

● *Prestation de services internationales* (service provider). The 'Service Provider Contract' concluded between a foreign company and a French client implies the obligation by the service provider to initiate the appropriate administrative formalities. A translated copy of an 'extract' of the contract must be submitted to the Labour Authorities under whose jurisdiction the client falls to substantiate the assignment in order to obtain the 'prior work authorization'. The foreign employer must complete a pre-printed '*déclaration de détachement*' (prior registration form in French), which outlines the nature, place, duration, and terms and conditions of the assignment. This document must be sent to the local Labour Inspection Office in France prior to the arrival of the assignee. The client in France is supposed to verify that the home company complies with French Labour Law (for example that there is equal treatment of French and foreign employees performing the same duties).

● According to the social security situation any '*salarié ou détaché*' worker from a country that has a bilateral social security agreement with France will be entitled to a social security 'détachment'. If the country does not, the host company has to declare the foreign employee at the URSSAF (Union de Recouvrement des Cotisations de Sécurité Sociale et d'Allocations Familiales) and pay the contributions.

▬▬ *Avis Favorable! (Approval)*

When the DDTEFP has approved the request, it sends the file to the ANAEM, which then authorizes the stay in France. The ANAEM then presents the file to the Minister of the Interior, who consults the world visa network and the police department before validating and transferring it to the French Consulate in the employee's country of origin, where the employee will apply for a *visa long séjour*. The visa will be marked *'espace Schengen'*. This means that the visa is valid in the countries that signed the Schengen Agreement but the visa only gives the holder the right to apply for a residence permit in France. Your *'titre de séjour'* in France allows you to travel freely among the Schengen states.

NB: Assignees and accompanying family members must remain outside of France while the French work permit application is submitted, processed and approved. They will then be required to make their entry clearance visa applications at the French Consulate of their country of residence.

The assignee can commence his or her assignment as soon as the host company has a copy of a valid passport, visa and work authorization from the Labour Authorities.

An application for a resident's permit filed with the Police Authorities is required for all assignments over three months. The application must be filed following the ANAEM compulsory medical examination and prior to the expiry of the long stay visa.

▬▬ *Beware*

Unlike a business trip (ie participation for a few days in meetings, seminars or conferences), a regular work assignment in France requires a work permit, no matter what the duration of the assignment, even if it is on a part-time basis.

Anyone holding a visitor visa will not be eligible to undertake a salaried activity in France. If the person does undertake a salaried activity he or she will be breaking immigration regulations and the organization employing the person will be committing a criminal offence.

In the event of an investigation by a labour inspector, the organization must be in a position to provide a copy of items relating to the foreign employee such as valid passport, visa, work and residence permit, and social security details.

Clandestine employment

By law, it is illegal to employ a foreign individual who does not have a work permit (French Labour Code: C trav.art.L 341–46). An employer who makes a false statement to the authorities in order to help a foreign individual to obtain a work permit will be sued (C trav.art.L 364–02).

The new law increases criminal, financial and administrative penalties (imprisonment and fines) against employers who employ workers in an irregular situation and enforces the controlling role of labour inspectors. Individuals and legal entities, or representatives thereof, also risk confiscation of their belongings. Furthermore, an employer having an irregular workforce in the company has to cover the cost of repatriating the employees to their home country. The foreign employees are also targeted. From now on, individuals will be forbidden to reside in France for up to five years and even a permanent ban is possible.

Specific situations

A person wishing to come to France independently (not sent by a company) begins the process at the French Consulate in his or her home country. The Consulate will ask for justification of the request for a *visa long séjour*.

Self-employed

- An independent professional project does not require a work permit but a *visa long séjour* from the French Consulate in the country of residence (upon proof of sufficient financial resources and medical and accident insurance coverage). Non-workers staying in France for more than three months are subject to the same obligations. If it is an independent business, the self-employed must register with the specific professional organization and the URSSAF before beginning to trade and invoicing clients. (Régime Social des Independants – RSI – www.le.rsi.fr.)

Special status

- 'Regulated' professions (doctor, lawyer, architect, academic researcher, etc) or artists must fulfil certain obligations. These are special cases. Only those foreign personnel with special qualifications may be employed in the French public sector.

- Permanent positions in the public service (*fonction publique*) are only open to French nationals, except for certain positions in higher education or research, medicine, etc, according to very specific regulations.

- Certain foreigners, such as members of foreign diplomatic and consular services in France, employees of international organizations and correspondents of foreign newspapers, have a specific status.

Talents et competences card

A permit marked '*Talents et competences*' is issued for a renewable three-year period to skilled non-EU nationals whose expertise and talents contribute significantly to the economic development of France and their own country. Such people might be scientists, intellectuals, those offering cultural and humanitarian expertise or talents, high-level athletes, etc. Individuals must have a pre-defined professional project which is evaluated by the French administration. Accompanying spouses are issued with a resident's permit *'vie privée et familiale'*.

LA FONDATION KASTLER

'The Kastler Foundation, located in Strasbourg, was created by the Academy of Sciences to fulfil two essential roles: To simplify the arrival of high level foreign researchers in France, and to maintain contact with them after they leave. Have a great stay in France!'
Professor Guy Ourisson

The underlying ideas with which the Kastler Foundation operates are mobility and access to knowledge and cultural exchange, all carried out from a very humanist perspective with the ultimate goal of international cooperation that was dear to Alfred Kastler. (See www.fnak.fr.) The European network of Mobility Centres exists in the member states of the EU.

Master's degree

New members of the EU (since 1 January 2007), who have obtained a Master's degree (or equivalent degree) from a French university or higher education institution no longer require a work or resident's permit. They must however be paid at least 1,900 euros and provide their future employer with a copy of their diploma and a valid passport or national identity card.

Non-EU nationals who have successfully completed an academic course in France may request a special temporary residence permit (*Autorisation provisoire de séjour* – APS) valid for six months. This entitles them to stay either to look for a job or to prepare their departure.

▅▅▅ *Trader's card*

All foreigners, except EU, EEA and OECD citizens, need a 'prior authorization to trade' issued by the préfet for the *création d'une entreprise commerciale ou d'un bureau de representation* – if they want to create or manage a commercial company or a branch office – whether or not they reside in France. The applicant must provide the necessary documents relating to the type of company, plus the usual identification papers. This procedure applies to the following positions:

● *directeur (gérant) d'une SARL* (director or manager of a limited liability company);

● *président du conseil d'administration d'une SA ou SAS* (president of a board of directors of a public limited company, or plc);

● *représentant de filiale d'une société étrangère* (representative at a branch office of a foreign company); and

● *agents commerciaux* (commercial representatives).

To obtain the visa requirements necessary for a specific investment, the applicant must contact the French Consulate in his or her country of residence. A commercial or industrial activity or trade requires registration with the Registre de Commerce et de Société.

▅▅▅ *Press card*

A non-EU journalist or correspondent in France for a foreign media has to apply for a long stay visa at the French Consulate abroad and submit a file for accreditation to the *Centre d'Accueil de la Presse Etrangère (CAPE)* in Paris. Holding a press card is incompatible with any other salaried position and a minimum monthly salary is required, substantiated by a bank statement. The press card forms an integral part of the resident permit file.

▬▬ Retired people

Retired people must justify their means of support, show proof of medical coverage, and may not be employed as a *salarié*: in a salaried position.

ASYLUM SEEKERS AND REFUGEES

France has a tradition of taking in asylum seekers and refugees. In 2006, France was the EU member country that granted refugee status to the highest number of applicants. France granted nearly a third of the total number of applications granted in the whole of the EU.

---

*L*iving in France

▬▬ Temporary residence permit – carte de séjour temporaire

Non-EU, EEA and Swiss foreign residents in France must have a *carte de séjour temporaire* (CST), if their stay in France exceeds 90 days. This permit may be obtained at the Préfecture nearest to your residence in France. Soon after your arrival, you must submit your completed dossier in exchange for a *récépissé de demande de carte de séjour* ('receipt for your request for a residence permit'). This receipt is valid for three months while you are waiting for your CST.

Your *carte de séjour temporaire* will bear the classification that corresponds to your situation: for example, *salarié, temporaire*, artistic or cultural profession, scientist, *étudiant, visiteur*. It is valid for a maximum of one year, and is renewable.

A *carte de séjour* with '*temporaire*' written on it allows the holder to work in France with APT.

NB: You should request a renewal two months prior to the expiration of your CST, at your local Préfecture or *mairie*, justifying your situation in France (for example, your professional situation, resources, domicile, tax status). Those in the *détaché* category with a provisional work permit (APT) will be limited to a 12-month *carte de séjour*, which is renewable.

CARTE DE SÉJOUR TEMPORAIRE

The following documents (original and photocopy) must be presented or sent for a *carte de séjour* at the local Préfecture (or at the Préfecture de Police in Paris):

- the applicant's identification papers and those of the family members accompanying the applicant (passports, birth certificates, marriage licence translated into French);

- *visa long séjour* issued by the Consulate and medical certificate issued by the ANAEM;

- proof of residence (rental contract, electricity bill or a letter from the person giving you housing); and

- three ID photos (full face, 3.5 × 4.5 cm, no head wear).

Each time you change your address you must declare the new address as soon as possible at the police station or *mairie* nearest to your new home. The new address will be printed on your *carte de séjour*.

Residence permit – carte de résident

After five years of continuous residence and employment in France with French social security, you may request a *carte de résident*, which is valid for 10 years and proves that you are well integrated into the French community and speak French. The list of documents required for this permit is available at the Préfecture nearest to your home in France.

AT THE PRÉFECTURE DE POLICE, DE PARIS

A written request for a *carte de séjour* may be sent to the *cellule postale* of the Préfecture de Police, by sending an application file. Three weeks later, you will know that your request is being processed when you receive two forms to sign and return to the Préfecture by post. Of course, it will be necessary to verify your identity and about four weeks later you will be asked to appear in person with your passport to pick up your *carte de séjour* at the bureau indicated.

When you have a *carte de résident*, you may work anywhere in France. This permit is renewable if you haven't been out of France for more than 3 years in a row over the past 10 years.

The foreign spouse of a French citizen may request a long stay visa, a *carte de résident*, after four years of marriage.

New set of rules for executives

The government wants to simplify the immigration procedures for the introduction into France of senior managers and their families, with a single unit of the ANAEM handling work and residence permits. Furthermore, spouses of top-level managers and salarie en mission are authorized to exercise a salaried activity in France as soon as they have obtained a resident's permit 'vie privée et familiale'.

A key reform will provide that all expatriate allowances will not be taxable in France for newcomers.

Nationality and citizenship

A national has a legal relationship with a state (the state's jurisdiction is applicable). A citizen has rights to participate in the civic and political life of the state once he or she reaches the age of majority (18 in France).

The five-year residence requirement for applications for French nationality can be reduced to two years for those who either successfully complete a two-year French educational curriculum or provide a particular service to the country, or are citizens of a country where French is an official language.

BECOME FRENCH

By naturalization:

You may apply for French citizenship after five years of continuous residence in France (your *carte de séjour* will prove this). The administrative decision to grant a request is based on a thorough review of your dossier and proof that you have been successfully assimilated into French society (having mastered the French language, and shown an appreciation of the values of the Republic).

A person who has fully filed a demand of naturalization receives a receipt when the file is registered at the Préfecture of residence. After that an investigation is carried out to check the person's loyalty to France. Each Préfecture is in charge of the naturalization process. Consent is then followed by a *décret* (publication) in the *Journal Officiel*. An official ceremony is held at the Préfecture to welcome new French citizens.

By marriage:

A foreigner can be given French nationality when married to a French citizen for a minimum of four years (the marriage must be registered by the French authorities at a *mairie* or consulate) and living together.

If your country of origin has not signed the Convention du Conseil de l'Europe (6/5/1963) you may hold dual citizenship.

Children:

- *Blood right* (droit de sang). A child born of at least one French parent is French at birth, wherever he or she is born.

- *Territory right* (droit de sol). A child born in France of foreign parents simply becomes a French citizen if he or she is in France on his or her 18th birthday and has been living in France for at least five years between the ages of 11 and 18. He or she can refuse French nationality between the ages of 17 and 19.

- A child born in France, if one of his or her foreign parents was born in France and has lived in the country, can acquire Fench nationality.

Apostille, Convention de la Hague du 5 Octobre 1961

APOSTILLE

This French word means 'certification of the signature' of an official document. It refers to the 1961 Hague Convention abolishing the requirement for legalization of foreign public documents. Certified documents with an *apostille* are accepted for legal use in the states that have signed this Convention.

For other countries, a foreign public document must be legalized by the Consular Officer of the country from which the document is issued.

To apply for French citizenship you have to obtain an *apostille* or legalization for your birth certificate.

▬▬▬*Accompanying family* – famille accompagnante

This is a special category for qualified personnel (*cadres*) who wish to have their families with them in France, and for whom the employer has fulfilled the necessary immigration requirements. The employer makes the request for visas for the accompanying family members (spouse and children under 18) with the work permit application.

Each family member must obtain a *visa long séjour*. The spouse's *carte de séjour temporaire* will be stamped '*visiteur*'. It does not give the holder the right to work as an employee.

▬▬▬*Documents for children under 18 years of age*

A *document de circulation* is granted to minors born outside France, which acts as a sort of identification card. It is needed each time the child returns to France after leaving the country. It is valid for five years and must be requested at the Préfecture by the parents, who need to present their *carte de séjour*, the child's passport and visa, and a schooling certificate (*certificat de scolarité*) if the child is over six years old.

A child born in France of foreign parents will be able to obtain a republican identification document (*titre d'identité républicain*) from the Préfecture, which will deliver *titres de séjour* to his/her parents. This document is a proof of identity and will enable the child to come back to France without a visa.

▬▬▬*Bringing the family to France* – regroupement familial

Every foreigner has the right to bring his or her spouse and children under 18 to France, when he or she has been a qualified resident for more than 18 months. One of the requirements for this is a stable employment position that is sufficiently well paid to support the other family members, who will be his or her financial responsibility.

The request for *regroupement familial* (deferred arrival of accompanying family members: spouse and children) is made at the ANAEM nearest to the home of the resident foreigner. The ANAEM verifies that there is adequate housing and a stable family income. Upon arrival, family members of 18 years or more must sign a compulsory 'contrat d'accueil et l'integration' (CAI) with the French State. The CAI commits them to French language and civic training sessions leading to a certificate. This is required for the renewal of a future residence permit. The decision regarding the family's entry into France depends on the results of a medical examination. The ultimate decision rests with the Préfet. Beneficiaries are issued with a resident's permit valid for one year.

Studying in France

Students

While promoting scientific, technical and academic exchanges, France has developed a strong economic and cultural presence in the world. Proof of enrolment in a school or university and proof of financial support will be required for the issuance of a long stay visa marked 'etudiant' by a French Consulate. In some countries, the procedures are online.

NB: A tourist or short term visa cannot be extended to a long stay visa either in France or any other EU country.

Students are permitted to work during their studies a maximum of 964 hours per year (60 per cent of legally working hours) once they have obtained a *carte de séjour temporaire* stamped '*étudiant*'. The exception is Algerian students whose legal status is defined by the Franco-Algerian agreement of 27 December 1968 and who are required to have a temporary work permit (APT). Students from private schools that do not provide student social security coverage are not eligible for work permits.

■ *Campus France*

This programme is designed to coordinate the French education systems in foreign countries, welcoming more foreign students to France by sharing knowledge. The ministries of National Education, Foreign Affairs, Culture and International Trade jointly created *Campus France* to promote French higher education abroad at educational fairs and exhibitions. Aiming to provide information and orientation, *Campus France* is the privileged point of contact for the 265,000 foreigners studying in France.

State grant holders – boursiers d'Etat

A grant may be given for study or training in France to the following:

● citizens of all the countries with which France has diplomatic or cooperative agreements;

● citizens of the overseas departments and territories;

● EGIDE manages French government international cooperation initiatives. This non-profit organization works with the state, foreign governments, international organizations and companies or research laboratories, to coordinate the administrative formalities and financing for students or trainees who have received grants in France. EGIDE offices in Paris and in different regions welcome people planning any kind or length of stay. See www.egide.asso.fr

Business *stages* (training periods) are for study; they may not be connected either to another professional activity or to a paid position.

The grant holders receive students' social security if they are under 26. If not, they may be covered by the EGIDE insurance.

The CNOUS (Centre National des oeuvres Universitaires et Scolaires) also assists foreign grant holders in France, provides many skills and activities and organizes international meetings.

PRESTIGIOUS PROGRAMME

- The Chateaubriand is to encourage Franco–American scientific relations. PhD candidates and postdoctoral students come to spend a year conducting research and discovering France and its intellectual resources (medical, economic, scientific, social and administrative). Public organizations and private businesses receive these *chercheurs boursiers* (research grant holders) and co-finance this programme with the *Ministère des Affaires Etrangères*.

- The Entente Cordiale Scholarship. This programme forges links between British and French through a one-year exchange of young professionals.

Trainees – stagiaires

France receives many young foreign trainees. They fill paid positions in French companies in order to acquire or perfect professional skills, or to learn French. Under the exchange or training agreements, their stay is generally less than 18 months.

The French Consulate in the home country, the ANAEM and the international student organizations have information on the programmes available and the required administrative procedures.

International exchanges organized by ANAEM

Agreements signed between France and ten other countries – Argentina, Canada, Hungary, Morocco, New Zealand, Poland, Senegal, Sweden, Switzerland and the United States – allow companies to invite foreign trainees aged between 18 and 35 who have professional experience in business for from 3 to 18 months.

The ANAEM coordinates the job offers and the requests for positions, in conjunction with its partners in the participating countries, and manages the administrative formalities between them. The trainees are paid according to their profession and benefit from the social security in the host country or from a bilateral agreement.

■ *An international career with AIESEC*

The AIESEC (International Non-Profit Association of Students of Business and Economics) recruits for French companies. They look for students or young graduates in more than 80 countries who will be paid for a temporary posting. AIESEC selects candidates according to the needs of the recruiting companies, and will complete the official formalities.

▬ *Registering at your Consulate* – carte consulaire

As soon as you arrive in France, you should register at your Consulate. Although it is not obligatory, it is useful for them to be aware of your presence in France, in case you have any problems or administrative questions during your stay. Your consular card will allow you to register to vote in your own country.

You may obtain it at your Consulate by presenting: proof of your nationality and date of birth; and your *carte de séjour* showing that your residence in France is legal.

All births, marriages, adoptions or deaths that occur in your family during your stay in France must be declared at the *mairie* nearest your residence. It is also a good idea to inform your own Consulate.

IDENTIFICATION PAPERS – PAPIERS D'IDENTITÉ

Your *carte de séjour* is your ID card while you are in France. Carry it with you at all times. The French are accustomed to carrying their ID with them, as it is frequently requested when entering public organizations or private companies, or even when writing a cheque at the supermarket. Be aware that, according to French law, any person found on French territory must produce his or her identification upon demand by the police. Both French nationals and foreigners are supposed to carry their identity papers at all times when in public places. A passport is regarded as a travel document, not a proof of residence.

Police record – extrait de casier judiciaire

If you are a resident in France regardless of your nationality and you are asked for a copy of your police record (for example, for a security clearance for travel or work in another country), you should ask for it at the Service du Casier Judiciaire, www.justice.gouv.fr/cjn/. Include your first name and surname, date and place of birth, and a copy of both your *carte de séjour* and your passport.

Lost or stolen identification papers

Should you have the bad luck to misplace your papers, or to have them stolen, you must report the loss immediately to the nearest police station. There you will make a *déclaration de perte ou de vol* ('declaration of loss or theft'), and be given a receipt. This will permit you to be *en règle* ('in accordance with the law'), while you are waiting for your papers to be replaced at your embassy or Consulate in France. The police should then tell you how to proceed.

You may also report your loss in writing to the Procureur de la République at the Tribunal de Grande Instance of the town where the loss or theft took place.

It is wise to keep copies of all your important papers (passport, visa, *carte de séjour*, diplomas) in a safe place. That way, if you do lose them, they are much easier to replace.

The most frequently requested documents

It is helpful always to have to hand the following:

● birth certificate translated into French (see your Consulate for a certified translation);

● copies of documents of which you should always keep the originals, for example, your CV and diplomas in French;

● justification of domicile, for example, a rental contract or letter from your landlord, or an electricity bill;

● ID photos (full-face, 3.5 × 4.5 cm, no head wear. French law says that both men and women must be bare-headed on identity photos);

● a few envelopes and stamps.

Sworn translators are listed at every *mairie*.

YOUR PAPERS PLEASE?

Your wallet will soon contain a whole pack of cards: *carte de séjour, carte vitale, carte de sécurité sociale, carte de visite, carte grise, carte bleue, carte navigo* (if you live in Ile-de-France)... and you have *carte blanche* to continue your collection of *cartes de France*!

SANS PAPIERS

The saying *'sans papiers'* without papers) refers to foreigners who are not legally entitled to be in France, 'illegal immigrants' or 'clandestines'. Someone who works without the relevant authorization is called an 'illegal worker' (and referred to as 'working on the black').

The legal structure of French companies

International business is now the norm for multinational companies and their branch offices, the PME/PMI (*Petites et Moyennes Entreprises/Petites et Moyennes Industries*, or small and mid-sized companies or industries), and public companies.

The foreign observer is often astonished by the diversity of legal structures employed in France to conduct commercial, financial or industrial business. Banks, for example, may be commercial companies, with private or public capital; they may be cooperative societies; or they may be specially regulated, like the Banque de France.

Structures such as the EPI (Établissement Public Industriel et Commercial), allow the state to exercise an industrial activity, for example, the SNCF (Société nationale des Chemins de Fer français, 'the National Train Service') or the GIE (Groupement d'Intérêt Économique), and give companies the opportunity to be part public and part private, without losing their autonomy (for example, the GIE Airbus).

The collaboration of state and private capital is a special characteristic of the French economy, which is known as an *économie mixte*. The state thereby reserves the ability to monitor strategic sectors such as the arms and energy industries.

▬▬ *Public companies*

A large number of French companies have, directly or indirectly, the state as their principal shareholder. Nationalization occurred in many sectors in 1945, and again between 1981 and 1982. These companies have unusual corporate structures. The board of directors includes representatives of shareholders, the workforce and other qualified directors. The state appoints the directors and the industries are monitored by one or more ministries.

Between 1986 and 1987, the tendency was more towards the partial or complete privatization of public-sector companies. There was a second phase in the 1990s. A third phase is currently under way, focused on the public services. France Télécom, no longer within the state monopoly, has become one of the European players in internet and wireless technologies. Air France and other 'semi-businesses', such as EDF, SNCF and La Poste, are under consideration. In effect, European directives are changing French law, and will be a death warrant for state monopolies. The balance between public interest and financial interests is at stake; the notion of a more dynamic and demanding 'client' or 'customer' is gradually replacing that of a 'user'.

> *'The nanny state is everywhere. The French tend to believe that the state knows best what is good for them.'*
> Diana Geddes (*The Spectator*)

The term 'public services' refers to activities of general interest which are carried by the authorities or by delegation. They assure an equality of access for all citizens, at the same cost.

▬▬ *Private companies*

Investors can choose between two types of status for their company: branch or subsidiary. The notion of '*société*' (company) is legal whereas the term '*enterprise*' (business) refers to the activity. A company may be constituted in a variety of different legal forms.

Organization and hierarchy

Each company bears the imprint of its founder and is unique in its conception. Its mission, its technology, its products and its personnel represent its heritage.

In France, the structure of a company is still very hierarchical, from worker, via employee, technician, supervisor, and manager, to director. The art of management has developed in France since the 1960s, when more companies began to compete internationally. Today, the trend in large companies is to increase efficiency by delegating greater responsibility to employees. Participative management and the recognition of merit are now important principles.

A new generation of bosses and new technologies imposed on all staff have reduced the amount of hierarchy. Even though the French remain somewhat ambivalent, for they have a natural sense of deference and respect for authority, they also have a tendency to constantly question the system.

French women represent more than 52 per cent of the population. The traditional separation of sex roles is changing, especially in business and social relationships. French businesswomen wish to be considered equal to men, but keeping their femininity and sense of freedom.

The words 'motivation', 'flexibility', 'quality', 'productivity' and 'profitability' apply equally to personnel and products. Recognizing that its personnel are a company's greatest asset, many company directors now give a great deal of thought to the management of their human resources.

NB: A chart showing the different legal structures of private companies is on page 355.

▄▄▄▄▄*Discover your company*

Most companies organize a formal introduction and welcome to facilitate the arrival of a new employee, regardless of his or her nationality. Some companies prefer to organize seminars once or more a year to present the company, while others give each new arrival a personal welcome.

You will probably have access to the official company documents, such as the annual report, the company regulations, the *bilan social* (social audit – obligatory for companies of over 300 employees), as well as other documents provided by individual companies.

● The *rapport annuel* (annual report) contributes to the public image of a company. The financial statements and statistics are of interest to the firm's partners and backers, and to the financial press.

● The *bilan social* provides an overview of the social structure of the company.

● The *règlement intérieur* (internal company rules) lists the general regulations for the company and the duties and obligations of the employees (hours, discipline, security and respect for the hierarchical system).

● The *intranet* is for many companies the finest of communication tools: it offers an up to date and dynamic presentation of the company to newly arrived employees instead of the traditional introductory book or internal notices.

● The *mémo* is the classic office message, for information and news.

● The *journaux d'entreprise* (company newspapers), sometimes online, give information and develop the company image.

You should get to know your new company, and introduce yourself to the various departments or services. To be at the right place at the right time, you will need to discover where everything, and everybody, is located.

■■■ *In the big companies*

Ressources humaines (human resources) and *communication* are the two services that assist new recruits and especially expatriates in settling into the new environment. Do not hesitate to ask for their help.

■ *Direction des ressources humaines (DRH)*

The concept of 'human resources management' is often preferred to that of 'personnel administration'. Other than managing the employment, recruitment, remuneration and training of all employees, the human resources department also assists the company's international members. It is usually responsible for welcoming, counselling and assisting expatriates with administrative or professional questions.

■ *Direction de la communication (Dircom)*

Within the company, the internal communication department is responsible for disseminating essential information and documents to the employees. The company publications will keep you well informed. The external communications department is responsible for public relations.

■■■ *Medical and social services*

The annual medical examination is designed to verify that employees are fit for work. When you are recruited for your job you will be given a medical check-up as part of the normal process.

Large companies have a doctor, nurses and a social worker to assist with health problems, or personal or family situations that may affect the employee's professional performance.

The doctor and the social worker are bound by professional secrecy. They are also there to inform employees – individually or collectively – on questions of health.

*E*mployee representation

There are three ways within the company that employee interests are represented. Their different priorities influence the social structure of the company.

■■■ *Personnel delegates* – les délégués du personnel (DP)

Since 1936, all companies with over 10 employees must legally have one or more employee delegates, each elected for a term of two years. Their responsibility is to present individual or collective claims relating to the application of the *code du travail* (labour law), collective labour agreements, and wages and working conditions in the company. They meet with the employer on a monthly basis.

After three months with the company, foreign employees are eligible to vote in the same manner as their French colleagues. They are eligible for election after one year with the company.

■■■ *Work council* – le comité d'entreprise (CE)

Since 1945, a company with over 50 full-time jobs is required by law to have a work council whose members are elected for two-year terms by two groups: management and non-management. The employer, the president of the work council, consults with the council regarding the organization and management of the company.

The *comité d'entreprise* is financed by the company. The budget depends on the number of employees on the payroll. Foreign employees are eligible to vote in the same manner as their French colleagues after three months with the company. They are also eligible for election after one year with the company.

The cultural and social activities available to employees and their families vary. They may include a company restaurant, company library, sports club, trips, outings, festivals or company gifts. Very large companies may offer property management and holiday centres for children.

The *comité d'entreprise* may work on various projects, such as the committees for health, security and working conditions (CHSCT), in conjunction with the employee delegates.

The elected employees, the employer, and health and safety specialists monitor working conditions and implement the measures necessary to prevent accidents in the workplace.

Some multinational companies have a European *comité d'entreprise*.

Union organizations – les organisations syndicales

A company with over 50 employees may have unions, which nominate delegates to bargain collectively with the company. Eight per cent of French employees are union members – the lowest percentage in the EU.

Given the evolution of working conditions within companies and the present economic climate, union representation and their demands have changed. There are four times fewer days lost to strikes now than in the late 1980s. Many unions have become more like partners, working with the company, concerned about the success of the company and job security.

Confrontations with management are now less a question of conflict than of constructive dialogue; except in those sectors undergoing drastic transformations, or in extremely protected sectors such as public companies. (Demonstrations and public transport strikes always receive massive press coverage when workers or travellers are left stranded at airports or railway stations.)

LA GRÈVE

In the Middle Ages, the *Place de la Grève*, located on the banks of the Seine near the *Hotel de Ville* (Town Hall), was where the condemned were executed and where labourers came to look for work. Waiting or looking for work was referred to as being on 'grève'.

Today, *la grève* is the strike. The right to strike was recognized in 1864 and written into the Constitution in 1946. Going on strike can involve partial or total cessation of work and often includes street demonstrations to attract public attention.

The diversity of union representation in France reflects various schools of thought. For example, the CGT, created in 1895, is of Communist tendency. Autonomous, independent or cooperative unions also have their place in the workplace. Only 5 per cent of the working population are union members, the lowest percentage in the EU.

REPRESENTATIVE UNIONS

CGT (Confédération Générale du Travail), created in 1895;

CFTC (Confédération Française des Travailleurs Chrétiens), created in 1919;

CFE–CGC (Confédération Française de l'Encadrement – Confédération Générale des Cadres), created in 1944;

FO (Force Ouvrière), created in 1948; and

CFDT (Confédération Française Démocratique du Travail), created in 1964; FEN (Fédération de l'Education Nationale); FSU (Fédération Syndicale Unitaire de l'enseiguement.

Company representation

Employers' associations and unions – les associations et les syndicats patronaux

The MEDEF (Mouvement des Entreprises de France) has represented companies (employers' unions and so on), of all sizes and in all professional sectors (including industry, commerce, the service sector, banks, insurance) in dealings with public authorities and employees' unions – mostly in collective bargaining negotiations – since 1945. It is a forceful, active organization, which uses various types of pressure, coordination and information to represent more than a million companies. The MEDEF International represents foreign companies abroad.

The CGPME (Conféderation Générale des Petits et Moyennes Entreprise) represents 500,000 companies, the UPA (Union Professionelle Artisenale) represents artisans.

Chambers of commerce and industry

France has 150 chambers of commerce and industry (CCI). The CCIs are public entities that represent all companies, and are run by company directors elected by their peers in manufacturing, commerce and service industries of their region (www.cci.fr).

The CCIs develop training and consulting programmes specifically adapted to the needs of the different economic sectors of their area. They also administer business schools (for example, HECs), and manage airports, ports and expositions.

World Trade Centres are located in most regions of France. They are managed by the local CCI and, as their name indicates, are responsible for developing international trade.

*F*oreign representatives

Foreign or bi-national chambers of commerce, most often in Paris, aim to develop economic relations between France and other countries. They are also a useful resource and meeting place for foreign expatriates. There are 86 French CCIs and 70 local delegates in 75 countries located abroad. They are a link between exporters and importers and the economic expansion departments of the French embassies.

▬ *The International Chamber of Commerce*

A non-governmental organization, the International Chamber of Commerce represents business interests worldwide and participates in the commercial, financial and monetary sectors. Founded in 1919, it encourages exchange and investment throughout the world. Its headquarters are in Paris.

*A*n outline of social legislation

▬ *Labour law – droit du travail*

The concept of the work contract originated in France in 1898. The *code du travail* governs working conditions, social protection and worker–employer relations. In companies with more than 20 employees, the legal working week is 35 hours. Each company negotiates with the relevant unions to decide on the best way to apply the law. This method of reducing working time (*RTT*, Réduction du Temps de Travail) over the year allows employees to have more flexibility and additional days off. Economic improvement in the year 2000 and technological tools have enabled the creation of new types of work from the start-up to the independent worker.

■ *Congés payés*

Employees have the legal right to two and a half paid working days off (congés payés) for each month that they have worked. For example, holiday rights acquired from 1 June 2008 to 31 May 2009 could be used after 1 May 2009. A full year's employment entitles the employee to five weeks of paid time off. Holidays may be taken in two or more periods in the course of the following year.

Congés or vacances, both words mean the same. The holiday (*vacances*) schedule is established between the employee and the employer to satisfy the needs of both. The employee has the legal right to time off for family events (marriage, births and deaths) where the family relationship is sufficiently close.

Collective bargaining (convention collective)

Collective bargaining completes the provisions of the *code du travail*. It is an agreement, by sector of activity or profession, setting forth the terms and conditions of employment. A company agreement, signed by the employer and the union delegates, or the work council, may also be included.

Collective bargaining and/or the company agreements give form to the work contract and set down minimum wages, pay changes, and the classifications and different categories of employment.

Since the law of 1971, all companies must allocate a percentage of their annual payroll to the continued professional training of their employees. A yearly plan is established to develop training programmes to increase employee skills, and also the competitiveness of the company. If the budget is not used, it is taken by the state. In addition, there are tax incentives for companies that invest in the continuing education of their employees at accredited institutions.

▬▬ *Employment contract* – le contrat de travail

The *contrat à durée indéterminée* (CDI) (a contract of unspecified duration) is the norm, although a *contrat à durée déterminée* (of specified duration) may be offered in special cases.

The written contract, or letter of engagement, defines the employer and employee, the employee's functions, position, salary, working conditions (location, number of hours to be worked, overtime, trial period) and any special benefits. It may also contain special clauses, and create additional obligations regarding mobility, confidentiality or exclusivity.

Any special conditions – benefits or limitations – make negotiation prior to the execution of the contract essential. If your employment contract is in French, you may request a copy in English.

▬▬ *Labour laws for foreign workers*

There are a number of different types of contract for the foreign worker in France:

● A *lettre de mission*, received in your home country. This sets out the terms of your French foreign assignment (pay, housing arrangements, length of assignment). Your original contract and coverage will be the same.

● A *détachement* (outside assignment). Your contract confirms your temporary placement at a branch office or in a foreign company. You may keep your original work contract and probably benefit from the international agreements that concern social security and taxes. These agreements have been signed between France and about 30 countries.

● A *contrat d'expatriation*. Your original work contract is suspended for an agreed and defined period. You will have signed an additional clause that specifies your working conditions and your pay in France.

● A *contrat de travail de droit local*. This is a direct recruitment by a French company, and is therefore governed by French law, especially in terms of social security. Your salary will be fixed according to the French market norms. (The minimum monthly wage SMIC is revised each year. It is currently about €1,310 gross per month for a working week (35 hours), an hourly rate of approximately €8.70.)

THE PAY SLIP – LE BULLETIN DE SALAIRE OU FICHE DE PAYE

The employer gives the employee a pay slip at the end of each month. The pay slip identifies the employee and the employer. The amount of the salary (gross) with the various deductions (social charges) is the net salary shown – the taxable amount. Salaries are paid monthly in euros by bank transfer.

Appeal – des recours

The *inspection du travail* (labour inspection), a century-old institution, monitors the application of labour laws in companies and may be consulted by employees as well as by employers.

The *conseil de prud'hommes* (arbitration tribunal) is a body specializing in labour law, which regulates disputes and conflicts between employers and employees. It is composed of an equal number of representatives from management and labour, all elected for five-year terms. Foreigners may vote in the same manner as the French, but are not eligible for the office.

Resignation and dismissal

An employee may resign at any time and for any reason – or for no reason – as long as he or she gives the proper notice period. The employer may dismiss an employee provided that such dismissal is grounded on a real and serious cause, whether it is for personal reasons (fault, professional insufficiency, etc) or for economic reasons. A dismissal procedure with a specific time line must be followed by the employer.

*S*ocial security

Created in 1945, after the Second World War, the French concept of social security was founded on the principle of national solidarity between generations and is based on a system of repartition (not capitalization). Everyone working in France must contribute to social security and everyone is eligible to benefit from the system. Contributions are collected by the 105 URSSAF (*Union de recouvrement de la Sécurité sociale et des Allocations Familiales*). The *regime general* covers employees in the private sector, the *regime autonome* is for the self-employed, the *regimes speciaux* are for workers such as civil servants (fonctionnaires) and railway workers, the *regime agricole* is for agricultural workers.

Financed by contributions from employees and employers, the *régime général* includes:

• *Medical insurance, maternity benefits, work accidents and disability* – assurance maladie, maternité, accidents de travail et invalidité – managed by the Caisses Primaires d'Assurance Maladie (CPAM) and coordinated by the Caisse National d'Assurance Maladie (CNAM).

• *Family allowance* – allocations familiales – managed by the Caisse d'Allocations Familiales (CAF).

• *Old-age pensions* – assurance vieillesse – managed by the Caisse Nationale d'Assurance Vieillesse (CNAV). Benefits are now always financed by a 'pay as you go' process.

• *Unemployment benefits* – indemnités chômage – managed by the ASSEDIC and the Union l'Emploi dans l'Industrie et le Commerce (UNEDIC).

The Couverture maladie universelle (CMU) is a basic cover for people on a low income. To qualify for this, foreigners must have been permanent residents in France for at least three months and have a resident's permit.

For the last 20 years, healthcare costs have risen and there is now, it seems, a chronic social security deficit. The reason is simple. There has been a reduction in the amount of time worked (due to longer studies and unemployment) and, therefore, a reduction in the amount of contributions. At the same time, increased life expectancy has increased costs as the population ages. It is a complex social and financial problem to which there are no simple solutions.

Expatrié ou détaché: *social security rules*

The types of coverage are determined according to the nationality of the expatriate and whether or not there is a bilateral social security agreement. The *'détaché'* remains affiliated to the social security regime of his country, providing the employer abroad applies for a certificate of coverage, while the *'expatriate'* is affiliated to the local regime, which can be supplemented by additional coverage according to the level of coverage granted by the host country and its healthcare costs. When an employee works in several European countries, the social security in the country of residence prevails.

Affiliation to the French Social Security

If you have a work contract in France, your employer must register with the social security office by completing a Declaration Unique d'Embauche (DUE) prior to hiring you. You must have worked 120 hours in the period of a month following your hire within the company, to be entitled to social security and benefits. A temporary number will be given to you by your local social security office: Caisse Primaire d'Assurance Maladie (CPAM), and this will be confirmed on your social security card.

SOCIAL SECURITY CARD

- Carte vitale

Your French social security number is a combination of 13 digits that identify your gender, date of birth, country of origin and your code. It will be listed on all your pay slips and your *carte vitale*.

- Certificate of coverage

SE (sauf Europe): Etats-Unis: SE 404–02, Canada: SE 401–01 (Québec SE 401-Q-201), Japan: SE 217–06, Turkey: SE 208–01, and so on

E (Europe)
- Series 100 (E 101, E 106, E 128): sickness and maternity benefits, 121: retired people;
- Series 200: retirement and pensions;
- Series 300: unemployment;
- Series 400: family allowance.

International social security agreements

Each of the 27 countries of the EU has its own system of social security, and the Community Regulation 1408/71 aims to facilitate the free circulation of European citizens in the Member States and in the EEA. It coordinates the different national social security regimes relating to healthcare, family policies and old age. The idea is that the rights acquired in one of these countries can be used throughout the European Union. The individual will be insured in the country where he or she temporarily works, subject to having forms E101 and E106, which certify the '*détachement*' (outside assignment), the length of stay and the right to medical services. The forms also certify that the contributions will be paid by the country that is sending the employee on an assignment.

- Prestations en nature, and prestations en espèce

The employee and his or her dependents (spouse, children), regardless of their nationality, will benefit from '*prestations en nature*' (reimbursements of medical expenses provided in public clinics, and of medication) upon presentation of form E128, which is filed at his or her local '*Caisse d'Assurance Maladie*' (Social Security Centre). The '*prestations en espèce*' (cash payments as a salary replacement) will continue to be met by the country of origin where the contributions are paid.

- European Health Insurance Card (EHIC)

If you are European and are only on a short stay in France, but require medical attention, you only need to provide EHIC form (formerly E111) and you will be reimbursed for your medical expenses under the same conditions as a French contributor.

In addition to the Inter-EU agreements, about 30 other countries have signed conventions or international agreements regarding benefits, including Canada, the United States, Japan and Korea. Employees who are nationals of one of these countries can maintain their usual social security system. The United States and Canada consider other nationalities – all agreements providing for pension schemes are coordinated, but they do not have exactly the same provisions in the area of healthcare.

You may receive services or benefits from French social security (paid for by the social security of your home country), if you can justify that you have acquired the right. The international division of the social security (CPAM – Division des Relations Internationales) will establish a dossier, assess your claim and issue a number to use for future claims.

Social security in your own country is responsible for providing daily payments (*prestations en espèces*) in the event of absence from work caused by illness or a work-related injury, or during maternity leave.

Reimbursement

Medical insurance refunds are part of your medical expenses (and those of your dependents) when you are unwell. Between 40 per cent and 100 per cent of your medical costs will be covered, depending on the treatments necessary.

A memory *carte vitale* with all your health and social security data is the reimbursement system. The doctor and pharmacist will transmit an electronic healthcare form to your social security centre. You may receive payment by direct transfer to your bank by sending a *relevé d'identité bancaire* (RIB) (your bank account information) the first time you request a refund (see page 286).

Retirement

The pension fund (*caisse d'assurance vieillesse*) provides retired people with financial support redistributing money collected from the active population. The amount received will depend on the number of years worked. Where there is an international agreement, insured time worked in a foreign country is credited to your pension. All employees must be enrolled in one or more pension plans, in addition to their social security coverage.

The system of complementary insurance for upper-level employees (*cadres*) is managed by the AGIRC (Association Générale des Institutions de Retraite des Cadres).

Based on systems in Great Britain and the United States, pension funds are being introduced in France to guarantee sufficient income to retired people. These will be in addition to the basic social security benefits and additional insurance.

Family allowance

Family allocations are made monthly to families with more than two children under 16, or, if they are students, until they reach their 20th birthday. Allocations are also made before and after the birth of each child, as long as the mother has been regularly examined by a doctor during her pregnancy, and if the child has regular check-ups after birth.

Following certain international agreements, and according to your personal situation, you may benefit from family allocations if your family lives full time in France.

Additional insurance – mutuelles complémentaires

Basic social security insurance coverage may be supplemented by an additional insurance policy, known as a *mutuelle*. Some employers have collective agreements with an insurance company, which enable them to offer their employees an additional policy at low cost.

A *mutuelle*, depending on the contract chosen, may make up the difference between the actual cost of the medical care, and the percentage paid by social security. Any medical care that has been partially paid for by social security qualifies for completion of the cost by the *mutuelle*, as long as the policy payments are made.

Taxation – fiscalité

Income tax – les impôts sur le revenux

Income tax was introduced in France on 13 July 1914. The rate was just 2 per cent!

As a resident in France (or as an individual who has spent at least 183 days working or residing in France over the course of a fiscal year or over 12 consecutive months), you will have the privilege of paying French taxes. Agreements between France and some other countries have limited the possibility of double taxation – that is, paying tax in France and in your own country. A non-resident is taxable only on French source income. If you work simultaneously in two countries, you should enquire at your local tax office in your country of residency. Stock options are taxable as income. Some companies offer assistance in filling out tax forms or the tax office in your area will advise you.

- Deductions may be taken for family dependants according to the number and age of those dependants living with you.
- A small deduction is possible for domestic help, and for charitable donations.
- The actual tax imposed 'revenue net imposable' is based on the final total after deductions, and varies from 0 per cent to 40 per cent.

NB: Married couples (or those recognized as a couple) must file a joint income tax return.

- There is a supplementary social security tax, the CSG (*contribution sociale générale*) to which was added the CRDS (*contribution pour le remboursement de la dette sociale*) in 1996. These new taxes are intended to reduce the social security deficit. It is applied to professional and personal assets.
- Wealth tax (Impôt de solidarité sur la fortune (ISF) is an annual tax payable on the value of your assets (>770,000 euros) as at 1 January each year. Your wealth tax return must be filed by 15 June.

▬▬*Declaring income* – déclaration de revenus

The declaration of income is obligatory and must be made in May of each year; the form entitled '*Votre Déclaration de Revenus*' should be completed on the Internet or sent to your local tax office. You may obtain the form at your local *mairie* for your first declaration.

NB: As France has over 100 reciprocal agreements with other countries, it is unlikely that you will be able to avoid making your contribution… and a fine of 10 per cent is added to late tax returns!

If you work in more than one country, you should have asked your local tax office how best to benefit from international agreements concerning double taxation. Foreign income should be declared on a special form.

THREE OR TWELVE PAYMENTS – MENSUEL OU PAR TIERS

Income tax is not deducted at source. It is up to you to make the necessary declaration and, subsequently, payment. Payment of taxes is traditionally made three times a year in France (15 February, 15 May and 15 September) but monthly payments, which avert the agony of making three large payments, are becoming more common. You may choose the system you prefer. The amount of the payments, whether monthly or in thirds, is based on the amount paid the previous year. Monthly payments are made over 10 months, from January to October, by automatic deductions from your bank account. The remaining debt (*solde*) is paid in November and December based on the actual amount due.

▬▬ *Residence tax* – taxe d'habitation

Taxe d'habitation varies according to the commune in which you live and the value of the property. It is paid annually for the residence you occupied on 1 January, even if you leave a few weeks later! You will receive a single tax notice including television licence fee by post giving the date and payment due.

▬▬▬ *VAT, or value added tax* – TVA – taxe sur la valeur ajoutée

TVA is an indirect tax applied to products and services; it varies from 5.5 per cent to 20.6 per cent and will soon be adjusted to the European norms. TVA on newspapers, for example, is 2.1 per cent. Tax is included in the prices that are marked 'TTC'.

PARIS CAC 40

The French version of the New York Dow Jones, the Frankfurt X-Dax, the London Footsie or the Tokyo Nikkei is the Paris CAC 40 (*Cotation Assistée en Continu*). It is the stock market indicator calculated by the *Compagnie des Agents de Change* and is based on the top 40 Companies listed.

*T*he rhythm of life

Since ancient times man has found various ways to count the days and measure the passing of time, from interpreting the shadow cast upon the sundial to looking at a watch. The French today can consult the multilingual clock at the Observatoire de Paris: 08 36 66 36 36. This talking clock – a feminine voice announcing the even minutes and a masculine voice giving the uneven minutes – gives the official time in France. The clock is programmed until 25 September 2088.

In France, as in most of Europe, the clocks go forward one hour in spring in the last weekend of March (*l'heure d'été*), and go back again in the autumn in the last weekend of October (*l'heure d'hiver*).

Throughout France, on the first Wednesday of each month, a siren will be set off at precisely 12 noon in a public building. Do not

be alarmed, this is a test siren only used in case of unusual circumstances such as natural disasters. Other sirens are for the police or
the fire brigade.

24 hours a day

There is a certain non-stop rhythm to the day in big cities. The rush
hour begins as workers hurry to their offices; they may have a meeting
at 9 am (9h), a working luncheon at 1 pm (13h), a conference at 4 pm
(16h) and a drink with work colleagues at 7 pm (19h). Then, if they are
not too tired, they may meet friends at the cinema at 9.30 pm (21h30).
(24-hour time is used.) Some would do well to heed the French saying
– 'ne cherchez pas midi à quatorze heures' ('do not look for noon at
2 pm') – that is to say, do not over-complicate your life!

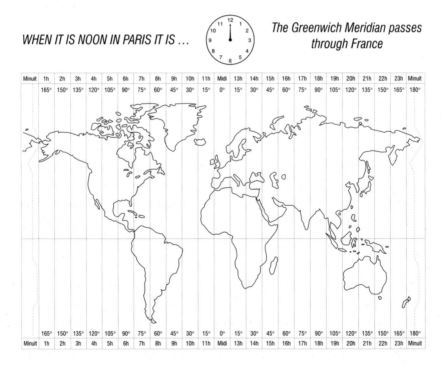

WHEN IT IS NOON IN PARIS IT IS ...

The Greenwich Meridian passes
through France

Other expressions relating to time are '*remettre les pendules à l'heure*' ('set the time'), which refers to calling someone to order.

Dates are written as they are said: *vendredi 8 août 2008, le 08.08.2008*, or simply *8.8.08*.

When people arrange a rendezvous *en quinze jours* (15 days), they mean 'in a fortnight', or 14 days (2 weeks). By *en huit jours* they mean in exactly one week (7 days).

▬▬ *Working days, holidays and the 'May bridges'* – jours ouvrables, fériés et ponts de mai

There are six opening days in the week, the seventh, Sunday, is a day of rest, except for those obliged to work, perhaps in public services and in shops. *Jours ouvrables*, are the six opening days while *jours ouvrés* are the five working days, Monday to Friday. (The words *ouvrable* and *ouvré* derive from the words *ouvrier* and *oeuvre*.)

IN A 365-DAY YEAR

There are:

- 271 full-time working days;
- 52 weekly days off;
- 11 public holidays;
- 30 paid holidays;
- 1 solidarity day (for the benefit of the elderly and handicapped).

An employee working full time will work 1,607 hours and be paid for 1,600 hours.

There are 11 official holidays in France. If they fall on a Tuesday or a Thursday, workers may *faire le pont*. This means that a 'bridge' is made over the weekend, allowing four days' holiday. The month of May has three official holidays (1 May, 8 May and Ascension Day Thursday), which shorten the working week. Some years, if the calendar is generous, France slows down in May because of the *'ponts de mai'*.

WRITING NUMBERS

When writing it by hand, the French cross the number 7, to distinguish it from the number 1. Americans and British people should heed this difference when writing down their request for a wake-up call, otherwise they may find themselves being woken up at 1 am instead of 7 am by an overzealous French hotel clerk.

When writing the figures for a sum of money, the numbers come first followed by the sign denoting the currency: 500€. In France, 200,000 euros is written 200.000€. A space or a comma can change the price of a contract!

UN AN OU UNE ANNÉE: THE WORKING YEAR

- *L'année civile*: the calendar year is from 1 January to 31 December.

- *L'année fiscale*: is a fiscal year of 12 months.

- *L'année scolaire*: a school year starts in mid-September and is divided into three terms (*trimestres*) with two months' summer holiday.

- *L'année universitaire*: the academic year has two terms (*semestres*).

See Chapter 9 on *loisirs et temps libre* (pastimes and time off).

*P*rofessional ways and customs – us et coutumes professionnels

▬▬ *Being a* cadre – *a peculiarly French concept*

The term *cadre* does not refer to a profession, but, rather, to a position in the hierarchical system. The idea of *cadre* dates from the 1930s when it had a military significance. Today, it covers various sectors, but always implies the idea of managerial or technical responsibility. It is possible to become a *cadre* by having specialized knowledge, holding a university diploma, having studied at a *grande école* (highly competitive university) or having a solid professional experience, which would make promotion within the company possible.

Although *cadre* is not defined in the *code du travail* (labour law), there is a special pension plan, the *caisse de retraite des cadres*, for employees of this level. Collective agreements generally define the work contract of *cadres* in matters of a trial working period, or three months' prior notice for a departure, or overtime.

▬▬ *Protocol*

The popular image of a *cadre* includes such accessories as *portables* (telephone and computer), *cartes de visite* (business cards). At the office he wears a suit and tie and she wears a tailored suit. It is acceptable to dress according to your activities. Often, Friday is a 'dress down day' in companies.

The French are somewhat formal in their manner of address, using *monsieur le président* and *monsieur le directeur*, for example. It is acceptable to address someone as *monsieur* or *madame*. (*Madame* may be used for all women, regardless of their marital status.) It is becoming more common for women to introduce themselves simply by their name, as in: 'Je suis Anne Dupont.' The

US managerial style has seduced some French companies. First names and the '*tu*' form are usually used between peers, but less spontaneously with superiors in the hierarchical system.

> '*Your working language may be English but understanding and speaking French will give you access to information and networks that help you to succeed.*'
> Catherine le Yaovanc

THE DIFFERENT LEVELS OF CADRE

Cadres de maîtrise (supervisory staff), *cadres dirigeants* (high management), *cadres supérieurs* (senior executives), *cadres moyens* (middle-management), *cadre fonctionnel* (staff executive), *cadre opérationnel* (line manager), *cadre stagiaire* (management trainee).

At the office, colleagues shake hands (or kiss if they are close friends) upon arrival, and sometimes on departure. The handshake, a brief warm gesture or a habit, only lasts a second. This apparent formality can be surprising to foreigners, one of whom said: 'Every morning, everyone shook hands with me as if I were new that day.'

Tu or *vous*? First name or surname? There is a delicate balance between hierarchical rules, company customs and current social practice. You will soon learn with the help of your colleagues, who will doubtless be delighted to initiate you into your company's particular way of doing things.

Business correspondence

Reports, letters or inter-office memos have a special format and use specific forms of address and courtesy. Signed documents are important as they may be used as a reference or serve as proof in time of need.

Most professional French contracts bear the words *lu et approuvé* ('read and approved') before the date and the signature. However, the increased use of e-mail has led to the emergence of a more brief and direct style.

The office

Offices have undergone various architectural changes. You will find companies with plant-filled open-plan offices with 30 people in the same area, or small individual offices with closed doors. (In the case of the latter, you should always knock and wait to be invited before you enter.) A computer with internet access, a private telephone line with voicemail, a mobile phone will allow each person to manage his or her time and correspondence. The *cadre supérieur* is usually assisted by a *collaboratrice* (personal assistant) and sometimes a secretary.

The French concept of time

'Man's time is a pleated eternity.'
'Le temps des hommes est de l'éternité pliée.'

Jean Cocteau

People live on average 25 years longer now than they did in 1890. We have time-saving gadgets and we travel quickly... but still the French are often *débordés, stressés, pressés* or *en retard* (over-worked, stressed, in a hurry or late). This is not new. In the 18th century, Voltaire wrote, *'Les Français arrivent tard à tout, mais enfin, ils arrivent.'* ('The French arrive late for everything, but in the end, they arrive'); in other words: *'Better late than never.'* 'Mieux vaut tard que jamais.'

The notion of punctuality is perhaps a question of culture, but it also depends on the individual. There are punctual French people who are precise about time and are always early, while some are always racing against the clock and yet somehow manage never to miss a plane; others, meanwhile, follow the course of the sun and have a very flexible idea of time, keeping people waiting in desperation.

According to the proverb, 'Time is money'. In business that is indeed true, but the French sense of time is not always rational or profitable. Some do not count the hours, but do know how to give of their precious time – it adds to their charm! The notion of time is sometimes flexible, and sometimes considered urgent. Meetings are delayed and timetables must be altered for various reasons, and schedules are upset. Those who run out of time have to rush.

Obviously, you should make a great effort to be punctual for a meeting which you have been asked to attend, especially if it is with a VIP; lateness might have serious consequences.

> *'The ultimate luxury is time: time we take, and time we give.'*
> Laurence Benaïm

▬▬*A working day*

Flexible working hours allow you to manage your work day at your own pace. In most large companies, employees have a badge that gives them access to the office, and also registers their time of work. Some employees start early, work late, and think nothing of the long hours spent at the office, commuting or away on business. Leaving the office at 7 or 8 pm in the evening is not unusual for the career-minded employee who has serious responsibilities.

The autonomy of some positions allows for more personal schedules. For example, some may work at home one day a week to concentrate on the creation and writing of a special report. Working on the computer at home (*télétravail*) is becoming more common.

▬▬ *Coffee break and lunch* – pause café et déjeuner

Coffee breaks are a ritual. In the morning and the afternoon people gather to chat about the weather and other goings-on, and to gossip.

The French usually consider the working day in two parts – the morning and the afternoon. The midday meal, even if it is taken on the run, is part of the rhythm of the French day, instilled since childhood. It is traditional in France to eat three times a day. Many companies have their own employee restaurants, or offer *chèques repas* (luncheon vouchers), which are accepted in most cafés or restaurants as payment for a meal. In some shops, they may be used to buy food.

DRINKS

Les pots d'entreprise (drinks at the office) are friendly get-togethers (either in small groups, or in more formal, larger gatherings) intended to foster a company spirit. A personal event, a business success or a special day may all be used as a pretext to gather over a glass of champagne or orange juice.

▬▬▬*Meetings: decisions, consultation, information* – réunions: décision, concertation, information

You may be summoned to a formal meeting with a clearly stated agenda. The objective, place, number of participants and the chairperson will set the tone. Formal meetings range from board meetings and legal discussions with business partners to the annual company conference. The latter called, rather pompously, a *convention*, or, less respectfully, the *grand-messe* ('high mass') is an event designed to inspire the employees with the company's ambitions.

Other meetings take place on a weekly or monthly basis, usually on the same day of the week, at the same time and with the same people. These meetings are designed to discuss department or team management, to bring files up to date or to develop projects.

For some people meetings at which no decisions are made may seem futile; to others, however, they are an occasion to exchange ideas and methods of working, to discuss and to reflect, until the next meeting.

Meetings in France rarely start on time to allow for late arrivals. As a result, they often last until the business at hand has been exhausted.

In international companies, the telephone, videoconferencing and e-mail make long-distance meetings possible, avoiding time-consuming and expensive travel.

▬▬▬*Conference, symposium, forum* – conférence, colloque, forum

Round tables and debates are gatherings that bring together specialists in a professional sector with well-known experts to discuss economic, scientific or technical questions.

These meetings, often held outside the company, are also a place to meet new people, and to exchange ideas and business cards over drinks. You will probably make new acquaintances whom you might meet again at the next conference, or with whom you might remain in contact by telephone.

▬ *Business lunch or working breakfast –* déjeuner d'affaires ou petit déjeuner de travail

The business lunch is a French institution. It is common to conclude an important affair in an environment that is more favourable than the office. To invite a business associate to share an excellent meal is believed to improve any professional relationship. A friendly atmosphere encourages discussion about business with the dessert, *entre la poire et le fromage* ('between the fruit course and the cheese course').

Different businesses have their own strategy and rituals, according to the business in hand, including the date, the number of guests and the placing around the table. Selecting a suitable restaurant, sufficiently well known for its menu, its service and its ambience, is of great importance.

Working breakfasts are generally held from 8.30 to 10 am with coffee and croissants, or a buffet (and the dossiers) at hand. These friendly, informal meetings are designed to take advantage of the high levels of energy experienced in the morning. Business dinners are less popular as they make the working day too long and tiring but it is another way to conclude an agreement, and the day, agreeably.

Once agreement has been reached, a special procedure is begun for the creation of the contract, which must clearly state the terms of the agreement. The French are often thought to be too formal and Cartesian in this area, ever anxious to put all the details down in perfect French.

▬ *Looking for information*

If you need professional information for your work, you might consult the internet, where you can gain access to a multitude of professional databases. Also, it is worth trying the following:

By joining a club or an association, you can develop your business network. It is *à la mode* and there are many possibilities, including business networks, sports clubs, university groups from professional or international schools and private circles (some *very* private). Influential networks facilitate entry to the worlds of finance and politics. Generally, annual membership fees have to be paid, and for some groups it is necessary to be sponsored by one or more members. The purpose and activities of these groups are varied, but there is usually a social aspect; many of them organize conferences, dinner debates, seminars and travel.

All professions have their *salons*, or trade events, some of which have professional conferences and debates with special pre-opening-day sessions reserved for companies.

● *Who's Who*, the British directory of VIPs since 1850, has a French version. It lists a favoured 20,000 French people with important specialities or functions (only 10 per cent of them are women!). Since the entries are chosen, and cannot be purchased, this is a valuable reference.

The accompanying spouse

'I found it difficult to no longer be professionally active. I organized my time into three types of activity: settling in, tourism and networking to develop professional projects.'
Edith, Canadian

Professional mobility and an international lifestyle offer many opportunities, but also lead to complex career choices for couples in which both partners work. For couples with children, the dates of transfer may not always fit in with family events or the school calendar. Today, some daring men are following their wives on foreign assignments, but it is usually the other way round.

In some situations French law permits an accompanying spouse to work. However, the *carte de séjour 'visiteur'* (residence permit) assumes that the accompanying family will be dependent. The spouse may, however, create an independent profession, if he or she has the necessary qualifications, diplomas, resources and the work is declared to the authorities. There are non-profit organizations helping to find a job to create career opportunities.

NB: Undeclared work, with non-payment of taxes and social security contributions, is *travail au noir* (moonlighting), and is illegal.

It may be necessary for a spouse to have a meaningful occupation during his or her stay in France in order to avoid a blank in a CV, which could be prejudicial to a career. Depending on your aims, your interests and your talents, you can look for personal or professional activities. Here are a few suggestions:

- enrol in a programme of study or training, which may perhaps be negotiated in the expatriation project of your spouse;

- learn a language (French, for example!), or improve your computer skills, or gain other professional skills that you will be able to use later;

- become a consultant or trainer (for example, technical, scientific or linguistic);

- create and write documents for advertising or communications;

- become a correspondent for a foreign magazine, newspaper or publication – with a computer, e-mail and the internet, there are many possibilities.

Professional or academic networks will help you discover the various opportunities available.

*F*or further information

Le Robert & Collins Eng/French, French/Eng Dictionary of Management, Business, Finance, Law (Dictionnaires le Robert)
Centre des Liaisons Européennes et Internationales de Securité Sociale (CLEISS), www.cleiss.fr (in different languages including English)

Websites dealing with formalities, practical information about daily life and law:

www.apec.fr

www.finances.gouv.fr

www.egide.asso.fr

www.pratique.fr

www.service-public.fr/etranger/info-eng.html – administrative forms are available online. The 'CERFA' logo figures on all official forms with a reference number

www.legifrance.gouv.fr/ – legal regulations

www.anaem.social.fr/defaut.php3 – French immigration office

www.travail-solidarite.gouv.fr

www.minefi.gouv.fr – Ministry of Economy and Finance

www.campusfrance.org, www.edufrance.fr/ – student gateway

www.club-international.org/cijp/index2_anglais – cultural and friendly activities and cultural exchanges between French and foreign students

www.ameli.fr, www.cleiss.fr/international.html, www.dwp.gov.uk – social security

www.impot.gouv.fr: taxes, www.douane.gouv.fr/menu.asp?id=498

www.europa.eu.int/eures/home.jsp?lang=en

www.oecd.org/eco/surveys/france

4 A few words about the French language

'I love all accents, it is that saltiness which makes the difference from the written word.'

'J'aime tous les accents, c'est le sel de la parole et la seule différence qui la sépare de l'écriture.'

Pierre Jakez Hélias

A French conversation

'It is a game of pruning shears where each clips the voice of his neighbour as soon as it sprouts.'
Jules Renard

What do foreigners think?

'I like to take part in a relaxed conversation in French, but, as soon as the discussion speeds up, everything goes too quickly. One speaks, the other agrees with short words, nods of the head, or interrupts to give his argument, or impose his opinion. They both speak at the same time and barely listen to each other.'
Michael, British

'The French speak while thinking. They speak on all tonal levels: softly and loudly, as if they were changing their mood. They do not control themselves or censure themselves.'
Hiroaki, Japanese

'It is a language of gestures and words which have a tone, a rhythm, a melody, but sometimes the way of speaking is too categorical.'
Helen, Dutch

*T*he French language

Every day, you will need to communicate with the French people around you, to speak to them and to find out information. Will you dare join in the conversation and speak a few words of French? You may be hesitant. It seems difficult, and it can be distressing, but rest assured that most French people will really appreciate your efforts to speak their language. Unfortunately, the French are not renowned for their language skills and many will not be able to help you, by addressing you in English. Do not interpret this as a lack of interest; take it, rather, as an invitation for *you* to try a little French.

French is a complex language of over 85,000 words, but they are not all essential. Victor Hugo, the writer and poet, used the most extensive vocabulary in his literary works, but the majority of us, according to our age, and our cultural, professional or social level, only use a vocabulary of about 2,000–3,000 words.

French is the mother tongue of 80 million Europeans living in France, Belgium, Switzerland, Luxembourg, Monaco, Andorra, Val d'Aoste (Italy) and Val d'Aran (Spain). Canada has seven million French speakers of whom six million live in the province of Québec. French is also the official language of 200 million people in 31 African countries. It is spoken in Lebanon, and in Haiti, the Seychelles, Madagascar, Mauritius and in Louisiana (the name of which was given in memory of Louis XIV after the discovery of the Mississippi river in 1862 by the Norman Robert Cavalier de la Salle. In New Orleans more than 200 streets have French names). It is the 19th most widely spoken language in the world.

French is one of the official languages of the UNO, UNESCO and OECD international organizations, and the most translated language in the world after English. Along with Italian, it is the diplomatic language of the Vatican. It is also the official language of the International Olympic Committee, in honour of Pierre de Coubertin, the creator of the modern games. Even the *Union Postale Universelle* (the universal Postal Union, which has 191 member countries) communicates in French.

Some foreign writers adopted France and its ways up to the point that they even wrote their novels in French. Examples include Julien Green, Andreï Makine, Nancy Houston and Hector Bianciotti.

▬▬ *Evolution*

'Because the word itself is a living creature.'
Victor Hugo

By the Middle Ages, the Latin language of Roman Gaul had been transformed – via the different regional dialects – into two main language groups. The *langue d'oïl* and the *langue d'oc* ('oïl' and 'oc' both meaning 'yes') were spoken in the north and the south respectively, the *langue d'oïl* having been influenced by the Germanic language. In the 16th century the French spoken in the Ile-de-France would become the official language when schooling was declared mandatory in 1881 by Jules Ferry. This was the language that would unify the French.

World War One brought together soldiers from the different areas of France. In order to understand one another, they had to speak French.

@ *VIENT DU LATIN*

@ comes from the Latin 'low circle' (*à rond bas*), which means minuscule (*bas de casse*). It was used as an international typographical sign for about two centuries in Europe, when it was usually put on top of the first line of address on official and diplomatic documents. It is now reigning supreme on the internet as a clever sign translated into English as 'at': @ home in France (*chez vous en France*).

In recent years, the expansion of French borders has paradoxically encouraged or reinforced the use of regional languages and dialects. People from the different regions want to affirm their particular cultural identity, and Basque, Breton, Corsican, Flamand, Occitan and the Germanic dialect spoken in Alsace are all recognized as regional languages. From north to south, France has retained a large number of accents. These are mostly heard in the countryside. It is certainly part of the charm of the provinces, but it is not always easy for a foreigner, or even a French person from another region, to understand. Radio and television journalists speak 'standard' French.

As with other languages, written French follows strict rules. The 26 letters of the alphabet, and the accents, are used to write the words, which obey a complex grammatical structure, with all the usual exceptions to the rules. Each year, new words in common spoken and written usage are added to the dictionary.

New words

'Language has always been a country of exile for immigrant words.'
Alain Rey

French, in common with all living languages, borrows words and expressions from other languages around the world. It adapts the apt or pithy from the worlds of business, science, technology, sport, advertising and politics. Thus, certain Anglicisms and their derivatives have,

---

THE DICTIONARY SESSION AT THE ACADEMIE FRANÇAISE

'The Académie Française remains, regardless of what one might say, a pretty feather in the cap of the French community.'
Pierre Mille

'The Old Lady of the Quai de Conti' is an institution founded in the 17th century by Richelieu. Its 40 members, three of whom are women, are called 'the immortals'. Valérie Giscard d'Estaing, former President of France, was elected in 2003. François Cheng, a writer, poet and calligrapher, born in China, became the first Asian academician in 2002. Assia Djebar, Franco-Algerian, was elected in 2005. According to the statutes of 1635, 'The principal function of the Academy will be to work with all care and diligence possible to give clear rules to our language and to render it pure, eloquent and apt for the use of the arts and the sciences.' Every Thursday morning since then, the academicians work on updating the dictionary of the Académie Française.

L'Institute de France houses the Académie Française and four other research and art academies under its golden dome.

Other than the Académie Française dictionary, there are other less academic editions, of all sizes, for young and old. The Maison du Dictionnaire in Paris is an amazing bookshop, with over 5,000 titles covering all subjects and languages.

with time and persistent use, become an integral part of French, and words such as *square, paquebot, wagon, station, rail* and *tunnel* have enriched the French vocabulary. Some words have kept their original spelling and pronunciation (*weekend, babysitter, hold-up*).

Some fervent defenders of the French language propose French equivalents to these Anglicisms, for example, *baladeur* instead of 'Walkman', *ordinateur* instead of 'computer', *logiciel* instead of 'software', *styliste* instead of 'designer', *équipe* instead of 'team', 'Startup' is preferred to *jeune pousse* (young bud), *mel* or *courriel*, a word from Québecois, instead of 'e-mail'. 'Fax' is quicker to say than *télécopie*, and 'rollers' sounds more hip than *patins à roulettes alignées*. Since computers (*ordinateurs*) 'speak' English, and the internet has invented its cyberspace jargon, the task of the French language defenders is very difficult.

▬ *French first names and surnames*

A certain number of surnames are derived from first names – Marie, Thomas and Richard are the most common. In France, there are approximately 900,000 different surnames, of which the most common are Martin, Bernard, Dubois, Thomas, Petit, Robert, Richard and Durand. Garcia, a name of Spanish origin, is however more common than Dupont.

Family names have been official in France since 1539. They were originally based on the name of a place (M Delille, for someone from Lille), a physical trait (M Legrand, for a tall man), a profession (M Boulanger, for the baker) or a family relationship (M Cousin). A French woman retains her maiden name as her legal name regardless of her marital status.

Since 2005, parents have been able to choose the 'family name' that they wish for their child: either the name of the father or of the mother, or of both as a hyphenated name. This choice, made at the birth of the first child, will apply to all children born of the same family.

At the time of writing, the most popular first names are Clara, Emma and Maëlys for girls and Mathis, Enzo and Mathéo for boys.

'France' is a feminine first name, and was very popular during the 1950s. Until 1994, only saints' names or historically symbolic names were officially accepted as first names. All first names are now authorized as long as they are not ridiculous or prejudicial to the child. A nickname given to children is seldom used outside of family or close friends. An exception is Zizou, a nickname for the famous footballer Zinèdine Zidane. During wars the French called British soldiers 'Tommy' because the name Tom was common in England. Americans were nicknamed Sammies, with Uncle Sam in mind.

ANGLICISMS AND GALLICISM

Check up, best-seller, brainstorming, jogging, loft, clip, cash, lobby, manager, ferry, copyright, stress, people, hacker, collector, interview, jockey, joker, label, shopping, design, high-tech, sponsor, gadget, vintage, turnover, best of, must, mailing, package, stand by and *zapper* are just some of the English words in the French dictionary. There has also been a transformation of French words into English – for example, *mousserons* into 'mushrooms', and *contrée* into 'country', while *rendez-vous* and *menu* have kept their original form. These are 'Gallicismes'. The unforgettable presence of the Normans in England is shown in the motto of the Royal Family '*Dieu et mon droit; Honi soit qui mal y pense*'.

'X' IS NOT ONLY THE 24TH LETTER OF THE ALPHABET

It is also the symbol for an unknown quantity in algebra, and is used in expressions such as *porter plainte contre X* (to bring a suit against person or persons unknown), *accoucher sous X* (to give birth without declaring the names of the mother), and *X fois* (countless times). And why is the Ecole Polytechnique called the 'X'? It is a legacy from the last century when mathematicians were known as the 'X' (the speciality of the school is mathematics).

▬▬ *Masculine and feminine*

The French language differentiates between the gender of nouns. The articles *le*, *la*, *un*, or *une* before a noun specify whether it is masculine or feminine. This can be essential to the meaning. For example, La Bourgogne is the region and le Bourgogne is the wine. The names of most French cheeses are masculine. The rules of French grammar impose the masculine over the feminine when both are referred to in the same sentence. For example, *'les garçons et les filles sont charmants'*, there is no feminine agreeing 'es' for the plural of 'charmant', even though it directly follows the 'girls' noun, and even if they are more charming than the boys!

In 1986, there was an effort at a ministerial level to impose a feminine form on the names of certain professions that had only existed in the masculine, probably because these trades had traditionally only been accessible to men (for example, *peintre* (painter), *chercheur* (researcher), *professeur, chauffeur de taxi, écrivain* and *ministre*). Today, the French are comfortable saying *'madame la ministre'* instead of *'madame le ministre'*. To the horror of the Academie Française, the Minister of Education has created a feminine form for its professions, and 'un professeur' now has the feminine equivalent of 'une professeure'.

Once upon a time (*il était une fois*), *la foi* and *le foie, le voile* and *la voile,* defy the rules of logic! Consider also *le lycée* (Greek) and *la faculté* (Latin).

Other trades are applied to both sexes equally: *un* or *une journaliste, le* or *la secrétaire, un* or *une photographe. Une personne* (a person) or *un mannequin* (a model) may be either a man or a woman.

To be a *couturier* (a dress designer) is a prestigious job for a man, but the feminine form, *couturière*, refers to a more humble seamstress. Incidentally, if you are invited to the *couturière* of a play, you will be going to the dress rehearsal at which the last stitches are added!

*T*he keys to communication

*'French is like a great organ, lending itself
to every nuance, from the gentlest sounds
to the most thunderous.'*

'Le français, ce sont les grandes orgues, qui se
prêtent à tous les timbres, à tous les effets, des
douceurs les plus suaves aux
fulgurances de l'orage.'

Léopold Sédar Sengor

The French, lovers of rhetoric and logic, love to talk. They use metaphors to debate and like to prolong the pleasure of conversation when they have the time. They know how to communicate by hinting, in a roundabout way, using an indirect style of communication, which sometimes leaves the listener guessing at what has been left unsaid. These subtleties sometimes lead to misunderstandings – it is best to interpret these with humour.

The French frequently use different levels of speech – for example, the language of the teashop and of the neighbourhood café – in the same conversation. The meaning depends on the context, the listener and the desired effect. In the same sentence, they may use a literary style into which they may let slip a few risqué expressions.

'Language is the DNA of culture.'
Gilles Vigneault

Written and spoken language have different styles, depending on the generation. French can be separated in several distinctive forms: legal, advertising, internet, and so on. Each trade has its professional jargon. Computer scientists, doctors, bankers, mechanics and even the insurance representative have a very specialized language.

Some universities or schools cultivate their own style and have adopted a special vocabulary. One school will use sporting expressions, another military phrases or technological terms. It is a way to create team spirit and to identify with the school.

The directors of a company may also adopt a particular style of expression. Some speak in the first person, using *je* (as in 'I decided'), while others, less managerial, prefer *nous* ('We have decided'). It depends on their strategy.

To speak in public, or with the press, politicians learn some set phrases in order to convince, to twist or to deflect an embarrassing question. Some have even acquired the art of replying to everything with a *langue de bois* (a 'wooden tongue'), that is to say, without saying anything at all.

The language of the young reflects passing fads inspired by ideas from various countries, or from musical styles. Their behaviour and language are often indecipherable to other generations, and especially to their parents. *Verlan* is the phonetic reversal of words (for example, *fou* becomes *ouf*, *fête* becomes *teuf*, Paris becomes Ripa), and is popular in some suburbs. Text messages sent by mobile phone could be a mysterious language: Ri129 (rien de neuf)!

In the 1950s, the working-class neighbourhoods of France's capital spoke a highly colourful and frank form of slang or *argot*. *La langue verte* was a ribald language whose familiarity and triviality sometimes made the listener blush.

AN UNDERSTATEMENT – *A* LITOTE

'Je ne suis pas mécontent' ('I am not unhappy') means 'I am happy', or *'Ce film n'est pas mal'* ('This film is not bad') means 'This is a good film'. The negative form in this case is used to express a positive feeling… with moderation.

'What the French–English dictionary doesn't tell you is that half the time merci also means 'thanks but no thanks'. Say you're offering a French guest a glass of wine and she says 'merci'. Does she mean 'yes please' – or 'no thank you'? If you're in luck, she'll also use a gesture that makes her meaning obvious, like placing her hand over her glass. But if she simply smiles and says 'merci', you have to rely on intuition, or inflection.'

Meg Bortin, IHT At home abroad

▰▰▰ *Deciphering gestures and mimicry*

Language is a mixture of expressions – words, gestures and silences – and, as such, it may be a source of incomprehension or misunderstanding. Body language, gestures and facial expressions all have their own meaning, expressing feelings and reactions (mostly of satisfaction or impatience), or revealing emotion that is not necessarily verbalized.

The expression *'tenir ses distances'* means 'to keep one's distance', but two French people speaking spontaneously will instinctively hold themselves close to each other or further apart, depending on whether they are friends, or are in a hierarchical relationship. The tone and rhythm of speech also varies according to the individual, the circumstances and the region.

It is easy to recognize a friendly, bossy or angry French person; the facial expression, tone of voice and gestures will often be revealing. Hand movements supplement the words and reinforce or diminish their meaning. Hands in pockets suggests a certain casualness. On the other hand, very busy hands indicate excitement or passion. The five fingers also have their code: one thumb up (as well as for hitch-hiking) means 'OK', but the thumb is also used to indicate the number one. By adding the other fingers, the French also count all the way to five. The fingers, hands and fists move in all directions to express themselves. With a little time, you will soon learn to translate each person's sign language!

'Americans hear only what is said, the French hear first how something is said, what is left unsaid or what is incorrect. The French prioritize relations.'

Pascal Baudry

▰▰▰ Bonjour *in daily life*

'Bonjour monsieur, comment allez-vous?' ('Good morning sir, how are you?') and *'Salut, comment ça va?'* ('Hi, how's it going?')

VOUS *OR* TU

'They always know whether to call someone *vous* or *tu*, but they can't explain it.' Jake

- The *vous* form denotes a certain distance, while the *tu* form is more familiar. In doubt, use the 'vous' form.

- *Vous* is used with *madame* or *monsieur* when the relations are hierarchical, respectful, or when speaking to strangers. *Pardon, madame. Pourriez-vous m'indiquer ou est La Poste* (Excuse me madam. Could *you* please show me to the post office?)

- *Vous* plus the first name is often used in professional relationships where there is a difference of age or in a formal context, as with a client or administrator.

- *Tu*, and of course the first name, is reserved for friends, people of the same generation and colleagues. It is used with family.

- Adults use *tu* automatically with children. Teachers establish the rules according to the age of the children at the beginning of the year. Small children use the *tu* form with their teachers, older children use *vous* with their professors.

are obviously not said to the same people, nor in the same tone of voice. The first is respectful, the second familiar.

The French often shake hands to greet one another (on arrival and departure), touch each other on the arm when speaking, and kiss. People frequently pass each other anonymously in the metro, but sometimes a friendly bus driver will greet his passengers. It is normal to say *bonjour* to your neighbours or to the *concierge* without necessarily shaking hands.

When entering a shop it is considered courteous to greet the shopkeeper and tell him or her that you would like to look, then the over-eager salesperson will not press you to buy something. *Merci* and *au revoir* ('thank you' and 'goodbye') are also appreciated even if you have not bought anything.

There is a good deal of *bon* (good) in French:

● *bon* (good); *bonbon* (confectionery – twice good); *bonheur* (happiness); *bonjour* (good day); *bon courage* (be brave); *bonne chance* (good luck); *bonne journée* (have a good day); *bonne route* (travel safely);

NB:

● *bien* (well); *bienvenue* (welcome); *bientôt* (soon); bien sûr (of course);

● biens (estate, goods).

*L*earning French

'What is my favourite language? French and Spanish have been a mixture in my life [and] I switch from one to the other just like moving from the kitchen to the lounge.'
Victoria Abril

Understanding and speaking the language of the country in which you live is obviously the best way to fit in. Your environment offers you the chance to immerse yourself linguistically. Take the opportunity to speak, without restraint, and to learn French, without being a perfectionist. Remember, you probably already use a certain number of French words and expressions – think about *rendez vous, café, chef, cordon-bleu, pâtisserie, apéritif, carte blanche* and *je ne sais quoi, faux pas, pied à terre*.

If you have children, they will probably be impatient to have play-mates; little ones seem to be more receptive to all learning situations. If they feel secure, they will dare to speak without worrying about either their grammar or their accent. 'Stop speaking English, daddy. You don't speak like my friend's parents', says little Thomas to his dad after school.

Learning French is undoubtedly more difficult for adults who can be held back by preconceived ideas about the language, or by unpleasant memories held over from school.

Where to learn

'To learn French painlessly, learn it at the dinner table. Food and language are closely related.'

'Le français sans larme, c'est à table qu'on l'apprend. Cuisine et langue sont liées.'

Jacques de la Cretelle

French is taught by more than 900,000 teachers in the world.

Numerous centres for adult language training offer a range of stimulating teaching formats. There are intensive courses in small groups, evening classes or e-learning for those who have already mastered a certain level of French. It is sometimes possible to attend a first class without further obligation, in order to find the level and the method which suits you, or to make sure that the reputation of the school is justified.

Seek recommendations from those who have personal experience, or from the local Chambers of Commerce, the Alliance Française and private schools. Some schools offer diploma courses leading to a recognized diploma or certificate.

To complete your training, watching television and listening to the radio are good ways to improve your understanding of spoken French. The internet and CDs also allow you to attune your ear to French and make rapid progress.

Another idea is the 'exchange of knowledge' type of class in which you might ask for two hours of conversation and offer, for example, a badminton session in return.

ALLIANCES FRANÇAISES

The Alliance Française Foundation, the ambassador of French language and culture, has woven a network of more than 1,000 centres in 133 countries throughout the world to encourage a friendly dialogue between people. These French-language centres allow visitors to discover France through its language and culture prior to living there.

In France, the Alliance Française has 32 cultural and linguistic centres. Located in urban centres, it offers people of all nationalities, ages and occupational backgrounds courses at all levels in living French (economic, professional and cultural vocabulary) and events (conferences, film clubs, etc).

A LA SORBONNE

Known throughout the world, the French civilization classes offered by the Sorbonne in Paris attract many foreign academics who come and struggle with grammar, writing and elocution. For advanced classes, university professors of note give brilliant conferences for lovers of French literature.

'Like French students, I came to the café to study. As I listened one old man spoke to the other, suddenly I realized I understood every word they were saying.... I was no longer an anxious outsider looking in at an alien culture. I was part of the scene.'

A postcard from France

▬▬ *Interpreters, translators and 'public scribes'*

The language barrier may sometimes be a problem for important contacts. For example, the first time you meet your children's teachers, you might want to ask a friend or an interpreter to accompany you. This will help you establish a good relationship with the school, and will reassure you.

You can often use the telephone instead of writing, but sometimes it is impossible to avoid sending a letter. You could copy the format used in a letter you have received, or ask a professional translator, a colleague or a friend to help you.

EXAMPLES OF BEGINNINGS AND ENDINGS

While letters between friends may be spontaneous and informal, other types of correspondence follow certain rules. To apply for a job, the normal style is to send a CV with a hand-written letter. For personal letters, the French generally write by hand to show respect or warm thoughts for their correspondence.

There is no equivalent of the Ms form in French. The best option is to use *Madame* rather than *Mademoiselle*, which is rather old-fashioned.

- Business letters: Madame, … Veuillez agréer, Madame, l'expression de ma considération distinguée.

- Business letters: Monsieur le Directeur, … Je vous prie de croire, Monsieur le Directeur, à l'assurance de mes salutations sincères.

- To an acquaintance: Cher Monsieur, … Je vous remercie de l'intérêt que vous portez à mon dossier et vous prie de croire, Cher Monsieur, à l'expression de mes meilleures salutations.

- To an acquaintance: Chère Madame, … Bien cordialement.

- Between friends: Cher ami, … Bien à vous, *or* Amicalement, *or* En toute amitié.

Some cities have seen the rebirth of an ancient trade of the *écrivain public* (the public letter writer). These modern-day scribes will write any document, dossier or letter with which you need help. The Academy of Public Writers lists more than 200 writers under the heading *'Ecrivains publics'*; be sure to ask the price prior to ordering.

*D*eciphering codes

▬*Logos: modern emblems*

The traditional coat of arms of towns, regions and institutions have become logos. These symbols represent, in a modern graphic form, a personality, site or product. They are shown on official documents or stationery and create a memorable identity for business or advertising purposes. The logos of some *régions* and *départements* use the same colours – often blue and green – and this makes it rather difficult to tell them apart.

▬*Acronyms*

Acronyms are retained more easily than a long name and are often used in daily and professional life. Some no longer need an explanation:

- CH (Confédération Helvétique) for Switzerland
- PDG (Président Directeur Général)
- SDF (Stade de France, or *sans domicile fixe*, homeless)
- PACS (*Pacte civil de solidarité* – civilian agreement of solidarity, cohabitation, common law marriage)
- VO (original version)
- NDLR (*note de la rédaction*)

- PJ (*pièce jointe* – enclosure)
- HS (*hors service* – out of order)
- CQFD (*ce qu'il falloit démontrer,* equivalent to QED)

ASAP (as soon as possible) can lead to variations such as *aujour-d'hui sans attendre plus.*

Sometimes, personal initials become commonly used acronyms: VGE (former president of France Valéry Giscard d'Estaing) and YSL (the couturier Yves Saint-Laurent), and businesses such as LVMH (Louis Vuitton Moët Hennessy) enjoy such recognition.

SIGNS

You will notice that some signs have both letters and symbols. They announce the proximity or the entrance to a hospital (H), a parking-lot (P), the metro (M) or the regional express train (RER). 'RN' means 'route nationale' and 'CB' indicates that credit cards are accepted. WC of course indicates the toilets.

Abbreviations: 'Bobo fan de déco et de bio…'

French people, and particularly the young, seem to enjoy abbreviating words. The word *cinématographe* has been shortened over time to *cinéma*, and then to *'ciné*, while *photo* has replaced *photographie*. The *métro* was originally called the *métropolitain*, in 1900. *Bac* is quicker to say and write than *baccalauréat*. The same case may be made for *resto (restaurant), expo (exposition), geo (geographie)* and *philo (philosophie). Info, edito, pub, foot…*

'Successors to the socially minded sixties generation, the bohemian-bourgeoisie – the bobos – have held on to their parents' liberal values but combined them with an acquisitive, self-interested 80s materialism.'

Amelia Gentleman, 2003

'Bourgeois' refers to BCBG – *bon chic, bon genre* – the concept of the traditional conservative family.

'*Système D*', where '*D*' is for '*débrouillard*', has come to be used in reference to a very resourceful person, and is also the title of a monthly DIY magazine. It is said that the French will unravel anything to find a solution to a problem.

AZERTYUIOP refers to the French computer keyboard, as opposed to QWERTYUIOP, which refers to the universal or English keyboard.

Colours in everyday life

'*En voir de toutes les couleurs*' ('to go through all the colours', ie 'to go through hell') might apply to your daily life in France. As you read through this book, you will discover the meaning of the following colourful terms:

- *carte bleue, zone bleue, les 'bleus'* (French football team);
- *carte grise, matière grise*;
- *carte blanche, faire un chèque en blanc, nuits blanches*;
- *carte verte, numéro vert, itinéraire vert, classes vertes, espaces verts, doigts verts* or *main verte, billet vert* (dollar);
- *liste rouge*; and
- *pages jaunes, maillot jaune, carton jaune*.

Rose and Blanche are nice first names.

In a restaurant, the waiter will ask you if you would like your red meat *bleu, saignant* or *à point?* (almost raw, bloody or just done). *La viande blanche* (white meat) is pork, veal or chicken. You will have the choice between '*blondes*' and '*brunes*', which means cigarettes of Virginia tobacco or black tobacco. If you add a *rousse* ('redhead'), you will also have a beer.

On the Paris Métro you can go to Chateau Rouge, Chemin Vert, Maison Blanche or Porte Dorée stations.

Other colourful sayings...

'If the brain were really pink, nobody would ever be brooding over dark thoughts.'
Pierre Dac

Idiomatic French expressions often make use of colours:

● *le marchand de couleur* – a term used in the past for a paint sales representative;

● *donner le feu vert* – giving the green light, authorizing;

● *se mettre au vert* – going to the country, relaxing in the greenery;

● *marquer à l'encre rouge* – to mark with red ink, for a bad debt that is 'in the red';

● *se fâcher tout rouge* – to be red in the face with rage;

● *voir la vie en rose* – to see the world through rose-tinted glasses;

● *rire jaune* – an embarrassed or forced laugh;

● *avoir une peur bleue* – to be 'blue' with fear;

● *avoir les idées noires* – to have pessimistic and anxious thoughts;

● *écrire noir sur blanc* – to put something in black and white;

● *montrer patte blanche* – to show a white paw, in other words, to make a sign of recognition;

● *en voir des vertes et des mûres* – 'to see them green and to see them ripe', that is, to be confronted by difficult or shocking events;

● *annoncer la couleur* – to show your true colours, or to speak frankly.

*T*he French media

'Free communication of ideas and opinions is one of the most precious of the rights of man. Consequently, every citizen may speak, write and print freely; yet, he may have to answer for the abuse of that liberty in the cases determined by law.'
Declaration of the Rights of Man and of the Citizen, 1789

Freedom of the press is a fundamental right guaranteeing pluralism. The media bring the world to our door. The working population of France spends an average of 30 minutes a day reading a newspaper, one hour listening to the radio and three and a half hours watching television. The US working population spends an average of four and a half hours watching television and the Japanese five hours. Youngsters enjoy watching television on their computers and mobile phones.

France has some 200 press agencies providing the media with information. The AFP (Agence France Press), founded in 1835, is the world's oldest established news agency. It is at the head of a fantastic satellite network that broadcasts information non-stop 365 days of the year in 130 countries and territories. The dispatches go out in four languages to newspapers, radio stations and television stations, as well as to private clients, including international organizations, administrations, banks and companies.

The daily press is in intense competition with the 24-hour television news coverage. The weekly press allows you to complete your reading (with supplements, special editions), giving you a week in which to read it. The French are very keen on magazines, and new titles appear regularly (1,600 magazines monthly, weekly and quarterly).

Newspapers and magazines are sold at kiosks on street corners, at the *Maison de la Presse*, and at the newsagents. If you do not find the magazine you want, order it or subscribe to it. The kiosks in railway stations, airports and some metro stations offer a large array of magazines, as well as a few books, and snacks to munch on during the journey.

Public transport is a favourite place for reading newspapers, or books. You will often see commuters reading over the shoulder of a neighbour, spotting a word here and a headline there.

▬ *Newspapers*

More than 80 newspapers are published daily in France. Among the big dailies are those listed below. Most magazines and newspapers are also published on the internet.

■ *National daily newspapers*

● *Le Monde*, founded in 1944, is the accepted authority on domestic and international politics. It offers special supplements during the week (finance, job offers, books, art and theatre) and a selection from the *New York Times*. There are also *Le Monde d'Education* and *Le Monde Diplomatique*.

● *Le Figaro*, a conservative daily founded in 1854, has financial pages, and an eagerly awaited daily section of job offers, especially in the *Figaro Reússir* (Monday edition). The Wednesday edition includes *Figaroscope*, a very informative calendar of cultural events. On Saturday there are the magazines *Le Figaro Magazine* and *Madame Figaro*.

● *Le JDD (Journal du Dimanche)* is a Sunday newspaper and includes the magazine *Femina*.

● *Le Parisien*, a popular daily, offers several different editions for the suburbs of Paris, and *Aujourd'hui en France* contains similar information but is for the regions.

● *Libération*, a newspaper for the '1968 generation' was founded in 1973, and is a free spirit.

● *L'Humanité* is the Communist Party newspaper.

● *La Croix* is the Roman Catholic newspaper.

• The financial newspapers mostly read in the business world are *Les Echos* and *La Tribune*.

Daily free newspapers

• *Métro, 20 Minutes, Direct Plus, Direct Soir* (only distributed in big cities).

■ *Regional newspapers*

In the provinces, the local and regional press brings the local news to its faithful readers. *Ouest France*, the biggest regional newspaper in France, with 850,000 copies distributed.

MAP OF REGIONAL NEWSPAPERS

Source: Syndicat de la presse quotidienne regionale

● *Le Canard Enchaîné* (the title is a play on words for 'scandal rag'), founded in 1915, with no advertising to curb its independence, reveals or discusses the latest news with matchless satirical wit each week.

● and … *La Bougie du Sapeur Camember*: this newspaper, issued on February 29 on leap years only, was inspired by a cartoon character born on 29 February 1824.

■ *Only available online*

● www.rue89.com, which was launched in 2007;

● www.agoravox.fr; this website wants to be a 'media citoyen' and invite citizens to send articles to the editor;

● www.mediapart.fr;

● www.cafebabel.fr, which is available in seven languages.

Magazines

■ *News magazines*

Each week, fortnight or month, various general interest news magazines cover important subjects or social issues in their pages, their approach depending on their political or social position:

● *Courrier International*;

● *Le Point, Challenges* and *L'Express* interest middle-of-the-road conservative readers;

● *Le Nouvel Observateur* is on the Left;

● *Marianne* (with no advertising);

● *La Vie* and *Le Pélerin* are Catholic; and

● *Paris-Match* deals with people and happenings;

● *A Nous Paris* (free magazine).

■ *Business and finance magazines*

- *Capital Management*;
- *L'Expansion*;
- *Enjeux les Echos*;
- *L'Entreprise.*

■ *Women's magazines*

A number of magazines are aimed at women. They tackle different aspects of daily life and follow the yearly trends; some also deal with social issues:

- *Elle*: Since its beginning in 1945, *Elle* has always featured a woman's face on its cover, except for number 2887 on 2 May 2001, which featured a Tchadri to denounce the persecution of women in Afghanistan.

- *Marie Claire, Marie France*;
- *Cosmopolitan, Biba*;
- *Atmosphère;*
- *Vogue*; and
- *Femme Actuelle.*

■ *Men's magazines*

A few modern men's magazines are available, even though men love to read women's magazines.

■ *General interest*

The French press publishes various magazines on such subjects as travel, science and nature, health, arts and hobbies. They are very well researched, interesting to read, and a pleasure to browse through because of the quality of the reporting and the photos:

- *Géo*;
- *National Geographic*;
- *Maison et Jardin*;
- *Art et Decoration*;
- *Ça m'intéresse*;
- *Sciences et Vie*;
- *Selection du* Reader's Digest;
- *Terre sauvage*; and
- *Maisons Côté Sud, Côté Ouest, Côté Est*.

There are also numerous professional or technical (mostly computer) magazines. Estate agencies have their own press, as do gastronomes and theatre-goers.

The French also cater for loyal pop or rock fans with music magazines for every kind of interest.

Sports, professional and technical press

The sports press is extensive. As well as some general newspapers such as *L'Equipe* and *L'Equipe Magazine*, many sports have their own weekly or monthly magazine such as *Auto moto*.

Children's and youth press

Children's magazines aim for readers from 6 months to 16 years and hope to engage their loyalty with educational publications that evolve with the growing child. There are more than 100 titles including *Quoti, Le petit Quotidien, Popi, Pomme d'Api, Astrapi, Picoti, Toupie* and *Tobbogan*.

Video games are the passion of young teenagers, and youth magazines therefore face tough competition. Some publications remain popular, including *Mon Quotidien, Le Journal des*

Enfants, Mikado, Okapi, Phosphore, Talents, Géo Ado, Les Clés de L'Actualité and *L'Actu*.

Information websites also exist for teenagers such as www. asapfrance.info.

FOREIGN NEWSPAPERS AND BOOKSHOPS

The kiosks in airports, large railway stations and some newsagents offer foreign titles, including dailies (allowing for the difference of time zones) and news magazines. *The International Herald Tribune* is the newspaper of choice for most English-speaking people in France.

In Paris, the Centre Beaubourg offers a large range of foreign newspapers, which can be read at their library.

The libraries of some foreign organizations have a lending service, and foreign language bookshops can be found in the biggest towns throughout France.

A few newspapers written in English and published in France by the English-speaking community can also be found:

- *French News;*
- *Brit Mag;*
- *The Connexion;*
- *Paris Time;*
- *FUSAC.*

Radio

> '*The radio marks life's minutes, the newspaper the hours, the book the days.*'
> Jacques de Lacretelle

The radio has a special place in French life in the morning from the first waking moment till arrival at the office. Many people listen to the radio while they are commuting by car.

The FM frequency offers numerous local stations. Most stations are specialized in order to develop listener loyalty to compete with the general interest stations. There are six national radio stations such as Radio France (France Inter, France Info, France Culture, France Bleue…), Europe 1, RTL and RMC. The French international radio station Radio France Internationale can be heard worldwide. Some foreign stations can be received in some areas, including the main BBC stations.

Television and radio

'The French talk a lot at meal times and like to be up to date with world news.'
Saori

Television is the most popular medium in France, especially with elderly people and children. Private or public, the channels are in bitter competition.

● The public channels, France 2 and France 3 are general interest. France 5 is a daytime channel with an educational orientation. A Franco-German network, Arte, transmits cultural programmes in the evening on Channel 5.

● There are two private channels, TF1 and M6.

● Canal Plus, BBC and CNN are just three of the many subscription (cable television) channels. Themed channels on subjects such as sport, news and cinema are available on cable and satellite.

● France 24 and TV5 offer French programmes to foreign stations under the label France Monde.

Viewers may choose between films, documentaries, sports, music, variety, game shows and news programmes, which are carefully monitored to see which are the most profitable. Television, like radio, broadcasts economic and political programmes during peak hours (interviews, face-to-face, round-tables), aimed at enlivening the exchange of ideas. Special logos –10, –12 and –16 provide information to parents.

Some regions in France, especially those near to the borders, can receive transmissions from Belgium, Luxembourg, Germany, Switzerland, Italy or Spain.

You will be able to receive foreign programmes by subscribing to cable television. If your neighbourhood is not connected, or not scheduled to be connected for cable service, you will need a satellite dish to receive transmissions directly via satellite. The dish can be fixed to the roof, a wall, or a balcony, and you will be able to find out more information at one of the satellite networks.

EURONEWS FROM LYONS

If you are connected to cable, Euronews, which has been based in Lyons since 1993, is a European news channel that broadcasts in seven languages in conjunction with the other countries of the EU. Euronews offers a wider perspective on the world, with a focus on European information from business to sport.

The television schedule is printed in the daily newspapers and there are also weekly magazines. The best known is *Télérama*, which offers literary and film reviews, while *Télé Loisirs* and *7 Jours* are also popular.

Not all video players are compatible with French television, which is equipped with a system called 'SECAM3' (other countries have a system called 'PAL'). The *multisystème* can get around the problem, but some tapes will only be shown in black and white. Check on this point with a specialized television shop. You may find home video very useful for seeing programmes from home or for catching British and US films, which are often broadcast in English very late at night. You can also borrow CDs from the local public library, or rent or buy them.

NB: You must pay an annual *redevance* (television licence) once a year with your residence taxes (if you have a television). If you have several televisions at the same address, you will only be required to pay once.

Centre d'Accueil pour la Presse Etrangère (CAPE)

CAPE is the orientation and meeting centre for the international press. It welcomes correspondents newly arrived in Paris and foreign journalists sent to cover a particular event or investigate a specific aspect of French life. The centre organizes press conferences or debates by French and foreign figures on headline issues in the national and international news.

PRESS CLUB À PARIS

Since the 19th century, side by side with their French colleagues, foreign journalists have witnessed both the good times and the tragedies.

The Association de la Presse Etrangère à Paris (APE) was created in 1944 to facilitate the work of journalists of all nationalities; under the guidelines of the freedom of information, they remain totally independent.

'Being a foreign correspondent demands a formidable capacity for adaptation... the discovery of a new culture. And Paris is not an easy town! Yes, she is beautiful, feverish and captivating. But Paris is also capricious, temperamental, and prone to administrative problems. Paris is also a thousand unanswered questions.'

Tuulikki Muller (APE President, 1994)

There is also a French–American Press Club in Paris for English-speaking journalists, created in 2002 under the aegis of the French–American Chamber of Commerce.

*F*or further information

The Oxford Companion to French Literature (Oxford University Press)
Les Mots Anglais du Francais, Jean Tournier (Belin, 1998)
Les Faux Amis de l'Anglais, Frédéric Allinne (Belin, 1999)
Dictionnaire des Mots d'Origine Étrangère, Henriette et Gérard Walter (Larousse, 1998)
www.int.com/athomeabroad
www.alliancefr.org/ – Alliance française
www.francophonie.org/
www.afp.com – press agency
www.radiofrance.fr/ – gateway for public radio
www.pariscope.fr – weekly events in Paris
www.francemag.com, www.livingfrance.com – Monthly magazine
www.frenchnews, www.theconnexion – Monthly English newspaper
www.ape.fr – Association de la Presse étrangère, www.cape.fr
Pardon my French, Charles Timoney (Penguin, Reference language, 2007)
The Story of French, Jean-Benoît Nadeau and Julie Barlow (St Martin's Press, 2006)
Le Robert & Collins Eng/French, French/Eng – Dictionaries of Management, Business, Finance, Law
Americans in Paris – A literary anthology, Adam Gopnik (The Library of America, 2004)
Paths to Contemporary French Literature, John Taylor (Transaction Publishers, 2004)

5 *Home comforts*

– accueil tout confort

*'Countless are our lives
and our chance abodes.'*

'Innombrables sont nos vies et nos
demeures incertaines.'
Saint-John Perse

*W*here?

There are detailed maps of every town in France, often free at the local tourist centre or *mairie*, or for sale in bookshops and newsagents. Local town maps will show the *quartiers* and *arrondissements* with the streets listed alphabetically to help you find your way.

Before choosing a place to live, make enquiries about the town and its different areas. There are working-class and smarter neighbourhoods, tourist areas and business districts, each with its own special flavour. Some have cheaper rents, while others may be nearer to the shops, public transportation or schools. Explore the town and learn its layout before you go about choosing a location for your new home.

In town, there are *avenues, boulevards, rues, squares* and *impasses*, which bear the names of famous places, events or people. The most common are Victor Hugo, Jeanne d'Arc, Racine, Voltaire, Marie Curie, Jules Ferry, Charles de Gaulle, behind the traditional rue de l'Eglise or rue de la Gare.

Although it is easy to find an address by following the house numbers – even on one side and odd on the other – sometimes, even the even are odd: n° 20 might be followed by n° 20 bis, and n° 20 ter (20a, 20b), before going on to n° 22. In Paris, the Seine is a precious landmark as the house numbers always start at the river and grow higher towards the outskirts.

The first time you visit a friend in town be sure to note not only the exact address, but also the *digicode* (the security door code), the name or number on the *interphone* (the intercom), and the floor of the apartment, and the location of its door!

For security reasons, buildings are equipped with a *digicode* and an *interphone* to limit access to residents and invited guests. A number still have a *concierge* or *gardien* to maintain the property. The *concierge* offers many useful services to new residents, such as telling you where to find the shops and other places you need, or receiving packages and deliveries in your absence.

S*earching for a home*

■■■*Location, size and price*

The French spend almost one-third of their income on housing. More than half of them are home-owners and a tenth own a second home, such as a family house in the country, or an apartment at the seaside or in the mountains.

For a renter, finding a dream home that is comfortable, well situated and a reasonable price is not easy. In the bigger towns, rents are based on the number of square metres. In Paris, the average size for an apartment is 40 square metres for a 'two *pièces*' (two rooms, plus kitchen and bathroom), and this is considered ideal for a single person or a young couple. The rent is monthly and approximately €20–30 per square metre, or more in a 'better' neighbourhood.

In the suburbs or the provinces, individual houses offer more space than an apartment, with rents that vary, according to the quality of the home and the importance of the town and its amenities (whether it has a railway station, a cinema or a sports centre).

■■■*The classified advertisements* – les 'petites annonces'

'*Appartement, maison, villa*': the advertisements briefly describe the rental property, its size, its layout and its location. A *studio* is a one-room apartment with a kitchen area (which might or might not be *équipée*, in other words, equipped with a stove, a refrigerator and so on), a *salle de bains* (a bathroom with a *baignoire*, or bath), or a *salle d'eau* (a bathroom with a *douche*, or shower). 'F2', 'F3', 'F4', 'F5' represents the number of principal rooms, not counting the kitchen, bathroom or toilet. A *séjour double* is one big living room, which counts as two rooms. Unfurnished is totally empty whereas 'meublé' indicates that the apartment is equipped with the furniture and fittings necessary for daily life.

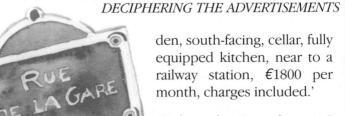

DECIPHERING THE ADVERTISEMENTS

'Appt. 180 m2, au 3e ét. comprenant salon, séj. dble, bur., 4 chbres, sdb, s. d'eau, ling., 2 WC, placards, cave et garage.'

'Apartment of 180 sq m, on the 3rd floor, including a lounge, a double living room, an office, 4 bedrooms, a bathroom, a shower room, a linen room, 2 toilets, cupboards, cellar and garage.'

'Rés standing: 3 p. 73 m2, séj., jardinet privatif, Sud, cave, cuis. aménagée – proche gare – €1800 cc.'

'Residence of quality: 3 principal rooms, 73 sq m, living room, minuscule private garden, south-facing, cellar, fully equipped kitchen, near to a railway station, €1800 per month, charges included.'

'Grd. studio "sous les toits" refait neuf, imm. ancien, salle de bns, WC, chauffage individuel, quartier du Marais – Paris – €1200.'

'Large one-room apartment, top floor (or attic), just redecorated, old building, bathroom, toilet, individual heating, a neighbourhood in the Marais area of Paris – €1200 per month.'

'Maison, 102 m2 meublé: 4 pieces, office, SdB et SdE, cuisine, garage, jardin. Quartier calme.'

'House, 102 sq m furnished: 4 principal rooms, office, shower room, bathroom, kitchen, garden. Quiet location.'

The *rez-de-chausée* (RdC) is the ground floor (the first floor for Americans), at street level. A *rez-de-jardin* is a ground-floor apartment, which opens on to a garden. An *ascenseur* – a lift (elevator for Americans) – or the stairs, lead to the upper *étages* (floors or storeys). The *premier étage* is the first floor (the second floor in the United States). The *cave* is the cellar, normally *au sous-sol* (underground). This is where you might find *le parking*, where you may rent a space for your car.

Special rental sections ('*Locations*') of the daily newspapers, or specialized publications, will give you an idea of the prices and help you make your choice. *Le Figaro* and the *International Herald Tribune* cover Paris and the suburbs, while the regional press cover the provinces. *Locations et Ventes, De Particulier à Particulier, La Centrale des Particuliers* cover property all over France (plus sections on cars and home furnishings for sale). There are also free local weekly newspapers, which you will find in some shops (for example, bakeries) and dedicated websites.

In Paris there are publications full of classified advertisements, which may be found free at many Anglophone centres in Paris (cafés, bookshops and so on), such as *FUSAC, Paris Time*. OVNI is the information exchange publication for Japanese in Paris and the French in Tokyo, with advertisements of all kinds, mainly property rentals.

■■■ *Other places to search*

● When you have selected a neighbourhood, you could ask *concierges*, or local shopkeepers, who hear all the gossip about available apartments.

● Property agents, preferably registered with the FNAIM (Fédération National de l'Immobilier), have websites. Estate agents and owners all request serious guarantees – an income three times the amount of the rent, plus a *caution financière* (someone who guarantees to pay the rent if you are unable or unwilling to make payment). The agency's commission must be clearly indicated. It is usually equal to one month's rent, or 10 per cent of the annual rent, and is due only when a lease is signed.

• The internet has online property lists and a rental transaction is directly between landlord and tenant, bypassing the usual agency fee.

• Associations of foreigners resident in France offer a welcome and comfort to their fellows, and also share information on available housing, including rentals, exchanges and apartment shares for short-term stays, as well as au-pair positions.

• Some employees benefit from the services of relocation specialists, who find apartments, and assist with installation and administrative questions.

• Seasonal rentals for holidays: numerous offers of short-term furnished rentals are published every day on the internet and are displayed by geographic areas. Beware when you pay for a reservation.

• Hotels: weekly or monthly rates are available in most hotels, which are classified by the Ministry of Tourism. A four-star hotel is very comfortable, while a two-star is comfortable; the staff usually speak English. Prices vary according to the number of stars.

• For young people, there are youth hostels and student housing networks – CROUS (Centre Régional des Oeuvres Universitaires et Scolaires) and CIDJ (Centre Information et de Documentation Jeunesse) – which give information and assistance.

When you do find an offer that interests you, you should make an appointment quickly (or, if a rental is listed with a day and time for viewing, arrive very early at the address given), and be prepared to make a decision on the spot. Good places do not stay on the market for long.

Rental/lease contract – contrat de location/bail

The bail describes the apartment, the rent, how and when the rent should be paid and revised, the amount of the deposit and the date on which the lease begins. Two copies are made and signed by the landlord and tenant. If it is requested the landlord should send a receipt free of charge for rental payment made. This is necessary not only as proof of payment, but also to give you the *justification de domicile* so frequently requested by the administrative services (to obtain a *carte de séjour,* to open a bank account and so on).

Sharing an apartment is becoming a common practice in France. Colocation two-room apartments are plentiful and landlords prefer to sign a contract with just one tenant. Even so, sub-letting (*sous-location*) is possible, if the landlord agrees.

The lease for unfurnished apartments is fixed for three years, but may be reduced to a year if personal or professional reasons are given prior to the signing of the contract. When the lease expires, it is automatically renewed for another three years, unless either the landlord or the tenant decides otherwise. The contract includes the following:

● *Les charges locatives* – these charges are in addition to the rent and are based on the previous year's costs for the maintenance of the building (*concierge*, cleaning and electricity for the communal areas, etc). At the end of the year the actual charges are calculated and the tenant is either reimbursed or sent a bill for the difference.

● *Le dépôt de garantie* – the deposit, usually one month rent, and kept by the landlord until the tenant leaves the apartment. It is returned after all money owing on the apartment has been paid (rent, repairs, utilities, etc).

● *La caution* – this is a guarantee by a third person who promises to pay any money owing on the apartment if the tenant is unable, or unwilling, to meet his or her obligations.

NB: This is a legally binding promise and should not be entered into lightly.

● *L'état des lieux* – prior to moving in, a complete inventory of the contents and the condition of the property is established between the landlord (or his agent) and the tenant. The *état des lieux* is signed by both parties and each keeps a copy. This is an important document as it meticulously describes the state of the apartment on entry, and will be referred to when the tenant leaves the property. If there is any damage, the *dépôt de garantie* is used to pay for any necessary repairs or cleaning.

● *Une reprise* – sometimes a previous tenant will have installed fixtures, or renovated the apartment, and may try to sell these additions to the next tenant. The latter is not obliged to accept the proposal and should only do so if it seems worthwhile.

● *Départ et préavis* – the tenant should give the landlord three months' *préavis* (notice) before leaving the property. This should be sent by *lettre recommandée avec avis de réception* (registered letter). If the tenant is transferred by his or her company, or becomes unemployed, then the *préavis* is reduced to one month. At the end of the lease, the landlord may reclaim the apartment, but only if he or she is able to prove that it is for personal use, or that it is to be sold. The tenant must be given six months' notice of this.

NB: Residence tax is charged (with the television licence fee) to individuals who occupy a property at 1 January of the year.

*R*ent or buy?

Let's say you have visited France many times for business or holidays and you have fallen for the Latin, Celtic, Nordic, or, in one word, French charm. Then it is time to realize your dream: owning a lovely home somewhere in the country of Descartes, Voltaire,

Balzac. The country that is twice the size of Great Britain and 17 times smaller than the United States or China, 8 times bigger than Switzerland and 30 times smaller than Russia, but the largest country in the EU.

▬ *Overview*

Buying a holiday home or a permanent residence, a house or a flat, requires a lot of thought. French law may seem tricky, and it is! So you need to be guided step by step on financial issues to define your budget, on legal aspects according to your family situation (taxation, inheritance, etc) and on the practicalities (appointing a *notaire*, preferably a bilingual one).

When you have found the ideal region and location with the help of an estate agent – and be sure the agent holds a *carte professionnelle* – you have to conclude an agreement with the seller. On signing '*le compromis de vente*' – the initial agreement – you pay a deposit of around 10 per cent of the purchase price. All the conditions of the transaction must be presented in writing, such as the description of the property and the means of purchase. Make sure a clause (called *conditions suspensives*) is inserted stating, for example, that the transaction is subject to a mortgage acceptance.

NB: As Independent Professional and Public Officer, the *notaire* has a monopoly on conveyancing (*vente de biens immobiliers*) and he or she is in charge of the deed of sale (*acte authentique de vente*). Fees are fixed by law and the buyer is free to choose his or her own *notaire*. If the vendor also appoints his or her *notaire* for assistance, the same fees are split equally in two ways. (www.notaires.fr gives helpful information in English.)

*H*ouse and personal insurance – assurances du logement et des personnes

Multirisques habitation insurance – a comprehensive insurance policy that covers fire, water damage, ice and storm damage and theft – is obligatory for all tenants. It also covers any accidents caused by family members to a third person.

Prior to signing an insurance contract written in French, you should have a clear explanation of the exact price and coverage, and should always compare insurance companies.

You must decide the value of the property you wish to insure (furniture, jewellery, etc). You should ask for help from colleagues on the subtle definitions of the guarantees.

On the contract will be your name, address, the exact coverage and exclusions, the date on which the policy takes effect and its duration, and the amount of the payments and taxes. If you have a chimney in use, it has to be cleaned once a year. The invoice will be your proof of having had this done. Beware! If your home is empty for more than 30 days per year, the insurance company might not cover it.

In France, as elsewhere, there are thieves. The *multirisques habitation* insures against theft, but has very specific conditions for reimbursement – you must have *portes blindées* (security locks on the doors), and *volets aux fenêtres* (shutters on the windows).

Vol complémentaire is an insurance contract that covers especially valuable possessions, such as artworks, jewellery or antique furniture. Keep the bill of sale on all valuables purchased or evaluated, and take photos of the objects insured. This makes it easier to prove the existence and the value of objects stolen in case you have to claim reimbursement.

As most thefts occur at weekends or when you are on holiday, take a few precautions:

- Never allow your letter box to accumulate too many letters. Ask the post office to forward your letters. Alternatively, the guardian or a reliable neighbour might hold them for you until your return.

- Ask a reliable neighbour to check your door from time to time, to make sure that it is locked.

If you do have the misfortune to be burgled, make a complaint at the local police station or *gendarmerie* – *'porter plainte contre X'* ('against a person unknown'). A copy of this *déclaration* is then sent to your insurance company by registered letter with an inventory of the stolen property.

M*oving in and moving out –* déménager et emménager

As a well-organized person, you have of course prepared your move. Children, depending on their age, will often willingly help with the packing, arranging their own particular treasures in such a way that they will easily be found on arrival.

▬ *Moving companies*

International removals companies offer a specialized service according to the volume of your possessions. Obtain several estimates made before choosing:

- *service total*: a complete service whereby the household objects are packed and unpacked by the shippers;

- *service standard*: the shippers wrap up the furniture and fragile objects, but the client takes care of the rest;

- *service économique*: the client is responsible for packing and unpacking the possessions in the containers, which are supplied by the shippers. Only the furniture will be dismantled and reassembled by the shippers.

The removals firm's liability will be based on the contract chosen and the declared value. Before paying the bill and signing the release papers, you should open all your boxes and check for damage.

CUSTOMS – LES DOUANES

- The French customs service wishes to discourage travellers from purchasing counterfeit (*contrefaçon*) or pirated goods. All thefts of industrial and intellectual property must be sanctioned.

- If you are settling on a permanent basis, a detailed inventory of the household goods and their value will be given to the customs office on arrival. Your car will be included if you decide to bring it. You will sign a document stating that all objects entering France are personal possessions and they must have been purchased more than six months in advance of your move to France. You will promise not to resell the objects for one year. Although you will not be taxed for normal household items, there are special conditions attached to certain items including plants, medicine, guns and artwork, as well as animals (depending on their species and size).

- When filing for a visa, you can at the same time ask for a change of address certificate.

▬ *Plugging you in and turning you on –*
installations et branchements

Electricity, gas and telephone installations involve personal con-tracts, and various connections. To speed up the process, contact the relevant office directly. The necessary connections will be made online or a technician will call by appointment to make the neces-sary connections.

PAPERS TO KEEP

- For ever and a day
  family papers (birth, marriage, divorce papers)
  property deeds
  school and university diplomas
  pay slips, work contract and certificate
  medical records (vaccinations, *carnet de santé*)

- For 30 years – bank records
  bank statements
  cheque book records

- For five years – tax records
  proof of payment, copies of tax returns
  proof of audio/visual tax (three years)

- For one or two years – household papers
  gas, electricity and telephone bills
  bills for repairs and work done on the house
  insurance evaluations

- For the duration
  rental contract and proof of rental payments
  guarantees and warranties

Gas is forbidden in many new buildings and only electrical appliances are accepted. The water meter and heating may either be individual or collective, and the cost may or may not be included in the *charges*.

Your bills for service and use (plus installation fees the first time) will be sent every six months or more frequently, depending on your contract for the electricity and gas. The bills give the due date for payment; your service will be cut off if you fail to pay on time. You may ask for automatic deductions to be made from your bank account, or sign a TIP (*titre interbancaire de paiement*), for a transfer from your bank. You detach the TIP form from your bill and send it with an RIB.

NB: French electricity is 220 volts and appliances have two-pin plugs. Some will require a ground plug. Remember to be careful of unprotected plugs when children are around. Needless to say, 220 volts requires certain precautions, such as not touching an electrical appliance when wet, and cutting the current when working on the wiring.

*D*IY

It is essential to ask the landlord for permission before carrying out significant changes, such as installing a shower, or knocking down a wall. However, you are entitled to decorate as you please (for example, painting, wallpapering, hanging curtains).

Before hiring a contractor to carry out work on your new home, it is customary to ask for at least two estimates (*devis*) in order to compare prices and services. The chosen *devis* must be signed by both parties and is a binding contract. At the end of the work, you will receive a detailed bill corresponding to the quotation you were given prior to the commencement of the work.

Your contractors will undoubtedly make some noise, and this is cited as the most difficult problem of urban living, before pollution or safety. If you are having lots of work done, or if you plan to have a party, it is considered polite to place a notice on the entry door of the building to inform your neighbours and apologize in advance for any inconvenience that may be caused. From dusk to dawn (in effect, after 10 pm), *tapage nocturne* (too much noise at night) may be reported to the police.

Decorating your home

The interior of a home expresses the personality of its occupants and their sense of comfort. The French usually have a few pieces of antique furniture inherited from their family, or found in an antique shop, and use these to form an eclectic mix with contemporary furniture, plants and books.

The average size of French apartments does not allow for a separate room for each activity. The living room is therefore also used as the dining room, the drawing room or the office. Children often share bedrooms.

Communications

The telephone

The telephone allows us to quickly solve daily problems and keep in touch, either directly, or via the internet, with friends and family. You may choose between various telephone companies for service, although the telephone lines remain under the control of France Telecom before connecting with another service. You may receive calls, or call out, regardless of which network is used; the telephone numbers stay the same, with only the prefix changing according to the server.

There is now enormous competition between servers, and costs and service vary. You need to decide which service best serves your needs. Mobile phones are used much more than fixed phones. The GSM is standard in Europe.

Each *département* has its own telephone directory. Listings are by town, in alphabetical order, and by profession in the *Yellow Pages*. Turquoise, green and pink pages give information about state services. If you wish to have an unlisted telephone number, you must pay a small monthly sum to be on the *'liste rouge'*. This will mean that your name does not appear in the telephone book.

A detailed telephone bill, listing all your calls with the first four digits of the numbers called, and the time at which the call was made, allows you to monitor your expenses. Be careful using numbers beginning with '08'. Numbers beginning 0800 to 0809 are free of charge, 0810 to 0821 are charged at the rate of a local call. All others have varying rates depending on the operator.

FRENCH TELEPHONE ZONES

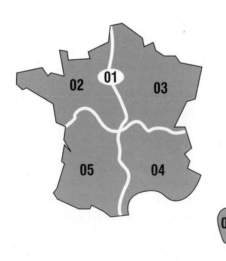

Country code: France, 33

Country codes were introduced in the 1930s with one number for each continent:

1	North America
2	Africa
3&4	Europe
5	South America
6	Oceania
7	Russia
8	Asia
9	Middle East and Southern Asia

This number was then personalized for each country, for example:

33	France
44	United Kingdom

If you do not have a mobile phone, you can always make your calls – local or international – from any telephone call-box. The instructions are written inside the box. However, you will need a credit card, or a telephone card, which you can buy wherever you see the sign *'télécarte en vente ici'* (at the post office, the *tabac* and in some newsagents).

You may also receive calls at a telephone call-box by giving the number of the box, which is inscribed on a little sign with a picture of a bell.

Internet

The internet is a source of information from all over the planet, and surfing the net has become enormously popular in France, as in other EU countries. If you have neither a modem nor a computer, you may connect to the internet at a *'cybercafé'* and surf to your heart's content for the price of a drink and a small service charge.

Since 1983 the French have used Minitel as a source of information and it still has a fan club.

Today 60 per cent of French households are connected to the internet. The most frequently consulted sites are for practical information, purchases, blogs, chat, managing personal finances, health advice and leisure activities. Requests for official documents such as birth or marriage certificates (if these events happened in France) can also be made via the internet.

The Post Office – La Poste et le Courrier

La Poste is yellow and blue with the easily recognized logo of a stylized bird. Its 17,000 post offices, 150,000 letterboxes and 90,000 postmen and women cope with billions of letters a year. La Poste is a public service enterprise with two functions – it collects and distributes letters and parcels. La Banque Postale offers financial services to its clients (cheque and savings accounts).

The opening hours of the post offices are usually 8 am–7 pm (in the provinces they usually shut for an hour at lunch-time). They are closed on Saturday afternoons, Sundays and national holidays. One post office is open 24 hours a day – the main branch on the rue du Louvre in Paris.

The cost of sending letters and parcels varies according to weight, destination and the service chosen – postage categories include *chronopost, colissimo, eurocolis* and *mondiocolis.* You may also buy pre-stamped airmail envelopes for every destination in the world. You can only use French stamps in France. Illustrated envelopes and special collection stamps are available in all post offices to decorate international correspondence; they are the same price as regular stamps and will amuse your correspondents with a little lesson on French history, art or geography. Stamps have been obligatory since 1 January 1849. The envelope dates from the same time and must now indicate the five-digit postal code for all destinations in France.

'In France the gardens are linear and the cinema queues are wandering. Complaining and not standing patiently in line is typically French.'

Pamela

The French are now learning to queue at the post office like the English! You will see a polite line of customers waiting their turn behind a restraining rope. However, it is still a good idea to avoid busy times between 5–7 pm when the post offices are packed with office workers.

You will easily recognize the yellow letterboxes in railway stations and airports, and elsewhere on the streets of every town in France. The letters are collected once or twice a day depending on the area. Within France, a letter arrives at its destination in one or two days. For other destinations outside France, it takes longer depending on the country and the service chosen.

LA FÊTE DU TIMBRE

Each year stamp collectors from all over France gather for a weekend to share their passion. To mark the occasion a special stamp is printed, showing a comic strip character, such as Tintin (2000), Harry Potter (2007), Mickey (2004), Droopy (2008 – in honour of Tex Avery, born in 1908)..

■ *Special service*

• *Lettre recommandée avec accusé de réception*: a registered letter with proof of receipt. The sender fills out a special form with the name and address of the addressee, and keeps a copy. When the letter arrives at its destination, a postcard is signed by the addressee, and this is sent back to the sender as proof of receipt.

■ *When you receive a registered letter*

If you are at home, the postman or woman will give you the registered letter or parcel, you will sign for it and the receipt will be returned to the sender. If you are away, the postman or woman will leave an *avis de passage* giving the date and times at which you may go to the post office with the *avis de passage* and proof of identity. You may send someone else to collect your registered letter by signing the back of the *avis de passage*. The person collecting your letter will be asked to show both your and his or her own ID.

■ *Forwarding your letters*

• Your *concierge* or neighbour can put your letters into an *enveloppe de réexpédition* – a special envelope available at the post office – write your temporary address and put the envelope into the letterbox. There is no charge for this service.

● Alternatively, you may ask the post office to forward your letters directly to your temporary address by signing an *ordre de réexpédition* for the duration of your stay or keep it until your return. There is a fee for this service.

POST OFFICE WORDS

Libeller une adresse is to write an address as follows:

Monsieur et Madame Dupont
3, rue de la Gare
13 004 Marseille

'13 004' is the postal code, with the first two digits indicating the department, and the next three digits indicating the town (or *arrondissement* for Lyon, Marseille and Paris).

Cedex – Courrier d'Entreprise à Distribution EXceptionnelle – is for the BP (*boîte postale*) and special deliveries (administrative and bulk rate).

'*Le cachet de la poste faisant foi*' means that the postmark proves the date on which the letter was posted. It gives the place, the day and the hour. The postmark is sometimes useful (for example, for proving that you made your income tax declaration prior to the due date).

■ *Change of address*

You should inform the following services as soon as possible of your new address (and this can be done online):

● the Préfecture, by going to the Commissariat de Police nearest to your new home; or the *mairie*;

● the social security office and the family allowance service;

● electricity, gas, telephone and water services;

- your bank;

- your insurance company (car and home insurance);

- your children's school;

- your consulate or embassy (if you are registered with them);

- magazine and newspaper subscriptions.

If you change departments be sure to change the *carte grise* for your car.

D*ogs and cats*

Many French people are fond of dogs and cats. Some count on the reassuring presence of their pets, and children consider them as playmates. However, man and beast must follow a few rules with respect to their neighbours and to the environment.

■■■■*Is your pet coming to France with you?*

Patte blanche: your pet must satisfy a few obligations, mainly for health reasons. Your airline company will explain the formalities required (vaccinations, especially anti-rabies, tattoo, recent certificate of good health) in order to pass customs.

In France, dogs and cats should have identification, by either tattoo or microchip. An EU pet passport will provide proof of vaccinations against rabies and replace international documents.

Walking the dog

Dogs must go out regularly to heed the call of nature and get some fresh air, but they must either be on a lead or walk at heel. They should wear a collar with your name and new address on it – easier to read than a tattoo – in case they wander off and get lost.

Dog owners have a civic responsibility not to allow their dog to leave any mess. There are a few places allocated to dogs' needs, but it is considered quite acceptable in French cities for the dog to use the gutter. However, if the dog does not use the gutter, its owner should clean up after it – that is the message from the city of Paris, which, in common with many other towns, now punishes careless dog owners with a heavy fine.

Wherever you see water flowing in the gutters, it is not yet another leak, but a matter of hygiene!

There is a great diversity of pet food available in supermarkets.

Travelling with pets

Dogs and cats may take the train with you, either in a basket, or on a lead, or with a muzzle if they are big dogs. The cost varies according to whether the pet is in a basket, or sitting on the floor at your feet. Dogs are not allowed into food shops, and some hotels refuse to accept them. Be sure to ask in advance when you make your reservations. If necessary, you can leave your pet in a kennel, or with someone who offers a boarding service; your vet will certainly be able to advise you.

Insurance

Pets may be partially insured by your comprehensive insurance policy; check the contract and add an additional clause if necessary.

━━ *Buying a dog or cat*

Choose your pet according to your lifestyle, the amount of time you spend at home, your weekend activities and the space you have. What sort of life will you be able to offer your pet?

When you buy a pet, the breeder should give you a bill of sale, specifying the date, the price paid for the animal and its identity. Thoroughbred dogs must have a pedigree and birth certificate, an ID tattoo and proof of vaccination. In some parts of the world, rabies is still a problem, so an anti-rabies shot is essential so that you can travel without worry.

If you find a dog or a cat lost in the street, inform the police or the *gendarmerie*.

CANINE CELEBRITIES

The French adore the characters from films and cartoons. Snoopy, Pluto, Dingo, Rantanplan, Milou, Belle, Rintintin, Lassie and White Fang (Croc Blanc in French) are all names given to pet dogs. Idéfix, Asterix's dog, is called Dogmatix in English.

Thoroughbred dogs should always be given a name starting with a letter of the alphabet corresponding to their year of birth. In 2008 it was the letter 'D', and popular names included Delta, Dotcom, Doggybag and Disco. In 2009 new dogs will be named Eclipse, Echo, Epice… The letters K, Q, W, X and Y are never used.

━━ *A farm in Paris*

If you live in or near Paris and your children like animals, visit the Bois de Vincennes, la Ferme Georges Ville, where there is a real farm of over five hectares, with cows, goats, sheep and donkeys, as well as an orchard with 50-odd varieties of fruit and a kitchen garden with raspberries and strawberries (they make jam in September). Fun and educational, the vegetable garden and farmyard reveal the talents of the green-fingered gardeners, or how wheat is transformed into a baguette.

*F*rench weather

'And what do you like, extraordinary stranger? I like the clouds that pass... over there... the marvellous clouds!'

'Et qu'aimes-tu donc extraordinaire étranger? J'aime les nuages qui passent... là-bas... les merveilleux nuages!'
Charles Baudelaire, *Le Spleen de Paris,* 1864

Halfway between the North Pole and the Equator, France benefits from a variable temperate climate. The longest river, the Loire (1,010 km), is the natural frontier that serves as a reference point for weather bulletins. North of the Loire is cooler and wetter, while the southern side is Mediterranean and, therefore, sunnier and warmer. Another break distinguishes east from west – regions facing the sea are more temperate, with sea breezes and ocean storms; rain generally comes from the west. The regions facing the mountains have a more continental climate, which is drier.

The best way to appreciate the subtleties of the seasons is to explore the different areas of France.

▬▬*Mother Nature's barometer*

The shortening days tell the migratory birds that it is time to move on because winter is coming. Before there were weather reports, the passage of the wild geese and the cormorants was a signal understood by people who lived on the land. They observed the behaviour of the birds and animals, and watched the sky to predict changes in the weather. Some of their predictions have become sayings that are still used today, for example:

hirondelles volant haut,
le temps sera beau;
hirondelle volant bas,
bientôt il pleuvra.

(Swallows flying high, the weather will be fine; swallows flying low, soon it will rain.)

Watch out for the return of the swallows as it is said that their arrival heralds the spring. However, if you are not at your window on the day they return, you could always contact Météo France.

THE SEASONS

- Wet and fresh, March and its showers herald the spring. April brings the first hint of warmth, but it is not yet summer.

- June, July and August are the months of lovely, soft summer evenings. Sometimes the daytime temperature is around 30 degrees centigrade (in the 80s Fahrenheit).

- September and October are full of autumn colour – the 'Indian summer' is harvest time.

- November brings back the mist and fog.

- December, January and February are mostly cold and grey, but there are some bright winter days when the sun shines through the clouds. The ski resorts look for snow; the other regions experience snow storms from time to time during the winter months depending on the year. Christmas is seldom white below 1,000 metres (3,300 feet).

- From July to December, every day loses a few seconds of daylight, then, from January onwards the days get longer, up to the summer solstice on 22 June, which is the longest day of the year.

FRANCE'S FOUR SEASONS

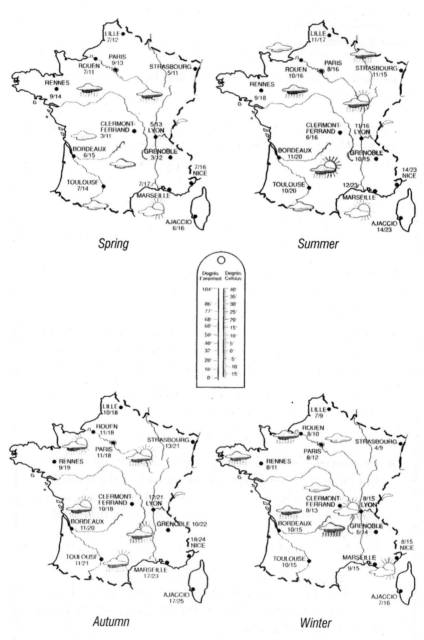

Spring

Summer

Autumn

Winter

Source: © Météo France (www.meteo.fr), *Libération*: 20 March, 21 June, 23 September and 21 December 2000

*F*or further information

Paris-anglophone: The directory of the English-speaking world in Paris: book and online website

The *Yellow Pages* of each department's telephone books: France Telecom contains a supplement called 'Les pages info'. You will find maps (street names included), addresses for all the administrative services, public transport, hospitals, school information, museums, parks and gardens, etc

La Poste: www.laposte.fr
France Telecom: www.francetelecom.fr
www.citadines.tm.fr
www.frenchentree.com/
www.changement-adresse.gouv.fr/changementAdresse
www.fnaim.fr, www.Exchange.com, www.homelink.org, www.papvacances.fr
www.notaires.fr
www.pagesjaunes.fr
www.meteo.fr
Renting or Buying a Property in France – Bilingual edition – De particulier à particulier (www.pap.fr)

6 *Buyer beware!*

– consommateur averti!

*'There are certainly many things
that money cannot buy.'*

'Il y a certainement un tas de choses
que l'argent ne peut acheter.'
Ogden Nash

*M*oney and currency

▬▬*The euro: single currency of the EU*

For the first time in history, several EU countries have agreed to share the same currency – the euro. Euroland is composed of 15 countries: Austria, Belgium, Finland, France, Germany, Greece, Ireland, Italy, Luxembourg, the Netherlands, Portugal, Spain, Slovenia, Malta and Cyprus. Since January 2002, people in these countries have had euros in their pockets. Great Britain, Sweden and Denmark have not adopted the euro, preferring to wait and see!

▬▬*A brief history of the Banque de France*

For nearly 200 years the Banque de France has had the exclusive privilege of issuing money. The other financial establishments created at the same time were given the name of '*crédit*', '*comptoir*' or '*société*' (for example, Crédit Agricole, Crédit Lyonnais, Société Générale).

The Banque de France is the Treasury and the bankers' bank. Since 1994, it has functioned independently of political power and is governed by the Conseil Général (composed of the members of the Conseil de la Politique Monétaire and an elected representative of the bank's employees). A *censeur* or his substitute, named by the Minister of Economy and Finance, attends the Conseil Général meetings and has the right of veto.

Today the Banque de France has prime responsibility for the manufacture and circulation for the euro in France. The Governor of the Bank is involved in European Monetary Policy, lead by the European Central Bank (ECB) in Frankfort-am-Main in Germany, and in its application nationally.

As the Central Bank, the Banque de France monitors the banking system, safeguards the public interest and centralizes all information concerning private and commercial funds. Prior to opening a new bank account, a bank must consult a central database to verify that a prospective client does not have an *interdit bancaire* (a banking bar, forbidding them to write cheques anywhere in France). The Banque de France also exchanges vast sums of foreign currency.

In order to control the economic forces of the country better after the shattering upheaval of the war, the French banking system was reorganized in the 1940s. Since that time, all commercial banks are obliged to register with the AFB (Association Française de Banques).

The evolution of the legal structure has permitted the unification of banking businesses under the heading *'établissements de crédit'*, with different statutes: *banques commerciales* (commercial banks), *mutualistes/cooperatives* (mutual/cooperative societies), and *sociétés financières* (finance companies). Banks manage the circulation of money and keep the wheels of the economy turning.

France has the second largest banking network worldwide after the United States, with 500 credit institutions abroad and many branches of foreign banks in France.

▬ *Opening a bank account*

A payment of over €1,500 (salary, rent, etc) must be made by bank transfer or cheque, so you will need to open a bank account as soon as possible after your arrival in France. Foreigners may have a 'resident bank account' if their family residence is in France and the greater part of their work is in France.

Having chosen your bank, you will need to show proof of identity, your *titre de séjour* and proof of your income. You will then make your first deposit in your new account.

THE EURO: PILE OU FACE, RECTO-VERSO!

The Euro is the single currency for 15 countries in the European Union – and others! All eight types of euro coins (€1, €2, 50c, 20c, 10c, 5c, 2c, 1c) have the same 'tails' side, which shows the money's value, but the 'heads' side of the coins are different in every country. French euro coins have three different 'heads':

- A tree surrounded by a hexagon that reads: *Liberté, Egalité, Fraternité*.

- The sower (*la semeuse*), a symbol which formerly appeared on the French franc and is often used on stamps. After the French Revolution, the image of the sower became almost sacred.

- The face of Marianne.

With all three of these symbols, one also finds the 12 stars of the European Union as well as the letters 'RF' for *République française*.

The seven types of paper bills (€5, €10, €20, €50, €100, €200 and €500) all come in different sizes and colours. Robert Kalina, an Austrian artist who designed the front of the euro banknotes, said, 'I had the idea of bridges linking the nations and peoples of Europe together, and of windows and doors through which one could look towards the future.'

On the reverse of each bill is a map with the seven colours of the rainbow, as well as 'euro' written in both Latin and Greek script, a map of Europe, the 12 stars of the European flag, the initials of the European Central Bank, and the signature of the current president.

HOW DOES ONE KEEP THEM STRAIGHT?
THE EU HAS TRICKS

The bills seem identical across Europe, but a careful look reveals that each bill carries a code particular to its country of origin: a letter, followed by 11 numbers. If your bill has the code U25147068458, it's French; if it has the code X032711243, it's undoubtedly German. The letter U and the number 5 is for France (5 is a checksum obtained by adding the 11 numbers together to arrive at a single digit). Germany's code begins with X with the checksum of 2.

'Yuro' is the Japanese word for euro. It's also the name of a French–Japanese baby born on 1 January 2002.

The bank will offer numerous services. Do not hesitate to explain your needs and ask for advice on selecting the services best suited to your situation – current account, bank card and so on. Some banks authorize an overdraft (*un découvert*), with bank charges, of course. As current accounts do not produce interest, your banker will suggest various ways in which to invest your savings.

A FEW BANKING WORDS

Acquitter	to pay the sum owed
Agios	bank charges and interest
Date de valeur	date on which money is debited or credited to an account
Relevé d'identité bancaire (RIB)	bank account reference numbers
Relevé de compte	bank statement
Retirer	to withdraw
Solde de compte	balance of account
Verser	to deposit
Virement	transfer

Types of account

● *Compte joint/compte commun* – a joint account opened in the names of two people, married or not, allowing either one to make full use of the account. Both parties are equally responsible for the account and any debts incurred.

● *Compte avec procuration* – a written proxy given by the holder of the account to another person. This is an act of confidence as the procuration allows the bearer to withdraw and deposit money and write cheques. The holder of the account always remains responsible for the account.

Cheques

It is not advisable to sign a *chèque en blanc* (blank cheque) as it might easily be lost or misused. A signed cheque is valid for one year and eight days. To postdate a cheque is strictly forbidden.

It is also forbidden to make a cash purchase of more than €3000. The safest way of paying for a private purchase is to request a 'closed' bank cheque.

● *Chèque de banque* – a bank cheque is issued by the bank on behalf of a client guaranteeing the payment for one year and eight days. For large purchases, a bank cheque may be requested rather than a certified cheque.

● *Chèque certifié* – a certified cheque is guaranteed by your bank and the money is set aside for eight days.

● *Chèque sans provisions* – a *chèque en bois* ('wooden' cheque) is a cheque for which there are insufficient funds. The bank grants the 'careless' person 30 days to make good the debt. If it happens again, a penalty is added to the amount due and the person is listed as a bad payer on the *fichier national des chèques irréguliers* (national register of bad cheques).

▬ *Bank cards*

● *Carte de retrait automatique* – a card bearing the name of your bank allowing you to withdraw money at any time from a cash-point machine using your confidential code (PIN).

● *Carte bancaire de paiement (CB)* – a regular income will allow you to obtain a national or international bank card, or, depending on your salary, a *prestige* card. These cards carry an annual fee, but they do offer an array of services (for example, medical or legal assistance). Carte Bleue, Visa, Eurocard/Mastercard, and American Express are welcomed in shops worldwide. (The name and logo are shown on the door of businesses that accept each card.) Be careful not to leave the bank card receipt behind as it shows your account number, and you will need it to monitor your expenditures. A bank card is not a credit card, it is a debit card.

If you make purchases by telephone or by internet, you will often be asked to give your card number (16 digits) so that the seller can make a direct withdrawal from your account. If you key your pin number into a shop machine, no signature is required. You will not be able to verify the amount charged to your account until much later. Errors are possible, and credit card fraud does exist as does the unauthorized use of confidential information. You should therefore be very careful.

▬ *Cashpoint machines* – les distributeurs automatiques

The machines you can use will show the logo of your bank card or your *Carte Bleue*, and will give money up to your credit limit. This limit may be higher at your own bank, or one of its branches, than at other banks.

You may exchange money and buy currency at the bank, the airport, the railway station, at hotels and at *Bureaux de Change* in tourist areas. It is advisable to compare rates as they vary from one place to another.

▬ *Paying in cash*

Small daily purchases are usually paid *en espèce* or *en liquide* (in cash). Some businesses will accept payment by cheque for amounts of less than €15; however, cards may only be used for amounts over €15.

If you manage your finances on the internet a confidential PIN gives you exclusive access to your account. However, be careful not to disclose your confidential four-figure number. Although you must pay for these services, they may well save you time and money.

THEFT – BE AWARE!

Experienced pickpockets are quick to spot people who look lost or uncertain of their way, so be very careful with your wallet or handbag during the first weeks of your stay in France. The loss or theft of your bank cards or cheque book should be reported as soon as possible. Here are the three steps to stop payment (you are responsible for any loss until you take them):

1. Call the bank centre to stop payment. All bank cards: 08 36 69 08 08. Cheque books: 01 42 41 22 22 (8 am–11 pm); or 08 36 68 32 08 (Banque de France). You may ask for these numbers in any shop which accepts bankcards or cheques. You will be asked for the reference numbers of your cheques or card as well as your account number.

NB: Do not keep your PIN with your card; should there be a legal dispute, you will be held responsible by the bank for charges made to your card.

2. Report the loss or theft to the nearest police station.

3. Either go to your bank, or send a fax, or a registered letter (*recommandé avec accusé de réception*) to confirm your loss or theft, enclosing a copy of the declaration made to the police.

NB: You may only stop payment on a cheque when it has been lost or stolen.

Payment cards

● Company credit cards – department stores, finance companies and so on, compete with each other to offer their clients the best rates, instalment payments, or, for example, a special cashier to speed the passage of privileged cardholders in their store.

NB: Credit is highly regulated. An offer for special credit terms must mention the nature of the product and its price, as well as the duration and cost of the credit. The buyer has up to seven days to consider the purchase, and to cancel the order if he or she decides to do so.

● Discount cards – you can save money on products, trips or services if you have a *carte de réduction* (discount card), or a *carte d'abonnement* (membership card); the card pays for itself with your first few purchases. For example, it costs less if you buy tickets for 10 seats at the cinema than if you buy them one at a time – and you do not have to stand in the queue.

*S*hopping

The French try to be careful shoppers, and always compare the price of products. An average French family spends half its family budget on housing and food. The other half is spent on clothes, taxes, telephone and transport, and health and leisure, and, for some people, on savings.

Often found on the outskirts of towns, shopping centres have all sorts of shops and services – home furnishings, petrol stations, food, restaurants, boutiques, banks, post offices, cafeterias, cinemas, etc. Some have become the destination for family outings at the weekend. Customers are attracted by the variety of shops, and by the fact that there is free parking.

The *grandes surfaces* (supermarkets) sell all sorts of products, including food, clothing, household appliances, toys and stereo equipment. Although it is necessary to have a car to go to a *hypermarché* – a massive supermarket of over 2,500 square metres, and usually located outside of town – smaller supermarkets are found in most towns. The various supermarket chains regularly offer widely advertised discounts; you will undoubtedly find their adverts coming through your letterbox.

AT WHAT PRICE? UNTIL WHAT DATE?

Even if businesses are allowed to set their own prices, the law demands that they post their prices TTC (*Toutes Taxes Comprises*, or including tax).

The international bar code, although simplifying life for the shopkeeper, does not make it easier for shoppers to find the price of a product. The name and price of the product are identified by scanning at the checkout, where a ticket listing your purchases and the amount owed will be given to you.

You will find the following codes marked on perishable items:

- DLC – *date limite de consommation* (to be used prior to the date marked);

- DLUO – *date limite d'utilisation optimale* (best used by the date marked);

- fruits and vegetables must be displayed with the name of the variety, country of origin and size. Preserves and tinned foods must show the date of production.

Neighbourhood shops

The bakery is still the most popular shop in every French town and village, its irresistible aroma of freshly baked bread and pastries wafting into the street. The name *'boulanger'* is reserved for professional bakers who make and bake their bread themselves. Even today, local shopkeepers take the time to exchange a few words with their customers, offering them advice. The *caviste* (wine merchant) will recommend modest or great wines. The *boucher* will give you cooking hints as he or she cuts up your chicken and shares his or her favourite recipe with you. Pork is sold by the *charcutier*, whose original name was the *'chair cuitier'* (meat cook). Buying on the internet has not replaced going to the grocer's shop. The *épicerie* (grocery) and the *traiteur* are the best local shops making daily or last-minute shopping easier.

▬▬▬ *Traditional French markets*

'On Sunday, there are daffodils, and going to the market without a tie,
the shopping basket filled with leeks.'

'Le dimanche, c'est les jonquilles, le marché avec le col ouvert, le cabas
avec les poireaux.'
Robert Doisneau

The fruit and vegetable market is held once or more a week in France, depending on the town, and offers good-quality fresh products and the popular ambiance of a street market. The stall-holders are always eager to make a sale, and to make you smile while they serve you. Shopping becomes an amusing and relaxing Saturday or Sunday morning outing.

Some markets have earned a special reputation for their charm or specialities; they have become a local phenomenon where regulars and tourists meet.

▬▬▬ *The department stores* – les grands magasins

The department stores offer a vast array of fashion goods, luxury goods, household wares and linens, furniture and so on.

In Paris, the name *'grands magasins'* brings to mind the famous shop windows of Printemps, Galeries Lafayette, BHV and Le Bon Marché.

▬▬▬ *Signs and logos*

Each town has signs that inform visitors and locals about its past. In the 12th century, shops had special shields emblazoned with an image representing the trade within. Some professions have kept their old symbols even though logos have often replaced shields:

● the green cross and the caduceus – the winged staff of Mercury entwined with serpents – denotes *la pharmacie* (chemist);

- a notary is identified by the double shield above his or her door;

- the red 'carrot' is the legal sign for a licensed *tabac*. The sale of tobacco to anyone under the age of 16 is forbidden.

OPENING HOURS

Bakeries in France are open earlier and close later than banks. Opening hours are chosen by the shopkeepers and vary considerably depending on the business and the location. As a very general rule, here are a few examples:

- Bakeries, cafés and newsagents are the early birds: from around 7.30 am, you may order your hot coffee and croissant and read your newspaper.

- Open-air markets are usually open from 8 am to 1 pm, although covered markets are open daily, in the morning and afternoon.

- Shopping centres are open from 10 am to 10 pm, Monday to Friday, and Saturday from 9 am to 8 pm.

- In Paris, most shops are open non-stop from 9 or 10 am until 7 pm, Monday to Saturday; food shops open from 8 am to 1 pm, and then from 4 pm until 7 or 8 pm. Some department stores and hairdressers stay open later, until 9 or 10 pm, once or twice a week.

- Outside the Paris area, shops and services normally shut for lunch.

- Although there are many exceptions, most small shops and hairdressers are shut on Mondays.

- August is the month most often chosen for the annual holiday. However, shopkeepers often arrange holidays among themselves to ensure that there will always be some shops open.

- On holidays and for special events shops have different opening times according to the seasonal trade (*authorisation prefectorale*).

SPECIAL SHOPPING DAYS

Other than the *soldes* (January and July sales that offer bargains twice a year), the department stores invent special events all year, accompanied by advertising campaigns. The shop windows always anticipate the event:

- January   *soldes, mois du blanc* (the linen sales)
- February   decoration and household goods
- March   spring–summer fashions, and Easter
- April/May   sports and luggage, travel, Mother's Day
- June   Father's Day, marriages
- July/Aug   back-to-school sales
- Sept/Oct   winter fashions
- Nov/Dec   Christmas markets and winter sports

Mail order – vente à domicile

In France, there is a vast network of catalogue sales. Purchases may be made by signing an order form, or by telephone, the internet, Minitel or post. This form of shopping is practical and the delivery is usually rapid. Door-to-door selling is strictly controlled. It is illegal for a salesperson to take payment when the order is given, and the order may be cancelled within seven days if you change your mind.

U seful hints

▬ *Deposits and down payments* – arrhes et acomptes

To secure a reservation for a rental or to acquire a coveted object, you will be asked to pay about 10 per cent of the total amount in advance. Make sure that you read the agreement carefully – does it say *arrhes* or *acompte*?

An *arrhes* is a deposit to reserve a purchase or a service, but the vendor or the buyer may change his or her mind. If the buyer cancels the order, the deposit is lost; if the vendor cancels, the deposit must be returned, but doubled, as a form of compensation.

An *acompte* represents a binding contract, and is the first instalment of the total amount due. If the vendor does not keep the promise to sell, he or she must return the money paid, plus compensation. Payment, not a substitution, is the rule.

▬ *Discounts and rebates* – réductions

If the amount to be paid for a purchase is large, you may ask for a small reduction if you plan to make full payment on delivery. It is always worth asking!

▬ *Guarantees and after-sales service*

A *garantie commerical* is free and differs from one manufacturer to another. The shop stamps the guarantee with its name, the date of the sale and indicates the duration (three months, six months or a year, depending on the article), the limit of the coverage (spare parts and work, shipping, charges). The *garantie légale* is required by law and covers defects in the item's manufacture. A defective item must be exchanged by the vendor.

Some shops will exchange recently purchased articles as long as you present proof of purchase (sales receipt or bill). However, if the words *'ni repris, ni échangé'* (no return or exchange) are clearly indicated no exchange is possible except if the item was damaged when sold. This is sometimes the case with articles bought in sales.

■■■■ *Home delivery* – livraisons à domicile

Many shops will deliver to your home if the purchases come to more than a certain amount. Whether free or at a minimal charge, depending on the shop, this is a good service for frozen products, or heavy or cumbersome articles. Most perishables are marked with a date by which the item must be sold.

STANDARDS – LES NORMES

The label 'NF' is the official certificate of quality given by AFNOR (*Agence Française de Normalisation*). The label guarantees that an object conforms to existing safety standards.

For electrical appliances and toys, the logo 'CE' on the label indicates that the product is certified to conform to European standards.

On food products, the *label rouge* (red label) or 'AOC' (*appellation d'origine contrôlée*) indicates the top quality preferred by the French. Other labelling includes: AB (*agriculture biologique*) and VBF (*viande bovine française*).

The contents of a product must be clearly marked on the package – *café: pur arabica, décaféiné*; or *lait: entier, demi-écremé* (whole milk, low fat). You will soon recognize your favourite brands.

▬▬ *Repairs* – dépannages

You will undoubtedly find numerous leaflets coming through your letterbox offering *dépanneur à domicile*. These kinds of repair service have a bad reputation and are far too expensive. It is much better to have a personal recommendation. A local shopkeeper or the *concierge* of your apartment building should be able to direct you to a reliable professional repair service.

It is always a good idea to ask for a *devis* (an estimate) before hiring a repair contractor. The *devis* will state: travelling expenses, cost of work (charge per hour); price of the spare parts, if necessary; and how long the repair will take.

If the work is costly (above €150), and can wait a few days, ask two different contractors for an estimate, and compare their services and prices.

NB: To be legal, a *devis* must be signed by both parties before the work is started. It is better not to pay until the work has been completed, and then preferably by cheque, in order to keep track of the contractor.

▬▬ *Objets trouvés*

'Found' property in France is 'lost' property in Great Britain and 'lost and found' in the United States. Each culture has its own name for familiar objects that, through negligence, are left in public places. In Paris, around 750 objects are handed in every day to *Objets Trouvés*, 36 rue des Morillons.

▬▬ *Clean towns*

In big towns, the *poubelles* (dustbins or trash cans) are emptied daily. Some rubbish is recyclable, for example glass (bottles are rarely sold on deposit) and papers should be placed in special containers.

The *mairie* has a service for collecting heavy or cumbersome objects. Parisians have been using *poubelles* since 7 March 1884. The use of closed bins in which to throw rubbish, so as to keep the streets clean, was imposed by the Prefet Eugene Poubelle!

Home help – aide à domicile

If you are looking for a cleaner, ask the *concierge* of your apartment building or a neighbour. They will probably be able to recommend someone. You could also put up a 'help wanted' advertisement in the local shops. All helpers, full- or part-time, must be covered by social security.

Legal advice – conseils juridiques

Legal experts, barristers and notaries – jurists, avocats, notaires

Legal texts and regulations are not always easily understood by the uninitiated, and sometimes expert advice is necessary. Many *mairies* in larger towns, in conjunction with the Ordre des Avocats, offer free legal consultations or advice. Information and advice on family, labour or housing laws may also be obtained by telephone.

The Bar Association of Paris has created AARC (Avocats, Assistance Recours du Consommateurs) to advise and counsel consumers, and to settle small claims out of court for a small fee.

● *Avocats* specialize in defending the interests of individuals. Fees are based on a fixed price, the number of hours worked or on results. *Un avocat* is a barrister in the UK, an attorney or lawyer in the United States.

REMEMBER THE TIP! – POURBOIRE

Although bills in restaurants and cafés include the service charge, it is customary to tip certain people – delivery people, guides, waiters or waitresses in a café or restaurant, taxi drivers – approximately 5–10 per cent of the total, depending on the quality of the service rendered. A tip is a mark of appreciation – it is a custom, not an obligation. At the theatre, some usherettes do not receive any compensation other than tips.

The Christmas gift – les étrennes

This is usually given to those who have given daily or exceptional service throughout the year, such as postmen and women and firefighters. In December, they traditionally come to the door to wish you a Happy Christmas and give you a calendar in exchange for a banknote or a few coins.

At the start of the New Year, the *concierge* or guardian of your building receives a cash gift from the residents. The envelope containing the *étrennes* shows appreciation for services rendered and is more generous if you have frequently used his or her services (for example leaving your keys with the *concierge*, or asking him or her to pick up letters).

● *Notaires* register deeds in property transactions and wills, and advise on financial, professional and family questions. In France, a *notaire* fulfils many of the functions of a British solicitor (such as conveyancing), authenticates deeds, and manages successions and settlements. In the United States, this work is performed by an attorney. The Chambre des Notaires can give you a list of *notaires*.

● The *conciliateurs civils* assist in the resolution of minor conflicts – problems with the neighbours or with housing – outside the courtroom. They are to be found at the *mairie* and their services are free.

Social services

Each *département* of France has a social services department to help people who have some difficulty in managing family, professional or personal problems. The social services offer practical as well as psychological help. You may also ask them for advice on day care for your children. They are available at the *mairie*.

Other help

Numerous associations (for example, consumer associations) give advice, or defend, or protect the interests of individuals. Their legal services are available to their members.

Cars and traffic

Many French people own a car, or two. The second one is often a small car that is practical and easy to park in town.

Buying a car new or second-hand

Before buying a car, consult colleagues or neighbours who may be able to recommend a garage or a franchised dealer according to the kind of car you are looking for. Test one or more cars to assess your needs in terms of size, optional extras and so on. If you buy a popular French model, you will find it easier to maintain and service.

Garages often sell used cars. The owner of a garage might offer a manufacturer's guarantee on the used cars for sale, or his own guarantee. Compare offers in order to obtain the best price.

NB: A written guarantee must be signed in order to secure after-sale services. Any car between three and a half and four years old must undergo a complete service check-up (*contrôle technique*) of which the vendor should give you a detailed account. The service is obligatory, must be performed by a registered centre and is renewable every two years.

Some car owners advertise their cars for sale in the classified advertisements. Sometimes these people are connected with car companies, and may buy a new car every six months at a considerable discount. These bargains have only had one owner and are generally reliable. They have few miles on the clock, are in good condition and are still under the manufacturer's warranty. You should ask to have the car serviced before concluding the deal.

The price of a second-hand car is referenced to the *Argus de l'Automobile*, which takes into account the age of the car and assumes an average of 15,000 kilometers (about 10,000 miles) per year.

NB: Do not forget to buy insurance immediately. A registered letter giving the details on the car should be sent to the insurance company you have chosen, which will give you immediate coverage. (The postmark is proof of the date of posting.)

▬▬ *Renting a car*

Most car rental agencies are found in the bigger towns, at railway stations and airports. If you wish, you can rent a car in one town and leave it in another. Many options are available including unlimited mileage, insurance or unlimited rental period. Read the terms of the contract carefully. You might need to take out a complementary insurance especially if you travel abroad, or on the Cross-Channel ferry.

Some companies have special agreements with car rental agencies, and their employees benefit from special weekend, week or monthly rates.

The branches of French car manufacturers abroad also offer car rentals. This might be one good way to try out the different French car models.

In the larger towns, many people prefer to use public transport occasionally taking a taxi or renting a car for the weekend or the holidays. This is much cheaper than buying a car, and paying for car insurance, maintenance – and parking tickets!

Importing a car

You will not have to pay taxes if you bring a car into France that you have owned for at least six months (this also applies to any paintings or artworks!). It should be listed on the inventory you establish with the removal company. The car must be inspected by the Service des Mines within the first year you are in France. If necessary, you will be asked to bring your car up to French or European specifications. The *carte grise* (the car registration) is issued at the Préfecture or sous-Préfecture and licence plates (*plaques d'immatriculations*) must be changed according to the EU standard.

Maintenance and repairs

For a recent model, maintenance is performed by the dealer who sold you the car, according to the manufacturer's guarantee or warranty.

If you must have repairs done on your car, it is wise to ask the mechanic to give an estimate of costs first. This is called an *ordre de réparation* and ensures that additional work will not be done without your consent. The mechanic's bill should list the cost of work performed and the spare parts. The hourly cost of work must be posted in all garages – the price of emergency repairs is fixed by law.

Service stations sell all kinds of fuel – super, unleaded, *gasoil* (diesel) – and are able to carry out basic maintenance such as checking and changing the oil, batteries, tyres and so on. They are usually equipped to wash cars.

━━ *Driving licence* – permis de conduire

In every country the highway code for car drivers, pedestrians and bicyclists should be known and respected in order to prevent road accidents. The driving licence was first used in France in 1922. In 1992, it became a *permis à points* – a driver, over 18 years of age, who has satisfied the written and practical tests, is given a permit with 6 points. There is a probationary period before a driver is given a permit with 12 points. Each infraction of the law, according to its gravity, is punished by the loss of points, and continued offending will end in the loss of the driving licence. There is a special driving licence for bus and lorry drivers.

Apprentissage anticipé de la conduite accompagnée (AAC) makes it possible for youngsters over 16 to obtain a learner's permit. These beginners are recognizable by the sign shown on the back of their cars – a circle with two people. A circle with the letter 'A' in the middle means *jeune conducteur* (young driver).

The French drive on the right-hand side of the road. Anyone who has never driven in France should take the time to familiarize themselves with the traffic signs and a map of the country.

━━ *Car registration* – certificat d'immatriculation ou carte grise

The *carte grise* is obligatory. You must register your car within 15 days of purchase. Some garages take care of this task for you and give you your 'papers', sometimes even offering to provide you with the number plate.

You may obtain the *carte grise* immediately yourself by going to your *arrondissement mairie* in Paris, or the Préfecture of the department where you live, at the Service Carte Grise, armed with: a completed request form, your ID and proof of address.

For a new car, you will need the bill of sale and compliance given to you by the dealer. For a second-hand car you will need: the former owner's *carte grise*; the bill of sale from the former owner; non-lien affidavit from the Préfecture of the department where the car was registered, if the sale entails a change of department.

The registration request may be made by post by sending a stamped self-addressed envelope. Any future change of address must be given to the Préfecture immediately, even if the change occurs in the same department.

FOREIGN DRIVING LICENCE

- If your stay in France is less than 90 days, a certified translation of your driving licence or an international driver's licence will suffice.

- If you have a *carte de séjour temporaire*, you may use your driver's licence from home for one year (the duration of your first *carte de séjour*), but if you choose to extend your stay, you must get a French licence before the 365th day. If your country, or a state within your country, has signed an agreement with France, it is a simple matter of exchanging your licence, obtained before coming to France, for a French licence at the Préfecture of your *département*. (Fourteen US states are party to such conventions.) If you do not convert your driving licence to a French one within the first year of your residence in France, you will be obliged to take a driving test. Otherwise, you must pass an examination in French, with the assistance of an interpreter, if necessary. The Préfecture will have more information regarding your particular situation.

- Driving licences *permis à points* will soon be the same for all Europeans of the EU. Meanwhile, all EU driving licences are valid in France.

REGISTRATION NUMBERS – NUMÉROS
D'IMMATRICULATION

It is easy to tell where a car comes from as the last two numbers of the number plate are the numbers of the department where the car is registered. Some letters are reserved:

- TT   car in temporary transit;
- CD   diplomatic corps;
- CC   consular corps;
- E   military vehicle;
- K   embassy or consular personnel.

Insurance contract – contrat d'assurance

Car insurance is obligatory. An expensive insurance premium can be three times as much as the cheapest for the same coverage depending on the insurance company. Compare prices and services offered by several different companies before signing a contract.

The costs also vary according to the risks covered (insurance against all accidents, collision, individual accident, professional use and so on), the size of the car, the number of drivers to be insured and their driving experience. A person who has been driving for less than a year will pay a higher premium. On the other hand, women, who according to statistics cause fewer accidents than men, will obtain a discount from some companies. Any change in coverage required, even temporarily, should be reported to the insurance company.

To obtain a discount rate in France, you should present an affidavit from your previous insurance company certifying that you have not been responsible for an accident in the last two years. Your French insurance company will then accord you a reduced rate. An extra premium is imposed on drivers who have caused accidents.

Police d'assurance is the contract with the basic conditions and special options listed (risks covered, the amount of the payments, date at which the coverage takes effect and so on).

Attestation d'assurance is proof of insurance given when you subscribe to the policy. It is a small square certificate that you stick on to the windscreen.

If you are a non-EU citizen ask for the *carte verte* – an international insurance policy, which is free of charge, and extends the coverage of your contract to the countries listed on your membership card. Otherwise, you will be obliged to purchase a 'frontier-insurance', which guarantees minimum coverage.

▬▬▬*Emergency assistance* – contrat d'assistance

This kind of contract ensures emergency assistance at the time when the accident, or problem, occurs whereas an insurance contract is used after the event, when the cause and damage have been assessed) and pays the victim's damages. A *contrat d'assistance* offers immediate help, including medical repatriation, the delivery of medicines, emergency car repairs and so on. Many insurance companies now include a clause covering emergency assistance in comprehensive home or car insurance policies. Some bank cards also offer this form of assistance to their customers.

▬▬▬*Safety rules for adults and children*

As well as the obligation to wear a seat-belt at all times (one seat-belt per person or child), in the front and back seats, there are other laws regarding the safety of young children:

- up to nine months or 9 kilograms, babies must be transported in a baby basket;

- under four years of age, children must travel in a child's safety seat that conforms to European standards;

- up to 10 years of age, children must sit in the back of the car, in a special seat that allows them to be at the right height, and to fasten their seat-belts to travel in safety.

In France, a car driver's blood-alcohol level must not exceed 0.50 grams/litre – this is reinforced by numerous information campaigns. If you are stopped by the police and you are over the limit, they may immediately withdraw your driving licence for three days.

Traffic accidents – le constat

After a car accident, the damage is described in a *constat à l'amiable*. The report describes the accident in detail, and includes diagrams (showing the positions of the vehicles) and the circumstances of the collision or accident. It enables evaluation of everyone's responsibilities. The differing opinions of the drivers involved are noted under 'observations'. It should be signed by both parties. If there are witnesses to the accident, their names should also be included in the report. You should keep a photocopy of the report and send it to your insurance company by registered letter within five days. The reimbursement will depend on the coverage of your insurance policy and the result of any investigation.

NB: You must call the police if people are injured in the accident.

Car theft

Car alarms are a current option for dissuading car thieves. Some insurance companies require that the serial number of expensive cars be engraved on all the car's windows. This facilitates identification of a stolen car.

Many insurance companies offer an option for the contents of the car (*objets transportés*). Never leave valuable items exposed to the covetous eyes of passers-by.

As soon as you discover that your car has been stolen, you should make a complaint to the nearest police station and report the theft to your insurance company by registered letter.

SPEED LIMITS

In good weather conditions, drivers should respect the following speed limits:

- 130 km/h (80 mph) on the motorways;

- 110 km/h (70 mph) on the main roads;

- 90 km/h (55 mph) on a secondary road; and

- 50 km/h (30 mph) in a built-up area, or less depending on the road signs.

In bad weather conditions, such as rain, snow or fog, drivers are asked to *lever le pied* (literally, to take their foot off the accelerator), and reduce their speed to 50 km/h (30 mph) on a main road or motorway when visibility is less than 50 m (165 ft), to leave an adequate distance between their car and the car in front and behind them, and to signal well in advance of any change in position. Other speed limits are imposed near to schools, roadworks or building sites. During extreme cases of air pollution, speed limits are imposed and sometimes driving is forbidden.

A new system enables a fine to be charged to the owner of a car caught by a special camera.

It is an offence to use a mobile phone while driving.

PAPERS PLEASE – VOS PAPIERS S'IL VOUS PLAÎT

If you are stopped by the police or *gendarmerie*, you must show your driving licence and the car's papers: *carte grise*, insurance policy. If you are unable to show them on request, you will have to show them at the police station within five days and pay a fine. Photocopies are not acceptable.

▬▬ *Traffic in town: pedestrians and cars*

French drivers are not always very courteous to pedestrians and French pedestrians seem to have a tendency to be a little careless. Always cross the road via the marked crossings (pedestrian crossings are indicated by white stripes on the road). At traffic lights a green figure appears when it is safe to cross; when it turns to red, beware!

Some roads, especially near schools, are equipped with *ralentisseurs* (speed bumps), also known as *dos d'âne* (donkey's back), to slow down the traffic.

At 14 you can drive a moped if you have passed the traffic security assessment. You can prepare for this in a driving school. Head protection is compulsory.

Press campaigns and billboards promote road safety and the prevention of traffic accidents in an effort to educate young and old about sensible and safe behaviour on the road.

If you are lost, or have a problem of any sort, a policeman – either in the street or at the police station – will always be willing to help you.

▬▬ *Fines and tickets* – contraventions: amendes ou PV (procès-verbal)

The cost of contravening the highway code varies according to the gravity of the offence. The most serious will lead to a court hearing or even imprisonment. In town, parking causes the most problems, and breaking the rules will mean a *papillon* (parking ticket) on the windscreen.

If your car is registered outside France, and you are neither resident nor employed in France, you should pay your fines before leaving the country, or your car may be held at the border.

There is a good reason for paying fines quickly. If you pay a speeding ticket within three days, it is reduced; on the other hand, it becomes much more expensive if you wait a month before paying.

PARKING – STATIONNEMENT

Parking is strictly regulated in the bigger towns:

- *unilatéral*: restricted to one side of the street;
- *en zone bleu*: for a limited time;
- *horodateurs* or *parcmètres*: parking meters;
- *parking souterrain*: underground parking has unlimited parking time, the cost depending on the location.

Look for the signs on the ground or on signposts, they indicate the parking rules (parking meters, hourly parking disk, etc). Remember that a car may never be left on a public street for more than seven days at a time. In big towns, some parking at a special *tarif résidentiel* is reserved for the inhabitants of the neighbourhood (ask at the *mairie* for your application). There are also special places reserved for handicapped people and for deliveries.

A car may be removed or impounded if it blocks traffic or poses a hazard (parking on a pedestrian crossing or at a bus stop). When a car is impounded you must pay a daily storage fee, as well as a penalty for the removal. If unclaimed for 45 days, it is offered for public sale.

S ecurity and the police

━━ *La Police Nationale (Ministère de l'Intérieur)*

The national police force includes:

- Police Judiciare (PJ), the criminal investigation department;

- Service des Renseignements Généraux (RG), the intelligence division and Surveillance du Territoire (DST), the domestic counter-espionage department (which have merged);

- Securité Publique, who are responsible for maintaining public order and safety in the towns;

- CRS (Compagnies Républicaines de Sécurité) are the state security police, the mobile units well known for keeping order during demonstrations. They also do surveillance and rescue work in the mountains and at the seaside;

- Direction Centrale du Contrôle de l'Immigration et de la Lutte contre l'Emploi des Clandestins (DICCILEC), who control the airports, ports and frontiers.

In Paris, the Préfecture de Police is responsible for all police activity.

Many towns also have a *police municipale*, under the authority of the mayor of the *commune*, who monitors the application of municipal laws. The mayor is the Officier de Police Judiciare for small *communes*.

━━ *La Gendarmerie Nationale (Ministère de la Défense)*

The *gendarmes* are part of the military. They are mostly stationed in *communes* of less than 10,000 inhabitants. Their mission is to prevent, report and stop crime. They deal mostly with traffic offences (speeding, drink-driving, etc). The *motards* are the motor-bike police, who keep order and act as official escorts.

The *Garde Républicaine* goes on parade for special occasions, and also assures the public safety.

Interpol: the international criminal police organization

The headquarters of Interpol are at Lyon, where people of 50 different nationalities work to disseminate information between the police services of the 154 member countries. Interpol is a police organization supporting all organizations, authorities and services whose mission is preventing, detecting and suppressing crime.

Police help – allo! le 17

Any threat to public safety, whether an accident on the street or at home, or any form of disturbance justifies a call to the police. Their job is to help people in difficulty, to report the facts and, when necessary, dispatch emergency medical assistance.

Travelling

'*Imagination is the best means of transport in the world,*' said Roger Fournier, but to get from one point to another in France, and the rest of the world, you would do better to take a plane, train, boat, car or even a bike.

The need for professional mobility, plus weekend and holiday travel, has greatly increased daily and seasonal travel.

▬▬ *Travelling by car*

National, regional and departmental maps will help you find your way. In 1912, André Michelin, the father of Bibendum, succeeded in numbering all the roads in France. Milestones were inscribed with numbers that correspond to those on the road maps. He also had the clever idea of calculating the distance from Paris to other French towns. A small bronze plaque on the *parvis* of the Notre Dame Cathedral in Paris marks point zero for the calculations. There is now an internet site which will calculate the distance between any two of the 36,780 French *communes*, and will plot an itinerary both in France and in Europe. You may also make hotel and restaurant reservations.

Traffic and road conditions throughout France are constantly monitored by the services of road and traffic safety, and the regional information centres (traffic, roadworks, weather conditions).

In the tourist offices, the *mairies* or the newsagents, you will find maps for every town in France. Various online services provide detailed maps of the French *communes*. There are some 24-hour automotic petrol stations operated by credit card.

■ *Roads and motorways* – routes et autoroutes

'In France, the kilometer signs on the sides of the roads are merely there to encourage English tourists to use the metric system.'

Jeff

Signs are blue for motorways, yellow for national roads, green for departmental roads and white for commune roads. A green line beneath the words indicates a scenic route that merits a detour. These same colours are used on road maps. (www.autoroutes.fr)

Bigger towns served by national roads are marked by green signs; white signs indicate *communes* of fewer than 20,000 inhabitants, as well as airports, railway stations, etc.

The shape and colour of a sign has a special significance:

- round indicates an order;
- triangle indicates danger ahead;
- square gives information.

Only the stop sign is hexagonal, making it easy to identify even if it is dirty or covered with snow (a US idea).

- red always means danger;
- blue means a restriction.

Temporary messages include the following:

- *travaux* (roadworks);
- *accident*;
- *bouchon* (traffic jam);
- *déviation* (detour);
- *circulation fluide* (smooth traffic flow);
- *ralentir* (slow down).

■ *Toll roads* – péage

There are a few rare stretches of free motorway, but elsewhere the cost of toll roads depends on whether they are managed by a public or private company. Payment may be made by bank card or a pass. A few timid attempts have been made to reduce traffic jams by offering lower toll rates during non-rush hours.

■ *Rest areas on the motorway*

An abundance of rest stops are found along the motorway, allowing drivers to rest and recuperate. They offer toilets, telephones, service stations and sometimes information centres. You will find some pleasant picnic areas and restaurants, or perhaps shops selling useful travel goods such as maps, sunglasses, food and so on.

MOTORWAY NAMES

- Autoroute du Nord (A1)
- Autoroute de l'Est (A4)
- Autoroute du Soleil (A6–A7)
- Autoroute de Normandie (A13)
- Autoroute La Provençale (A8)
- Autoroute La Languedocienne (A9)
- Autoroute l'Aquitaine (A10)
- Autoroute l'Océane (A11)
- Autoroute La Catalane (B9)
- Autoroute des Deux Mers (A61)

NB: Remember that prices are always higher in these motorway shops than elsewhere.

In the summer, other services are announced along the motorway and are easy to identify:

- welcome centres for babies and their parents, with changing tables, a dining area, etc;
- sports equipment that allows travellers to relax and take a little exercise, try archery, or climbing, or simply freshen up.

■ *The 'crafty bison', or how to avoid traffic jams* – bison futé

During the mass exodus on long weekends or holidays, there is a special service for drivers called *bison futé* (the 'crafty bison'). The radio and press predict traffic conditions, hours and days to avoid, and advice on finding *itinéraires bis* (secondary routes), which are

BREAKDOWNS – EN PANNE

The motorway is equipped with roadside emergency telephones every 2 km. They are connected directly to the *gendarmerie*, which alerts an authorized repair service. There is a flat rate for this service, which is calculated by the day, whether or not it is a holiday, and depending on the time of day.

indicated by green and yellow signs. The significant comings and goings in French travel always coincide with the school holidays. *Bison futé* indicates the *jours noirs* (black days – very bad traffic), such as 31 July or 1 August (when *juilletistes et aoûtiens* travellers are simultaneously leaving and returning from their holidays), and the *jours rouges* (red days – bad traffic). The *jours oranges* days are those on which the traffic is less heavy. Traffic jams are forecast by hour, zone and length: 150-km traffic jams are orange, 1,200-km jams are red and (terrible thought) 4,800-km jams are black.

This information and advice is given in order to reduce traffic congestion. You may consult the internet, listen to the radio or stop by the information centres in the motorway rest stops, to obtain these traffic bulletins (www. infotrafic.com).

▬▬Travelling by rail

The SNCF (Société Nationale de Chemin de Fer Français) operates an extensive rail system connecting some 2,000 stations. The trains go everywhere in France, and beyond.

If you travel by train, it is wise to consider the calendar (long weekends as well as religious, national and school holidays), and to reserve and purchase your ticket in advance. Conversely, during non-peak travel periods, certain ticket services might reward your flexibility.

■ *Taking the train*

More and more people now commute to work by train. It seems that, morning and night, trains on some routes have become a second office, with travellers bringing files and laptops, stretching the work day right to the doorstep of their home. Sometimes, a fellow traveller with a mobile phone will be so indiscreet as to involve everyone else in his interminable conversations, while others read, play never-ending hands of cards and chat. The train is certainly a fruitful ground for sociological observations.

■ *Tickets and reservations*

You can check schedules and reserve and purchase tickets at station information desks and ticket counters, as well as at travel agents displaying the SNCF logo. You can do the same via the internet (www.SNCF.com). Your ticket will clearly indicate all the information necessary to find your seat – first or second class, car and seat number, and the date and times of departure and arrival.

THE TGV – *HIGH-SPEED TRAIN*

Since the 1980s, the *TGVs* (*trains à grande vitesse*) have won praise and commendations. They link a number of the larger French and European towns and cities. The TGV is operated by SNCF and now covers 31,840 km.

Eurostar (www.eurostar.com), the Cross-Channel high-speed train linking the UK to France and Belgium, runs up to 14 services a day from Paris to St Pancras Station in London and back, in 2.15 hours. The '*shuttle*' ferries cars and other vehicles 40 m (130 ft) below the Channel's surface.

Thalys links Paris and Brussels (in 1.25 hours) and carries on to Amsterdam (reached in 3.15 hours).

Reservations are required on an ever-increasing number of trains, including the *TGV*. The price will depend on the date and time you intend to travel. Even so, a pre-purchased ticket can be exchanged or returned for a refund at any time before the scheduled departure. If you miss your train, you can still cancel your ticket up to 30 minutes after its departure. A ticket for a train not requiring a reservation is valid for two months from the date of purchase.

Free train schedules are always available at the stations. The schedules change twice a year, once at the end of May and again in late November. Informative pamphlets are available in different languages. There are also attractively priced fares to tempt those who can travel during off-peak hours. You must do a little digging to find the best train at the right price.

Most of the *grandes lignes* (main lines) offer the services of a bar, restaurant car or snack cart. *TGV* trains also have telephones. If you are travelling with your family, some trains have changing facilities and play rooms. Children between the ages of 4 and 14 can travel alone on certain lines, as long as they are placed in the care of a steward.

The trains in France usually run on time, except on a few older lines or those currently being modernized. These offer all the charms of a real adventure.

Once on the train, you are responsible for your own bags, unless you check them in as *bagages accompagnés*. The SNCF does offer many other services, including car rentals upon arrival, hotel reservations, assistance for handicapped travellers and a door-to-door luggage service.

■ *Discounts*

Frequent or occasional travellers, a couple or a family, young (12–25) or old, the SNCF has a variety of discounts depending on the particular situation of each. Make enquiries at the railway station and compare the options.

The state initiated the following discounts:

● *famille nombreuse* – the reduction is based on the number of children (30 per cent off for three children, 40 per cent off for four, and so on up to 75 per cent off). The discount is given at the station when the tickets are purchased. Copies of the parents' and children's birth certificates must be shown to obtain a *famille nombreuse* card. This card also gives access to reductions on the metro, in some museums, swimming pools and so on;

● *congés payés* – employees benefit from a 25 per cent reduction on a round-trip ticket once a year (the employer fills out a special form for this).

VALIDATE YOUR TICKETS – COMPOSTEZ VOTRE BILLET

To validate a train ticket, you should stamp it in the yellow machine located at the entrance to the train platforms. When the ticket is inspected on the train, the validation will be checked to verify the station and the day on which the journey started.

There is an electronic information board in the station for the *grandes lignes*, showing the destination or departure town of the train, as well as its number, the time and platform on which it will arrive or depart. If you have a reservation, all you need to do is find the number of the carriage and seat. Railway personnel are available on the platforms before the train leaves to help you find your way. During the trip, they are also at hand to assist you.

■ *Welcome centres* – points-accueil

Railway stations and airports have *points-accueil* where receptionists (who usually speak English) are available to help travellers. Urgent messages can be broadcast from the centre and the *points-accueil* may be used as a meeting place.

Travelling by air

Air France is the national airline. The deregulation of air travel has opened up the skies of France to private and foreign carriers, and competition is likely to intensify. There are many different airlines, but Air France (www.airfrance.fr) has 800 daily flights to 200 destinations in France, in Europe and throughout the world.

Air France aims to win customer loyalty through creative, high-quality products and services, and offers a frequent-flyer programme with each flight contributing, eventually, to a free ticket or other benefit.

PLANÈTE BLEU

Children between 4 and 12 years of age may travel unaccompanied on domestic or international flights, as long as the airline is informed when the ticket is purchased. The child must have parental authorization, identification papers, and the documents necessary for leaving and returning to France, as well as the name of the person who will be meeting him or her.

Sea crossings

Numerous ferries carry passengers and cars from France to Corsica, Great Britain and Ireland. If you plan to take a ferry to Ireland or Corsica during school holidays, it is wise to reserve your place well in advance.

Taxis

In town, there will be a taxi rank on busy streets. There is always one in front of railway stations and airports, even though the long queues may be discouraging. You may also flag down a passing taxi if its light is on, indicating that it is available.

Your first encounter with the French will probably be at the airport, and with a taxi driver. You and your children may add up to more than three passengers and the driver may refuse to take you, because 'it's against the regulations to take more than three people', and might suggest that you take two taxis. However, before you do so, check to see whether there is a minivan available to accept your fare.

The meter will register a basic charge as soon as you get in the taxi. Each 200 metres or so, an additional sum will be added to the meter. Prices vary according to the time of day, the day and the zone. There is an extra charge if you pick up a taxi at the airport or a railway station; another charge is made for each piece of luggage. The driver may refuse to take you if your destination is out of his 'zone', or area – except to take you to the airport.

Some taxi companies offer a subscription service which gives priority to clients. Many taxis take credit cards, but they rarely take cheques.

The driver will ask you to pay the amount on the meter and he must give you a receipt if you ask for it. He or she will expect a tip of about 10 per cent; your generosity should be based on the service you get.

━━━ *Travelling outside Paris* – en province

Larger towns have their own private or public transport; all have buses and some also have metros (Marseille, Lyon, Lille) or tramways. It is cheaper to buy a book of tickets, or to buy a season ticket, than to purchase tickets individually. Ticket prices vary from one town to another.

Towns that do not have a rail service are linked by buses or coaches. You will find details on these services at the railway station or at the *mairie*.

▬▬ *Public transport in Paris*

Public transport in Paris is run by the RATP (Régie Autonome des Transports Parisiens) (www.ratp.fr) and the SNCF (Société Nationale des Chemins de Fer Français). Metro, bus, RER (Réseau Express Régional) and the suburban trains serve Paris and the region of Ile-de-France, which is divided into eight zones.

In the Ile-de-France region, you may purchase tickets and find information in the metro and train stations (metro, RER or SNCF). Some *tabacs* and railway stations outside of Paris also sell *carnets de tickets de métro* – booklets of 10 tickets.

When taking the RER or the suburban trains it is important to check the train's destination, as trains to various destinations use the same platforms. Be sure that you are on the right platform, on the right train and that you have the correct ticket!

Whichever means of transport you use, remember to keep your ticket until you leave the station at your destination, as inspectors will impose fines on passengers without the correct ticket.

◼ *The Paris* métro

White is the colour of the tickets and the logo of the metro that has been part of Parisian history since 1900. The *métro* stations are named after famous people and events, but only two stations are named after women – Louise Michel and Madeleine.

In the *métro* you will meet working people during rush hours, bands of children on a school outing, provincials visiting Paris for a trade fair, tipsy tourists, down-and-out musicians, people selling tawdry goods and cut-rate fruit, and the homeless, who will either be asleep or passing 'the hat' among their fellow passengers.

Regulars on the *métro* often seem blasé. They stare into the distance with vacant expressions, lost in their own thoughts; others are absorbed by their books and newspapers. During the rush hour, people are seldom courteous as they hurry to their destinations. Fatigue and nervousness often cause tension and people get cross

BUYING YOUR TICKET

- A *navigo* (yearly, monthly or weekly pass) allows you to use all forms of public transport as often as you wish. The price varies according to the number of zones covered.

- A *carte hebdomadaire* entitles you to a round-trip journey per day from Monday to Sunday.

- Tickets may be purchased in books of 10 (a *carnet*), or individually (more expensive).

- There are special prices for one or more days of unlimited travel. This is especially useful for visitors to the city.

- Bus, RER and train prices vary according to the distance covered; however, you may travel the 200 km (379 stations and 14 lines) of the *métro* system or ride on the bus from start to finish all for just one ticket!

very quickly; but do not worry, as there are also friendly passengers who will help you find your way if you get lost.

The *métro* is the quickest, cheapest and most reliable way to travel in Paris. It runs from 5.30 am until 1 am, with trains every two minutes during rush hours.

The métro *on automatic pilot* – Météor (Metro Est-Ouest Rapide) links the Bibliothèque de France to the Gare Saint-Lazare across the heart of Paris under the River Seine. Elegance and speed make using the *métro* a pleasure. One day, line 14 will pass through the Gare Saint-Lazare to the suburbs.

Many stations have been redecorated to reflect the history of the areas they serve. For example, the Louvre-Rivoli station offers a foretaste of the Louvre Museum. Some lines run above ground and allow you to see a little of Paris, before plunging back underground.

Some *métro* stations have street maps at the exit, which show you how to find your destination, either on foot, by bus or on another *métro*.

The police and the RATP keep watch over the *métro* and its passengers, and the French will take the *métro* late at night after the theatre or early in the morning without fear. Of course, it is, however, always wise to keep an eye on your belongings.

A MÉTRO *GUIDE*

Ask for a *métro* map at the ticket booth, or buy one of the street map books that also contain all the *métro* lines. Each line is shown in a different colour, with a number and the name of its start and finish (for example, Line n° 1: Château de Vincennes-La Défense, passing by the station Palais Royal-Musée du Louvre). There are also *métro* maps in all the *métro* carriages. On the platform you will see that the exit (*sortie*) is indicated in blue, and the connecting trains in orange.

RER: *Réseau Express Régional*

The RER, a frequent and rapid service, crosses Paris from east to west and from north to south with a few stops in between. Quicker than the *métro*, it serves many suburban stations. There are four main lines: A, B, C and D.

Signs on the platforms indicate the stations served by each train, and arrivals and departures. Some trains are non-stop and serve the main stations; others are slow trains, which stop at all the stations along the way. Times are also available at the ticket office. You may use your *carte orange* for some destinations on RER, while for others you will pay an additional charge.

Unlike the *métro*, the RER requires you to punch your ticket at the exit, as well as at the entry, in order to leave the station.

FROM PARIS TO THE AIRPORT

Airline, hotel and RATP buses run from Orly airport (14 km and 25 minutes south of Paris) and Roissy airport (25 km and 45 minutes north of Paris) to the centre of the city. There are also trains: Orlyval and the RER Line C go to Orly, while the RER Line B goes to Roissy. There are also buses that run between the airports.

■ *The bus in Paris*

The bus is a pleasant way to get to your destination in Paris and see the sights along the way. The buses run from 7.30 am to 9 pm and are less frequent than the *métro*, as they are often slowed by heavy traffic. To ride on a bus, you validate your ticket in the machine located by the door. A few buses run throughout the night.

PARISIAN RAILWAY STATIONS

There are six stations in Paris linked by buses and *métro* stations; each serves a particular region:

- Gare Montparnasse: west to Rennes, Nantes, Bordeaux (TGV Atlantique), Brest, Granville;
- Gare de l'Est: east to Reims, Metz, Nancy, Strasbourg, Luxembourg, Switzerland, Germany, Austria;
- Gare du Nord: north to Lille, Brussels (Thalys), London (Eurostar);
- Gare Saint-Lazare: west to Rouen, Caen, Cherbourg;
- Gare de Lyon: south-east to Lyons, Grenoble, Avignon (TGV Sud-Est), and Italy; and
- Gare d'Austerlitz: Limoges, Orléans, Tours, Pau, Perpignan, and then Madrid, Lisbon.

All railway stations except the Gare Montparnasse are classified as historical monuments for some part of their architecture (for example, the main hall and the façade of the Gare de l'Est, and the buffet of the Gare de Lyon).

■ *Vélib, bicycle rental*

Like Strasbourg, Lyon and Rennes, Paris offers a self-service bicycle rental system called *Vélib* (vélo + liberté). Parisians and visitors are delighted to cycle, picking up and dropping off bicycles throughout the city at different locations. To hire a bicycle, cyclists can select a one-day, weekly or annual pass. The first half-hour is free and a supplement is charged for additional time.

*F*or further information

Dictionary of Contempory France, Richard Alpin (Hodder & Stoughton, 1993)
The Riches of France, A shopping and touring guide to the French provinces (St Martin's Press, 1998)
Minitel 3616 NF

www.conso.net
www.aeroport.fr

www.adp.fr (Paris)

www.viamichelin.com, www.maporama.com, www.mappy.fr, www.vivalville.com

www.autoroutes.fr

www.code-route.com (driving licence exchange)

Paris in a Basket, Markets ,The Food and the People, Nicolle Aimée Meyer and Amanda Pilar Smith, (Köeneman, 2000)

7 *Youngsters*

E... enfants, élèves, étudiants

'There always comes a moment in our childhood when the door opens and lets the future in.'

'Il y a toujours dans notre enfance un moment où la porte s'ouvre et laisse entrer l'avenir.'

Graham Greene

*C*hildren and family

The family is a reference point in the patrimonial and religious traditions of France, an institution that has changed enormously over the generations. It is now less conventional. Unmarried couples live together, children are raised by single parents, and families can also consist of children from different unions. It is a sign of the times that civil marriage (created in 1792), which is often followed by a religious ceremony, has suffered from the new family order, which often prefers unfettered partnership to marriage. About 60 per cent of children born in France are born 'out of wedlock'. In 1970 a law replaced paternal authority with parental authority.

Men and women organize their private lives in a wide variety of ways in France. If you are living with someone, you can ask for a cohabitation, concubinage or common-law marriage certificate from your town hall, though you will still be considered as single, except for social security, social aid and the train company SNCF.

The PACS (Pacte Civil de Solidarité) is a contract, different from marriage, between two people whatever their sex and may be entered into between foreigners on condition they live in France. Established at the Tribunal d'Instance (local Court) the PACS introduces rights and duties between partners (involving, for example, issues of the status of joint wealth, equal share of household expenses, inheritance, tax, mutual assistance toward each other). As for married couples, the name of each person is reported on the original birth certificate of the partner (at the *mairie* of the place of birth).

In 2007 in France, 266,500 marriages were registered (as opposed to 140,000 divorces) and 102,000 PACS.

New lifestyles, professional and geographic mobility, and a leisure society sometimes disrupt family life. The vicissitudes of love are no longer taboo, and separations and divorce have increased in French society. Nevertheless, the family is still the essential reference, where children learn autonomy, and the shared responsibilities of men and women. The family is the safe haven in time of personal or economic need, and many young people live with their parents until they find their first job. Family feeling is seen in selfless sharing – the exchange of services, babysitting, loaning money or a car – and also in family celebrations.

A family with three or more children is considered to be a *famille nombreuse* (big family), which merits discounts in public transport or museum entrance fees. Young children almost always know their grandparents and, frequently, their great-grandparents, thanks to increasing longevity. Elderly people (seniors), living longer, and keeping their independence as long as their health permits, often play an important role in volunteer and cultural associations.

Happiness is a state of mind, and the French believe that it is to be found in good health, love, family, work, freedom, children or wealth.

A FRENCH MEAL

Taking time over a meal allows for family discussion about the events of the day, forthcoming projects and perhaps appreciation of the food served. Most French parents will try to teach their children a few good French habits:

- to stay at the table until the end of the meal without losing their napkin;

- to keep their hands on either side of the plate while waiting to serve themselves or be served;

- to use the left hand for the fork when using a knife, and switch it to the right hand when eating with it; only *frites* (French fries, or chips) may be eaten with the fingers!; the bread is placed on the table, next to the plate, where it waits to be nibbled, or used to push the peas on to the fork. When the food is finished, the knife and fork are placed together neatly on the plate while dessert is awaited!

253

▬▬ *A French upbringing*

Education and the rules of polite behaviour differ according to each family and its social and cultural level. Some habits will seem more or less strict to the foreigner, or certainly different. Do not hesitate to discuss your impressions; it is a fascinating subject of debate between people of different cultures and will allow you to understand the different values and points of reference that make French people what they are.

*A*BC *for the little ones*

▬▬ *Children born in France*

Congratulations! The birth of a child must be registered within three days at the local *mairie*. The declaration is made with the birth certificate, either directly at the *mairie* or with a representative who visits the maternity ward.

Parents may choose any name for their child, as long as it is not ridiculous or prejudicial to the child.

Since 1 September 1998, every child born in France of foreign parents receives a *titre d'identité republicain.* He or she automatically acquires French nationality at the age of 18, if he or she is then resident in France, and living permanently (or for prolonged periods) for at least 5 years from the age of 11. The child may also refuse French nationality, or make his or her first request for it at the age of 16.

▬▬ *Child care*

In the 1950s, the French economy, needing workers, facilitated the entry of women into the workplace by creating company childcare centres. Since then, most French women have wanted to have a job in order to guarantee their independence. In France, nearly half of employees are women and 78 per cent of them are aged between 25 and 49. Eighty per cent of women with one child work, compared to 50 per cent of women who have three children. Thirty per cent of women work part time (compared to only 5 per cent of men) and some big companies offer financial assistance for home childcare, thereby avoiding absenteeism when children are sick.

Although French towns have multiplied and diversified the available collective and individual childcare (*crèche, assistante maternelle, garde à domicile*), they remain insufficient for the needs of young parents.

● *Crèches* are day nurseries, usually run by the municipality. They receive infants from two months to three years, in nurseries equipped for small groups, under the supervision of a nurse and a teaching staff. They are generally open from 7 am to 7 pm, except at weekends and holidays. Parents pay according to their income.

● *Assistantes maternelles* are certified by the DDASS (Direction Départementale des Affaires Sociales) to care for one or more children over three months old in their own home during the day. Their salary level is fixed by the state.

● *Halte-garderies or jardin d'enfants* are places where children from three months to six years learn to socialize with other children. They also offer a meeting place for mothers who do not work, or who work part time, who may leave their children there a few hours a week.

● A *garde d'enfant à domicile* gives childcare at home for children under six years of age. Working parents who employ a nanny (nounou) may obtain aid from the CAF. This is called PAJE (*prestation d'acceuil du jeune enfant*) and pays the social security charges for the employee directly to URSSAF. The amount depends on the family's income. Part of the employee's salary may be deducted from income taxes. A 'garde partagée' implies sharing the nanny with another family and splitting the cost.

- There are also other formats, such as *mini-crèches,* run by parents, families or babysitters.

These forms of child care, municipal or private, are state-certified. For information about childcare in your area, enquire at the *mairie*, who will help you find the most appropriate solution or use word-of-mouth.

■■■■ *Which school for your child?*

While you are living in a foreign country, two cultures and two languages will certainly be an advantage for your child, but your situation will also mean that you have to make many difficult decisions about your child's schooling.

The choice of the language of instruction should be based on the age, self-sufficiency and scholastic level of the child and your location in France. The personality of the child should also be considered:

- Does the child want to learn French?
- Is he or she curious about the new environment?
- Does he or she go readily to others, adults or children?

And from your point of view:

- What is your own interest in French language and culture?
- What is the probable length of your stay in France?
- What are your plans for the future?

Do not hesitate to consult other parents who have faced the same problems. You could also seek the advice of child specialists, psychologists or teachers. It is obviously useful to prepare the child and, depending on his or her age, also include him or her in the decision-making process.

AGE	FRANCE	UK	US
2.5–6	maternelle	nursery school	nursery school
5–6		year 1 (infants)	kindergarten
	Ecole Primaire	**Primary School**	**Elementary School**
6–7	cours préparatoire/11ème	year 2 (infants)	first grade
7–8	cours elémentaire 1/10ème	year 3 (junior)	second grade
8–9	cours elémentaire 2/9ème	year 4 (junior)	third grade
9–10	cours moyen 1/8ème	year 5 (junior)	fourth grade
10–11	cours moyen 2/7ème	year 6 (junior)	fifth grade
	Collège (premier cycle)	**Secondary School**	
11–12	6ème	first form (year 7)	sixth grade **Junior High**
12–13	5ème	second form (year 8)	seventh grade
13–14	4ème	third form (year 9)	eighth grade
			High School
14–15	3ème	fourth form (year 10)	ninth grade
	Lycée (second cycle)		
15–16	seconde	fifth form (year 11)	tenth grade
16–17	première	lower sixth form	eleventh grade
17–18	terminale	upper sixth form	twelfth grade
	Université or classes préparataires		
18–20	Deug	Bachelor's degree	
20–21	Licence		
21–22	Maîtrise	Master's degree	

Exchanges with a French family offer a chance to become familiar with the language and the different customs. Whether they are experiments, or simply experiences, such exchanges may indicate to you whether or not your child wants to live a 'French adventure'.

Some private schools, mostly in the provinces, offer boarding for children whose families are far away; problems of separation, distance and the high cost often make this a difficult choice.

In order to participate in the regular curriculum, non-French-speaking children between the ages of 7 and 15 may take a special preparative class of intensive tuition for one year.

'On the first day we watched, intrigued, as all the pupils kissed their teacher, filed in [and] changed their shoes for slippers. At playtime, Luke was befriended by the football crowd. At home, there were tears all round. I was sorry he was upset. On Monday of the second week, he wanted to take the school bus... Then, on week three he demanded new slippers for school...'
Luke's mother

*F*rench school

The governing principles of French public education are that schools should be secular, free, mixed-sex and obligatory from 6 to 16 years of age. The *école maternelle* is not obligatory, but receives almost all children from the age of three and over.

Teaching establishments, either run by the state or private (under contract from the state), follow rules fixed by the Ministry of Education, which defines and controls school programmes. Private schools are often religious, usually Catholic.

The Ministry of Education is represented by a rector in each of the 28 school districts (*académies*), covering several departments, except for the Paris school district. The rector manages the establishments of higher learning in his or her school district. Each department has a school board responsible for the administrative and educational responsibilities for primary and secondary schools in conjunction with the school directors in the district.

An *école* is a school for elementary education, while an *école supérieure* or a *grande école* (such as HEC) is at the tip of the academic pyramid.

THE FRENCH SCHOOL SYSTEM

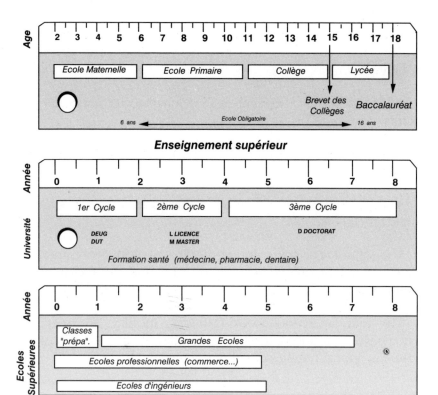

Age

2 3 4 5 6 7 8 9 10 11 12 13 14 15 16 17 18

| Ecole Maternelle | Ecole Primaire | Collège | Lycée |

Brevet des Collèges   Baccalauréat

6 ans ← Ecole Obligatoire → 16 ans

Enseignement supérieur

Année

0 1 2 3 4 5 6 7 8

Université

| 1er Cycle | 2ème Cycle | 3ème Cycle |

DEUG   L LICENCE   D DOCTORAT
DUT   M MASTER

Formation santé *(médecine, pharmacie, dentaire)*

Année

0 1 2 3 4 5 6 7 8

Ecoles Supérieures

Classes "prépa".   Grandes Ecoles

Ecoles professionnelles *(commerce...)*

Ecoles d'ingénieurs

Lille
Rouen Amiens
Caen   Nancy
Paris Reims Metz
Rennes versailles Créteil   Strasbourg
Nantes Orléans   Besançon
Tours Dijon
Poitiers
Limoges Clermont- Lyon
Ferrand Grenoble
Bordeaux   Aix
Toulouse Marseille
Nice
Montpellier
Corse

The school year

The school year is divided into three trimesters, with 36 school weeks (162 class days), and 16 weeks' holiday. The rhythm is roughly seven weeks of school, followed by two weeks' holiday:

- first trimester (September–December), with *Toussaint* (All Saints' Day) and Christmas holidays;

- second trimester (January–March), with winter and spring breaks;

- third trimester (April–July), followed by the long summer holidays (July–August).

The school year starts during the first week of September, the date dependent on the school's director and the rector of the school district.

The four-day school week (Monday, Tuesday, Thursday and Friday) was introduced in 2008. Wednesday is a free day, often dedicated to sports, hobbies or cultural activities.

Registering your child for school

The *carte scolaire* is the system whereby a child's school is determined by the child's address. However, parents may now send their children to the school of their choice.

A *dossier d'inscription* must be completed at the school office of the *mairie* for primary schools, and at the *rectorat* school service for secondary schools. You will need to supply the following documents:

- child's birth certificate translated into French, and passport;
- obligatory vaccination records or medical records;
- school report from preceding school, if applicable; and
- proof of residence (rental contract).

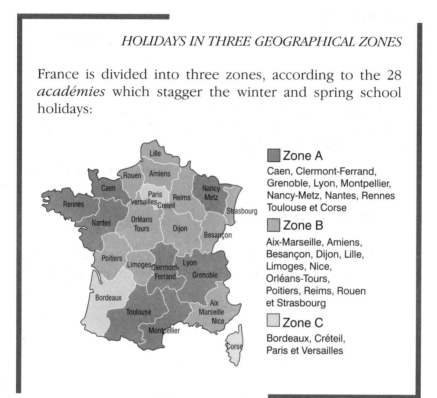

HOLIDAYS IN THREE GEOGRAPHICAL ZONES

France is divided into three zones, according to the 28 *académies* which stagger the winter and spring school holidays:

Zone A

Caen, Clermont-Ferrand, Grenoble, Lyon, Montpellier, Nancy-Metz, Nantes, Rennes Toulouse et Corse

Zone B

Aix-Marseille, Amiens, Besançon, Dijon, Lille, Limoges, Nice, Orléans-Tours, Poitiers, Reims, Rouen et Strasbourg

Zone C

Bordeaux, Créteil, Paris et Versailles

The *mairie* will give you a registration form, which will allow you to meet the director of the school before you register your child.

State schools are free and books are lent to the children. Other school materials are the responsibility of the parents, as are some school activities, such as outings. An annual medical check-up is performed at the school, after the age of six, to check vaccinations, hearing and sight.

It is considered courteous for parents to send a note to the teacher if the child is absent from school for a day. School attendance is obligatory for all children over six, and parents must justify any absence over two days with a medical certificate. A child aged between 6 and 16 can be registered in an *école publique* at any time of the year. In a private school, it depends on the places available.

SCHOOL INSURANCE

Insurance coverage for school and extra-curricular activities is recommended, in addition to your comprehensive insurance policy. It covers all risks, at school and outside school (outings, trips, holidays), 24 hours a day, all year, whatever the circumstances or location.

Parents' authorization

The director of the school will ask you to sign an authorization form for emergency medical care for your child, and also for supervised school outings.

Parents' associations

Parents, generally as part of an association, are annually elected to the school council (for primary schools), or the board of administration (for *collège* or *lycée*). These associations are of different political and ideological tendencies. They intervene on all questions of school organization, including school projects and management, quality of welcome for the children, the school canteen or school transport, if applicable. They are also responsible for informing the other parents and proposing services (such as school insurance).

The first day at school

The first day at school is always a big event for a child, and the younger the child, the fewer words he or she has to express any feelings. It is reassuring for the child to see the school and visit the classroom before school starts to see what it is like. He or she might also get to know other children in the neighbourhood who will be at the same school.

In nursery school, the child may go to class part time, in the morning or the afternoon, to get used to school life slowly. You are allowed to go into the classroom with your child before leaving him or her; children can take a special blanket or toy to cuddle at school in case of loneliness.

At the end of the day, the teachers are there to exchange a few words with you. If you would like a longer interview, you should ask for a meeting. A parent–teacher evening is held shortly after the start of the school term to introduce the class and its activities to the families.

◾ *A school day*

School hours are generally between 8.30 am and 4.30 pm, with two breaks of 15 minutes for recreation, and a lunch break of about an hour and a half.

In the morning and afternoon children go to school with their parents, or another authorized person. From primary school onwards, most children go to school by themselves. Children may be registered for the school canteen, and for the before- or after-school supervision (*garderie*), while waiting for their parents to come home from work. School meals are either prepared at the school, or delivered by a restaurant service. The menu is always on the notice-board for the parents to see.

Although there is no official uniform for state schools, most children and adolescents prefer to wear the same sort of clothes as their peers, and this usually means jeans, T-shirts or sweaters, a jacket, trainers, and a backpack, which serves as a satchel for their books. Junior fashion calls for accessories, such as badges and pendants, for the brief period of a season.

'The unofficial dress code is more sober in France, possibly because French kids have never been forced to wear school uniforms and therefore don't feel obliged to go wild, like Brits tend to whenever they get a chance to don civilian clothing.'
Catherine Sanderson (*La Petite Anglaise*)

A new law introduced in 2004 confirmed the principle of secularism, and forbids the wearing at school of symbols intended to show that a pupil is a member of a religion, such as a cross (for Christians) or headscarf (for Muslim girls).

*N*ursery school – l'école maternelle

French nursery school is financed by public funds. Most children from three to five years of age, and some two-year-olds, are happy to go to nursery school. Although it is an integral part of the primary school system, the nursery school is interested in the social adaptation of the child. This leaves time for the child to become accustomed to the idea of a teacher and a classroom, and to become familiar with a school-type setting.

The *école maternelle* is a rich source of adventure and discovery away from home. One hundred years ago, nursery schools were simply for babysitting, now they make use of all the new teaching methods to awaken a child's intelligence through play. Your child, along with other children, will gradually discover the French language in a stimulating environment. Depending on your choice, he or she will be preparing for a French or international education.

*P**rimary school: from* maternelle *to the* école elémentaire

Schooling is organized into three cycles, which include the standard subjects of French, mathematics, science, history and geography:

- *apprentissages premiers* – the first steps in learning are the *école maternelle* (3–5 years old) in the *petite* and *moyenne sections*;

- *apprentissages fondamentaux* – basic learning starts in the last year of *maternelle* and the first two years of elementary school (5–8 years old), in the *grande section* – CP, CE1; and

- *le cycle 'approfondissements'* – during the three years before *collège* (from 8–11 years old) in CE2, CM1, CM2, the children perfect their basic skills.

For the last few years, many schools have introduced foreign languages in CM1 and CM2, and this is now becoming common at that level.

School record and report – dossier scolaire et carnet de notes

The school record is a book in which the child's scholastic progress and teachers' comments are recorded annually, throughout his or her school life.

A *contrôle de connaissance* in each subject evaluates the child's progress (marks are given from 0–10, or 0–20, or from A–E). The *carnet de notes* reports the marks, and comments on progress.

KEY FIGURES AT SCHOOL

- *Le directeur/la directrice* is the director of the school who coordinates the work of the teachers.

- *Le professeur des écoles* is the teacher of the class, who might also be called *le maître* or *la maîtresse*.

- The canteen personnel prepare and serve the food at noon.

- The school health and educational counselling services help with personal or family difficulties.

Homework – devoirs du soir

There are no *devoirs* in elementary school, but the teachers often give a lesson or an exercise for the child to finish at home. Children do not generally like working alone, so you will need to encourage them. At *collège* or *lycée*, professors will expect children to work independently, in addition to doing class work.

The children have a *cahier de texte*, an agenda or log-book, which allows them to note the date their homework is due, as well as their schedule of classes and activities.

Students, or the mothers of your child's friends, may help him or her with homework or revision. This may be done on exchange basis.

Holiday homework – devoirs de vacances

Some parents, preoccupied with the scholastic success of their children, organize homework for them during the holidays. There are attractive and educational holiday workbooks, but everyday situations can be just as educational, including going shopping and working out money and change, reading a recipe and following the directions, and writing postcards, all of which are just as good as doing a dictation, and more fun.

■■■*Discovery classes* – classes de découverte

As part of a school project, children may go on an accompanied trip with the teacher and other activity directors for one to three weeks. They may go to the mountains, the seaside, the countryside or a cultural setting. These *classes de découverte* are organized throughout the school year.

Learning is adapted to the surroundings, with classes held in the mornings and discovery activities in the afternoon. Children are thrilled by this possibility to learn – outside the classroom; for most, it is also their first experience of communal living.

■■■*A break in the middle of the week* – Mercredi

At the elementary school level, there are no classes on Wednesdays, leaving over 200 free days a year, plenty of time for children to practise their leisure-time activities. Public and private clubs, and a few company clubs, offer numerous activities on Wednesdays and during the holidays, including music, theatre, manual arts, computing, foreign languages, cooking, dance, sports, etc. Some of the activities are held in schools, which are otherwise

---

SCHOOL OF GOOD TASTE – L'ÉCOLE DU BON GOÛT

In October, an annual 'taste week' is organized in schools everywhere in France to initiate children in the appreciation of the taste and smell of the food they eat. This idea, uniting chefs and teachers, reveals unknown cooking skills. A guarantee that tomorrow's consumers will be well informed, and do their bit to help maintain the French reputation for good taste!

unused on Wednesdays. Many museums organize activities and visits for children and adolescents.

Between friends, young children show a true sense of conviviality, always finding a pretext to invite themselves to play or even to sleep over on birthdays. It is up to the parents to become acquainted with each other through their children's friends.

*S*econdary school: from 6th to terminale

- *Collège* consists of the classes *sixième, cinquième, quatrième,* and *troisième*.

- *Lycée* consists of the classes *seconde, première* and *terminale*, with various options and branches depending on the aptitudes or ambitions of the student.

Collège *and* lycée

After elementary school, starting *collège* brings an important change of rhythm to school life. Students must learn to manage their own day, which is divided into class hours given by different professors. So much novelty is sometimes overwhelming.

The first foreign language is taught in the *sixième,* followed by a second language in the *quatrième*. At the end of four years of *collège*, there is an examination called the *brevet des collèges*.

At the end of the trimester, the teachers meet to evaluate the scholastic level of each student. Going on to the next class depends on the results of school work and the evaluation of the teachers.

━━ *European sections*

The creation of European sections in a number of *collèges* is designed to facilitate the children's acquisition of foreign languages. Intensive language classes should later enable the students to take other subjects, such as history or geography, in the language chosen.

These European sections are designed to integrate students in a plurilingual European environment.

━━ Lycée: *working towards a* baccalauréat

After the *troisième*, the student, parents and professors must decide the direction the student's studies will take. *Seconde, première* and *terminale* are the classes that lead to the *baccalauréat*

KEY PEOPLE AT THE COLLÈGE AND LYCÉE

- *Le professeur principal* is responsible for a class; he or she coordinates relations with the other professors.

- *Le conseiller principal d'éducation* (CPE) is responsible for enforcing discipline, and the rules and regulations of the school. He or she also supervises the class assistants (called familiarly *pions* by the students).

- *Le/la documentaliste* runs the CDI (Centre de Documentation et Information) of the *collège* or *lycée*. He or she counsels the students on their reading materials (books, newspapers, etc).

- The director of a *collège* is called a *principal*, whereas the director of a *lycée* is a *proviseur*.

- *Le service médico-social* (social worker and nurse) is the school health service. It is there for students who need help with personal or family problems.

269

and graduate study. There are various options for the *'bac'*, based on literature, science or linguistics. Other sections prepare the student for professional, scientific or artistic study.

The *bac de français* is given at the end of the *première*, whereas the other tests are given at the end of *terminale*.

▬ *Report card* – bulletin trimestriel

A report card is sent to parents at the end of each *trimestre* listing the student's average marks for each subject and the comments of all the professors or the school director. At the same time, a *carnet de correspondance* is a current record of the marks given for class work during the school year; this *carnet* must be signed regularly by the parents.

*I*nternational studies

Some state schools have international sections at the elementary, *collège* or *lycée* level for French children who have lived abroad, or for bilingual or foreign students. In the bigger French towns, these schools teach the regular national school programme, in addition to certain classes given by foreign teachers (history, geography, etc) in their various native languages.

When you enrol your child, you will be asked to provide the usual dossier, plus documents showing the child's level in French (such as school records, and essays). A test will be given to complete the evaluation.

Remedial classes are offered to children who have not completely mastered the French language. (Except where agreements exist between France and other countries, fees are charged for classes in the international section.)

International sections prepare students for various French exams, often the *baccalauréat* with an international option (which consists of tests in French and a foreign language), as well as for foreign diplomas, which differ according to the country.

Foreign schools

These private establishments provide the official academic programmes of their own country and prepare students for related exams. They are therefore not under the supervision of the French Ministry of Education. French language and culture are also taught, and some of the foreign schools are called *écoles bilingues* (bilingual schools).

'I' AS IN INTERNATIONAL

- At the CDI of the *International Lycée*, at Saint-Germain-en-Laye, there are 10 languages from which to choose. Books, videos and computers are available for reading, *zapping* and surfing. The documentation centre is an educational meeting place for many cultures: 2,000 students are assisted and counselled by the teachers, documentalists and parents from different countries, each with his or her own language and specialty. There is also an international kiosk and exhibition site that celebrates the artistic and cultural geography of the planet.

- At the *Franco–Japanese Institute*, Japanese children aged 6 to 15 follow the Japanese school programme. Their school year starts on 1 April, just as it does in Tokyo. In keeping with the international spirit of the school, French language and culture are taught and used during meetings with children from neighbouring schools.

▬▬▬*An international* baccalauréat

The Option International Baccalaureate (OIB) is a diploma offered by a number of schools throughout the world. In France, it is considered as a foreign diploma. There are some French and foreigners' schools in France with an international section leading to the OIB in order that students may follow studies abroad. Universities establish their own admission policies and evaluate foreign diplomas according to their own criteria. To establish academic equivalents, students should compile a complete dossier of their academic records (text scores and official documents).

Welcome to foreign students

Campus France is a service provided by the French Embassies to welcome and assist foreign students who wish to pursue their higher studies in France. You will find all the information necessary for organizing your studies (requirements, application forms, choice of university programme, etc). In order to avoid costly and perhaps unnecessary travel, you should start the registration process before leaving your own country through the Campus France website (www.campusfrance.org).

Registrations are made in January for the following university year. If your application is accepted, your registration will be confirmed after a French language test.

The French Government allocates a significant number of grants to foreign students.

The requirements for state grants (part of the university cooperative policy) vary according to the programmes.

For visa and *carte de séjour* information, see Chapter 3, p102.

H*igher education*

France has over 2,160,000 students and hosts 265,000 foreign students in a great variety of public and private schools of higher education. Some academic disciplines (*grandes écoles*, medical or law schools, etc) have special admission requirements.

The university registration fee and social security fee are minimal. Classes are free in state institutions; there are also some fee-paying private universities.

■■■ *Universities*

There are 87 universities in France, of which 13 are in the Ile-de-France region. Besides the traditional universities, there are other centres on the outskirts of towns.

Universities admit students who hold a French *baccalauréat*, or a foreign diploma, as determined by the individual admissions' policies.

The studies are divided into three cycles, leading to national or university diplomas (Licence, Master, Doctorat: LMD).

LA SORBONNE

In 1267, Robert de Sorbon founded a college for poor students. La Sorbonne became a university and bears the name of its founder. In 1906 Marie Curie was the first female University Professeur at the Sorbonne, and in France.

In May 1968, the Sorbonne was the symbol of student riots. Nowadays there are 30,000 students in one of the five universities under the Sorbonne umbrella. A branch of the Sorbonne was created in Abu Dhabi (EAU) as *La Sorbonne des sables*.

■■■ *The* grandes écoles

Since the 18th century, the *grandes écoles* have prepared the *cadres* – administrative, scientific and business leaders – for their place in the economic world, whether as leaders in government or private enterprise. Most of these schools accept non-French-speaking students and offer English courses.

These public and private schools offer a highly specialized course of study. Each has its own specialty and its own system of selection; they are all highly competitive, requiring an excellent scholastic record, *baccalauréat* with honours, and success in an entrance examination that is prepared over one or two years in the special *classe préparatoire aux grandes écoles* (CPGE).

■■■ *Private schools*

Some private schools, mostly teaching business, are accredited by the National Board of Education and their diplomas bear the Ministry stamp. Only state schools give state diplomas.

NB: The diplomas of other schools do not have official recognition, but they do have ministerial approval. It is advisable to compare the price with the quality of teaching, the reputation of the school and the value of its diploma.

*E*uropean programmes

The European dimension is increasingly important in the education and training of young people. This realization has led the EU to create and finance a European plan for scholastic and university cooperation.

A European credit transfer system makes it possible to combine credits towards three fixed levels of qualification (LMD: Licence,

Master's and Doctorate) obtained in any of the 32 participating European countries. See www.europa.eu.int/france.

Under the Socrates Programme, young European university students can study for six months in a university in another EU member state. Foreign languages are an essential means of communication for students of all ages, and it is especially useful to promote the study of the languages spoken in the EU countries. Cooperation and exchange projects between several schools on the subject of teaching are one of the objectives of the Socrates Programme.

THE MOST FAMOUS 'GRANDES ECOLES'

- Engineering:
  Ecole Polytechnique (called the 'X' by the cognoscenti)
  Ecole des Mines
  Ecole des Ponts et Chaussées (called 'les Ponts')
  Ecole Centrale
  Conservatoire National des Arts et Métiers (CNAM)

- Administration:
  ENA – Ecole Nationale d'Administration

- Management and business:
  HEC – Ecole des Hautes Etudes Commerciales
  ESSEC – Ecole Supérieure des Sciences Economiques et Commerciales
  Sup de Co – Ecole Supérieure de Commerce (ESC)

- Other specialties:
  Institut d'Etudes Politiques – Sciences Po and IEP
  Ecole Normale Supérieure: lettres et sciences – Normal Sup
  Ecole Nationale d'Agronomie
  Ecole Nationale Supérieure des Beaux-Arts

Cooperation and partnership are encouraged in high-tech research and development between universities and industry, and between business and the institutions of higher learning. This is why, within the EU, there are many possibilities for grants for schoolchildren and students to encourage the free flow of ideas and the mobility of young people.

ERASMUS

Since 1987 the Erasmus programme has offered the chance of experience in one of its 31 member countries. This popular programme also has a worldwide option. Erasmus The Mundus programme is dedicated to internationalizing European education.

---

*T*hings to know

━━*E-learning*

The impact of information and communication technology (ICT) has brought changes to learning and training. The internet is now a part of the daily life of pupils, students and teachers.

━━*Annual rites*

Bizutage (ragging and initiation rites) has been condemned by public opinion as excessive behaviour, and is forbidden by law in schools. Happily, other student initiatives are more useful, including the organization of forums, games and competitive sports, galas, conferences and debates, trips and so on. These events offer an excellent opportunity to learn about management.

Carte jeune

The annual *carte jeune* is for 12–26-year-olds, and is valid in many European countries. The membership card proposes reductions and special discounts in everyday life, including activities, transport, theatre and concerts, CDs and other items. It also gives access to an insurance service, legal aid and information. It is sold in train and metro stations and many shops. In Ile-de-France you can buy the *carte imagine 'R'*. See www.isic.fr.

Finding a job – petits boulots

Jeune au pair – international exchange programmes allow young men and women (traditionally more frequently women) from 18–30 years old to find a place in a French home. An *au pair* must be registered in a French language class for foreigners, for a period of 3 to 12 months. Social security payments are made by the family employing the student, thereby providing insurance coverage. The au pair is lodged, fed and receives pocket money and laundry service. In return, he or she works 5 hours a day or 30 hours a week (babysitting included). The application is addressed to the ANAEM and the DDTE, for an *accord de placement* (an agreement to hire an *au pair*).

Babysitting – looking after one or more children in the absence of their parents (after school, on Wednesdays, during the holidays, in the evenings, etc) is a responsible task. The responsibilities include preparing the children's meals and giving them their baths, and supervising them according to instructions given by the parents. The babysitter should always be given emergency telephone numbers for contacting the parents or getting other assistance. Babysitting agencies, and student or parent associations, regularly recruit people for supervising children. If these activities interest you, register with one of these groups.

'Winter on a beach remembers a shell. Thou faraway childhood.'
© Patrick Joquel

*F*or further information

Association of American Wives of Europeans (AAWE) Publications, BP 127,
   92154 Suresnes
Guide des études supérieures, Hors série (L'Etudiant) www.letudiant.fr
www.education.fr
www.onisep.fr
www.edufrance.fr
www.eduparis.net
www.transfac.fr
www.cnous.fr/etrangers/orientation
www.globegate.utm.edu/french
www.famili.fr
www.cidj.com, www.phosphore.com (high school, students)
www.socrates-leonardo.fr, www.planeterasmus.ne, www.info-europe.fr
www.studyrama.com, www.aiesec.org
www.fabert.com – list of private schools in France
www.france.english-school.org

www.cndp.fr
www.unesco.org
www.expolangues – cultural exchanges, traineeships, teaching methods
Moving to France with your Children, Angie Power
    (www.movingtofrancewithyourchildren.info/book/)
Paris with Kids, Valerie Gwinner (Open Road Publishing, 2007)
Fodor's around Paris with kids, 2nd rev edn (Fodor's Travel Publications,
    Inc, 2003)

8 *Let's talk about health*

'Health is like wealth, one must take care of it when it is good and be patient when it is bad.'

'La santé est comme la fortune, il faut la ménager quand elle est bonne et prendre patience quand elle est mauvaise.'

La Rochefoucauld

*T*he French and their health

The French are increasingly concerned about their health. Health sells newspapers and television and radio programmes, and this coverage in the media sometimes leads people to play doctor with their own health, randomly applying the advice given.

For the most part, minor health problems are a part of life and do not prevent people from going into the office or to school. There are 207,000 doctors in France, of whom 45 per cent are women, and there are as many specialists as general practitioners – the *médecin généraliste*, or family doctor. Male or female doctors can question you on private matters and ask you to undress without the presence of a female nurse. In France this is seen as a professional attitude which allows the doctor to arrive at a more accurate diagnosis. Medical competence and efficiency should allow for physical examinations to be carried out without embarrassment; however, you should not hesitate to talk about your fears or your modesty.

A more healthy lifestyle and medical progress, in conjunction with preventive care, regularly increase the average life span. In 2007, the average Frenchwoman lives to be 84.4 years old, and the average Frenchman to be 77.5. Because of this, health costs constantly increase and there is a chronic deficit in social security funds. France holds the record for the amount of medicine taken per inhabitant. Informative campaigns try to encourage the medical profession and consumers to be more responsible; mastering healthcare costs is a national problem.

Social security, which covers medical insurance, family allowance, work accidents and old-age pensions, is part of France's heritage. All contribute and, in turn, appreciate the right to receive benefits. *Prestations de nature* reimburse part of the cost of treatment, and the *prestations en espèces* are the benefits paid to a salaried employee for each work day lost due to sickness (see Chapter 3, pp 122–125).

C*hoosing a doctor*

Health is always a cause for concern, but France has an excellent medical network and offers all the special care necessary for any age.

Medical care is governed by two basic principles – the patient chooses his or her doctor and pays the fees. These fees are either set by social security, or unregulated, depending on the doctor's status; the doctor is responsible for his or her prescriptions, which are controlled by social security. All doctors are registered, as general practitioners or as specialists, by the Ordre des Médecins, which also monitors their professional qualifications and the ethics of the profession. Doctors are bound to professional secrecy by the Hippocratic oath.

You may therefore consult the doctor of your choice in the private sector (office, clinic), or the public sector (hospital, dispensary). You must register your family in order to follow your medical situation and receive full reimbursement of payments.

It is wise to find a 'good' doctor as soon as you are settled into your new home. Do not hesitate to ask the local *pharmacien* for a recommendation, as they are familiar with all the available health services in their neighbourhood.

Your local social security office (*Caisse Primaire d'Assurance Malade* (CPAM) can give you a list of doctors in your area and tell you their status.

Doctors also have patients who are in good health, mostly children, whose growth and vaccinations they monitor, as well as patients who play sports. (You may need to ask for a medical certificate before taking part in a strenuous sport.)

An increasing number of doctors speak English, as they regularly read British and US medical journals – your consulate will have a list.

The *médecin libéral* practises alone or in a group with fellow doctors. A name-plate at the entrance indicates the doctors' names,

> ### YOUR MEDICAL RECORDS
>
> Bring your family's health records with you to France – children's vaccination records, the results of recent examinations, plus any other information that might be useful to the doctor who cares for you.
>
> If you are under a doctor's care, ask your doctor at home to give you the name of a fellow doctor or hospital service in France with whom he or she might consult; also find out the generic names of your prescription medicines. If you wear glasses or contact lenses, do not forget your prescriptions in case you need to replace them.

status and medical specialties, and perhaps the consulting hours. All doctors have hospital experience and some add the words *'ancien interne'* (former intern), or *'ancien chef de clinique'* (former clinical specialist).

Some doctors work in a hospital in the morning and in their private practice in the afternoon, both to diversify their activity and to expand their knowledge. Doctors are required to inform patients by indicating their fees and their status in the waiting-room.

Conventionné, honoraires libres, non conventionné

● If the doctor is *conventionné*, the price of the consultation is fixed by social security and your reimbursement will be about 70 per cent; especially serious illnesses are covered at 100 per cent (after an agreement has been made with the social security). In other cases, your *mutuelle* (additional insurance policy) will cover the difference.

● If the doctor is *conventionné à honoraires libres*, the cost of the consultation varies, since *dépassement d'honoraires* (higher fees) is authorized. You will be reimbursed on the basis fixed by social security for a consultation, and your *mutuelle* will reimburse all, or a part of the rest, according to your contract.

● Two per cent of French doctors are *non conventionné*; the cost of a consultation with them is set by the doctor, according to his reputation. Social security reimburses a few euros, following a *tarif d'autorité* (a fixed rate); your *mutuelle* decides how much it will reimburse you – sometimes you end up paying the entire cost yourself.

● Patients using *médecines douces* ('alternative doctors', offering homoeopathy, acupuncture, etc) are reimbursed at much lower rates than those using other medical practices. However, a number of French people find these therapies effective in the treatment of minor health problems.

● For some medical care (such as physiotherapy, speech therapy, prosthesis, etc), the patient must send a *demande d'entente préalable*, indicating the treatment prescribed, asking for prior approval from social security. Unless your prescription is marked '*en urgence*', you must wait a certain amount of time. Your doctor will explain the procedure to you.

NB: Be sure to ask for the fees and status of the doctor before making an appointment.

▬▬ Consultations and home care

In the larger French towns, doctors rarely make house calls. In case of a serious problem you should go directly to the nearest medical centre, or dial 15 for emergency help. However, in smaller towns, the general practitioner divides his or her time between the office and house calls, when the call is justified. There are doctors on duty during the night and at weekends; their names and telephone numbers are posted on the door of the *pharmacie* or the police station and published in the local press. Alternatively, you could always call the local police station for the necessary information.

The *carte à puce vitale* has replaced the *feuille de soins* throughout France when the doctors, *pharmaciens* and the social security
are fully automated. The *carte vitale* is a genuine medical ID card
for all insured people, making reimbursement simpler and quicker.

A new 'carte vitale 2' with photo and chip is currently being
launched. Your local social security office will reimburse you by
direct bank transfer to your account. Your complementary insurance policy (*mutuelle*) will make a further payment, based on the
amount given by the social security; the amount will vary according
to the terms of your policy.

*H*ospital or clinic – public or private?

There are different types of public hospital: a *centre hospitalier
universitaire* (CHU) is a university medical centre and a *centre hospitalier régional* (CHR) is a general hospital in a medium-sized town.

Hospitals are divided into different departments, each of which
has a head doctor, respectfully known as *le patron*.

Some hospitals, formerly religious institutions, have remained
private. They receive patients under the same conditions as the
public service hospitals. Private clinics are for-profit institutions,
most of them have agreements with social security and complementary insurance funds, which give reimbursement for some medical procedures. Some have a good reputation for their medical or
surgical personnel, but often have less specialized medical equipment than the public hospitals. Others offer, and charge, for more
comfortable accommodation than is normally found in a hospital. It
is advisable to ask about the insurance status of the hospital before
accepting treatment.

In France, the public hospital is the standard reference in medical care. The departmental head doctors sometimes have a private practice within the hospital where they charge for their services. The public hospitals are run by the state with automatic payment agreements with social security. In Paris, they are managed by the *Assistance Publique*.

In public hospitals no discrimination is made regarding the sex, religion or culture of the nursing staff. Only their professional competence counts.

Your doctor has to recommend the specialist or hospital that has both the best care and the best accommodation. In most cases, if the hospital is *conventionné*, or state-run, social security advances the bulk of the cost of the hospital stay directly, leaving your *mutuelle*, or you, to pay the rest (*le ticket modérateur*), plus a small daily contribution (*forfait hospitalier*) if you want a private room, television or telephone.

Outpatient care – consultation externe

Public and private hospital doctors reserve most of their consulting for patients who have been hospitalized, but anyone may make an appointment at the hospital with an introduction letter from your family doctor.

Hospitals are equipped to perform scans and laboratory tests, and other highly specialized examinations. The test results are sent to the doctor who requested them.

A hospital stay

The evolution of medical care has greatly reduced the length of hospital stays. A certain number of long-term treatments, or minor surgery, are performed on an outpatient basis (*hôpital de jour*). The patient is then cared for at home by a medical team who work with the doctor in charge. This is known as *hospitalisation à domicile* (HAD).

Public and private hospital accommodation varies. You may request a private room and a telephone or television. A booklet will be given to you when you enter the hospital, listing all the rules and regulations, as well as the hospital services available. You will be more comfortable if you take along your own pyjamas, dressing-gown, slippers and other personal items.

*S*ome medical and paramedical specialities

Medical care is now so highly specialized that your personal doctor is the best guide to finding the appropriate specialist, should you need one.

MEDICAL RECORDS – DOSSIER MÉDICAL

A hospitalized patient always has medical records concerning his or her health – clinical observations, test results, X-rays, etc. The patient can ask that the records be sent to a doctor, or the doctor may consult the records at the hospital. It is the responsibility of the patient's personal doctor to explain to him or her what the records indicate.

Except in an emergency, the patient's written consent is required for all important medical care. For children under 18 years old, the legal guardian must sign for the child. The doctor should, of course, explain the proposed surgical procedure and its possible risks to the patient, in writing if necessary.

▬▬ *Gynaecologist* – gynécologue

Specializing in the care of women, gynaecologists are regularly consulted for check-ups, contraceptive advice and pregnancy. Some are also obstetricians, and many are themselves women.

If you plan to have a baby in France, as soon as you know that you are pregnant, announce your happy news to your local social security office and to the CAF (Caisse d'Allocations Familiales). You will receive a *carnet de maternité*, which will give you all the medical and insurance information necessary. A first prenatal examination is required before the fourth month of pregnancy, followed by monthly examinations until delivery. Two scans will be made to verify the baby's development.

Antenatal care is covered 100 per cent by social security. At the clinic or hospital, a midwife working under the supervision of a doctor will help you prepare for the delivery and give you any advice you need. Women who have followed the prescribed prenatal care are eligible for a *prestation d'accueil du jeune enfant* (PAJE) (monthly payments from the CAF), from the fifth month of pregnancy until three months after the birth of the baby.

At birth, the baby receives its own *carnet de santé*, which guides the parents in the care of their baby – growth, feeding, vaccinations, etc. Several check-ups are obligatory during the baby's first few years.

Working women benefit from a 16-week *congé de maternité* (maternity leave), which is usually taken 6 weeks before and 10 weeks after the birth of the baby. They will receive daily social security benefits for the duration of their leave. New fathers are also very happy to benefit from the two weeks of paternity leave.

▬▬ *About abortion*

Since 1975, French law *'la loi Veil'* authorizes abortion for a woman who makes her definitive decision after consultations with a doctor who informs her about the medical risks, then with a social worker. A foreign woman has to prove her legal status in France before being allowed an abortion.

▬▬ *Psychotherapist* – psychothérapeute

Family or professional problems are the primary reasons for consulting a psychologist, who is able to evaluate the difficulties and suggest appropriate treatment, or simply reassure the patient.

If you are anxious or depressed, the following specialists may be able to help you:

● *psychologue* – a certified psychologist has a university degree and practical training in the mental health of children and adults;

● *psychiatre* – a psychiatrist is a medical doctor who has specialized in mental disorders (he or she can prescribe medicine);

● psychoanalysts – there are many psychoanalysts in France, who offer counselling to troubled individuals. Psychoanalysts adhere to different schools of thought, and generally belong to an association.

These specialists are either private (with an office), or public medical-psychological consultants (at a hospital or dispensary). In the public sector, consultations and care are covered by social security. For private care, only consultations with a psychiatrist are reimbursed. It would be wise to ask your doctor, or others in whom you have confidence, to help you find appropriate help.

▬▬ *Physiotherapist* – kinésithérapeute

In France, the *kiné* treats osteoarthritis, respiratory and neurological problems. Most are in private practice. A prescription from a doctor and the prior approval of the social security office are necessary for reimbursement for the services of a physiotherapist *conventionné*. Some physiotherapists practise a *théraphie manuelle* (osteopathy).

▬▬ *Speech pathologist* – orthophoniste

Learning a second language is sometimes more difficult for children who have a problem acquiring vocabulary or pronouncing words. A few appointments with a speech pathologist, prescribed by a doctor, may help them get over their problems and make progress.

▬▬ *Dental surgeons and orthodontists*

The dental surgeon may be identified by the brass name-plate on the door, but you should make an appointment. As with doctors, it is a good idea to ask for recommendations before choosing a dentist. Social security may approve payment for orthodontics for children under 12 years of age.

In an emergency, there is always a dentist on duty somewhere nearby.

*N*ursing care

If you need an injection, or a bandage changed, or any other prescribed treatment, a State Registered Nurse will either come to your house or see you at his or her office.

The chemist's shop – pharmacie

You can only buy prescription medicines at one of the 23,400 pharmacies in France. The *pharmacien* wears a *caducée*, or a name tag to distinguish him or her from the assistants. As a qualified doctor of pharmacy is bound to professional secrecy too, he or she may advise you and suggest non-prescription medicines for minor health problems and will also explain their correct use. You will need a doctor's prescription for other medicine, and for some products you will be asked to give your name and address. Your prescription will state the length of the treatment and sometimes the words '*à renouveler*', which will allow you to renew the prescription.

Not all medicine is reimbursed by social security. Those that are, are registered on your *carte vitale* or have a coded *vignette* (price tag).

Medicines are always marked with a *date de validité* (valid until …), and include an instruction sheet explaining the contents, the therapeutic qualities, the dosage and precautions for use. Of course, you should always follow the doctor's directions regarding the use of the medicine. Medicine comes in boxes, tubes or bottles for adults, children and babies; it comes in liquid form (syrup, injection or phial) pills or powders, and sometimes suppositories, when other forms are not tolerated by the patient. The *pharmacien* may also prepare medicine according to a formula supplied by the doctor.

Prescription drugs should, of course, be stored out of the reach of children. Do not throw them away when you have finished with them, but return them to the *pharmacien*, who will pass them on to a charitable association.

There is always a *pharmacie* on duty, day and night and on holidays. The address will be published in the local press, posted on the door of all the *pharmacies*, or at the local police station. There are *pharmacies* that are open 24 hours a day, 365 days a year in Paris.

AT THE PHARMACIE

You may purchase syringes, bandages, contraceptives, condoms, beauty and toilet products, as well as baby food (powdered milk, cereals, jars of purée). These baby foods are also available at the supermarket.

In the autumn, if you go out picking mushrooms, the *pharmacien* will be happy to verify that they are of the edible variety.

*E*mergency – 24 hours a day

Hospital emergency services

Emergency hospital care is available in at least one hospital in each area, where doctors and surgeons are on call 24 hours a day. It is always useful to know the address of the nearest emergency care centre to your new home, just in case.

Anywhere in Europe – allo! le 112

Use this number to contact the multilingual European emergency services by mobile (GSM).

Emergency medical help – allo! le 15

In France, 15 is the permanent, free number to call in the case of a medical emergency. The SAMU (*Service d'Aide Médicale Urgente*) is usually located in one hospital in each area. A doctor will meet all requests for urgent medical help, with advice, a doctor's visit, by sending an ambulance, or organizing whatever other assistance the situation requires. The SMUR (*Service Mobile d'Urgence et de Réanimation*) are qualified to give first aid.

The police – allo! le 17

You can always call 17 – the telephone number for the police – where a direct connection with the emergency services will rapidly transfer your call.

The fire brigade – les pompiers: allo! le 18

Firefighters in France are qualified to give first aid in an emergency. The fire brigade is an extremely efficient public service reserved for really serious emergencies. Firefighters are highly esteemed by the French public for their sense of duty and availability. The number 18 will connect you to the nearest fire station to your house. In certain cases of personal negligence, the fire service may charge a fee.

SOS médecins

In most big towns, there is an SOS medical service with doctors on call 24 hours a day. They make house calls for serious health problems. A doctor (*conventionné*) will arrive rapidly after your call.

Poison centre

When a toxic product has been swallowed, call 15. First aid will be given by telephone, while you are waiting for the doctor to arrive. Ask your *pharmacien* for the telephone number of the service nearest to your home.

▬▬*Ambulances*

Ambulance services are private and their services are expensive. A medical prescription is necessary in order to be reimbursed by social security. Of course, in emergencies when you call the police or the fire brigade, the patient is transported to the hospital by the emergency service.

▬▬*About death*

When a person dies, a doctor certifies the death and the under-takers (*pompes funèbres*) can take charge of all the required procedures such as death certificate (*acte de décès*), burial certificate (*autorisation d'inhumer*), which is delivered by the authorities (at the *mairie*), and repatriation if the family wishes.

In Paris, Père Lachaise cemetery has many graves of artists, writers and other famous people such as Molière, Marcel Proust, Jim Morrison and Oscar Wilde.

*H*ealthy children

General practitioners and paediatricians look after sick children, and also monitor the growth, weight and motor development of babies in good health. If need be, they will design the child's diet, suggesting vitamins if necessary. In France, a daily dose of vitamin D is prescribed for children up to the age of three years.

As with all healthcare professionals, ask for recommendations for a good paediatrician who will take the time to listen to you and your child, and build a solid relationship with you both.

■■■■ *Health records* – carnet de santé

In France, babies receive a *carnet de santé* in which their medical history is recorded. Prenatal and delivery conditions are noted, then results of the postnatal tests, childhood illnesses, growth chart, vaccinations and so on. The *carnet de santé* is confidential. It is completed by the doctor during visits, and it belongs to the parents. If the school (or anyone else) asks for it, it is preferable to give them a medical certificate.

■■■■ *Medical visits*

In the course of the first six years, obligatory free visits are scheduled to monitor the child's development. A visit during the first week after birth, at 9 months, and at 24 months, gives you the right to a medical certificate allowing you to receive family allowance.

■■■■ *Vaccinations: obligatory and recommended*

In France, the only obligatory vaccinations are for diphtheria, tetanus and poliomyelitis (DTP), and the BCG, which immunizes against tuberculosis. Other vaccinations are highly recommended by doctors, but parents may decide themselves whether their child should have whooping cough, *ROR* (measles, mumps, rubella), or anti-haemophilia vaccines.

Vaccinations may be given by the paediatrician, the family doctor, or the PMI (Centre de Protection Maternelle et Infantile), who will record them in the child's *carnet de santé*.

Proof of vaccinations is required for registration at the *crèche* and at school. If they were given before your arrival in France, do bring a medical certificate with you.

▬▬ *Childhood illness*

Winter and spring in France can be cold and wet (especially in the northern part of the country), and provide a fertile breeding ground for the seasonal infections often caught by children at the *crèche* or at the *école maternelle*.

Contagious illness, such as measles, mumps and rubella, may now be avoided, thanks to vaccinations. Many schools have a yearly outbreak of chickenpox, a contagious viral infection.

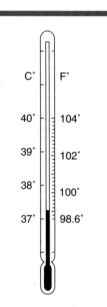

C°	F°
40°	104°
39°	102°
38°	100°
37°	98.6°

CULTURAL DIFFERENCES

Centigrade/Fahrenheit

If you have children with you it is very likely that a *pharmacien* or doctor will want to take their temperature at some point; it is French practice to use the centigrade scale. Some use thermometers rectally, which gives a more reliable reading, especially in children.

Tooth Fairy or Tooth Mouse?

If your child loses one of his or her milk teeth in France, tell him or her to put it under the pillow and during the night a mysterious but nice mouse, *la petite souris*, will come to collect the tooth in exchange for a euro coin or a bonbon.

If you sneeze

A vos souhaits (God bless you).

Domestic accidents

Taking a few simple precautions will make your life safer. A new home is a place to explore, but it also holds many dangers for inquisitive little children. If you do have an accident, call 15 at once. In the case of poison, it is important to give the name of the product and the quantity taken. This will enable the doctor to diagnose and treat the problem quickly.

DANGER! In France, electricity runs on 220 volts, so be sure to install safety covers on the electrical outlets if there are small children in the house.

Mother and childcare centres

Every town in France has a PMI (Centre de Protection Maternelle et Infantile), where free medical care is given to children under six years of age. They are run by a group of paediatricians, educators, psychologists and childcare specialists, who monitor the child's medical, social and familial development.

Children in hospital

A child needing specialized medical attention may have to go into hospital. The specialists in their white lab coats (blue or green in the operating room) must seem frightening to children all over the world. Whenever possible, you should try to explain to children, even if they are very young, why they are going into the hospital. Depending on their age, they might help prepare their own suitcase, choosing a few toys and clothes, a favourite book or blanket to reassure them at a difficult time.

The *carnet de santé* or medical records should be given to the doctor in charge, so that he or she will be aware of the child's medical history. Many hospitals have a few 'parent and child' rooms

available, allowing the mother or father to stay with their child during hospitalization. In other hospitals, visiting hours are very flexible and parents are encouraged to visit as much as possible in order to give reassuring cuddles. Most hospitals have a psychologist available to help parents and care-givers, and, above all, to listen to the questions and fears of their young patients.

Thanks to the generosity of patrons and the general public, some children's hospitals have formed an association to run a guest house for parents whose children are hospitalized. Near to the hospital, this warm and friendly place is designed to welcome and lodge families who live far away, in the provinces, or abroad.

'*P*revention is better than cure'

The social security works hard on initiatives and information campaigns to inform the general public about preventive care.

> ## CLOWN DOCTORS
>
> To put a smile back on the face of children in hospital is the aim of the association Theodora (Clown Doctors). It was founded, in Switzerland in 1993, by André and Jan Poulie in memory of their mother, Theodora. The Clown Doctors have been established in France since 2000, and they are affiliated to the Theodora Foundation, active with its professional artists in nine countries. These smile merchants are welcome in six French hospitals to visit children each week and bring them dreams and fantasies. You can reach them on contact.france@theodora.org.

A check-up

All salaried staff have a compulsory medical check-up every two years. A free medical check-up is available once every five years for other people. The patient, or the family doctor, will be informed of any symptoms or abnormalities discovered, so that further tests may be carried out if necessary.

Some companies give their *cadres* a medical check-up, including state-of-the-art tests, to detect problems early and keep their employees in good health.

Stop smoking

It is against the law to smoke in public places, including the workplace, hotels, bars and restaurants. Some people still refuse to acknowledge this law, but, if caught, they risk a heavy fine.

━━━*AIDS* – SIDA

The campaign says, 'Prevent AIDS'. In the absence of a vaccine or an effective treatment, only prevention can stop the spread of AIDS. Condoms are sold in the *pharmacie* and in dispensers in public places (secondary schools, on the metro, etc).

Information campaigns try to influence the sexual behaviour of young people. Counselling and anonymous free AIDS tests are offered in many medical centres throughout France.

*M*ineral water: do the French put water in their wine?

The French are simultaneously the world champions in the production and consummation of wine, and of mineral and spring water – nearly 145 litres of bottled water are drunk per year, per person! Plenty of water is essential for good health, but there is now also evidence to suggest that a glass or two of wine a day is beneficial for the arteries (the French paradox!).

'*Mettre de l'eau dans son vin*' is a commonly used expression, which means to dilute the alcoholic content of your glass with water; in other words, to dilute your demands and soften your affirmations.

Some French towns, such as Vittel or Evian, originally built their reputation on their mineral spring waters. There are 105 spas in France, certified and *conventionné* by the social security department, and popular for their therapeutic water cures. Some chronic illnesses benefit from these treatments, which may be reimbursed by social security.

Other spas have a reputation as natural health centres for beauty and relaxation. *La thalassothérapie*, always supervised by a medical team, has many uses – enhancing your diet, providing rest and

relaxation, or forming a part of beauty treatment. Sea resorts and thermal spas obtain their designation from the Ministry of Health.

French tap water is constantly monitored. Its taste may vary from one place to another, but it is always safe to drink. If, in exceptional cases, the water is unsafe, the fact is announced loud and clear.

*F*or further information

Health-Care Resources in Paris (WICE, the Women's Institute for Education) Community Health Care Committee, 20 bd Montparnasse, 75015 Paris

Centre de Vaccinations Internationales

www.messageparis.org (ABCs Motherhood in Paris)
www.sante.fr – Ministry in charge of health
www.sante-jeunesse-sports.gouv.fr
www.frm.org – Foundation for Medical research
www.doctissimo.fr
www.hon.ch – health on the net
www.pheur.org – European Directorate for the quality of medicines and healthcare (Pharmacopée européenne – Strasbourg – France)

9 *Leisure and pleasure*

– loisirs et temps libre

'To be capable of intelligently occupying leisure time is the ultimate product of civilization.'

'Être capable d'occuper intelligement ses loisirs tel est l'ultime produit de la civilisation.'

Bertrand Russell

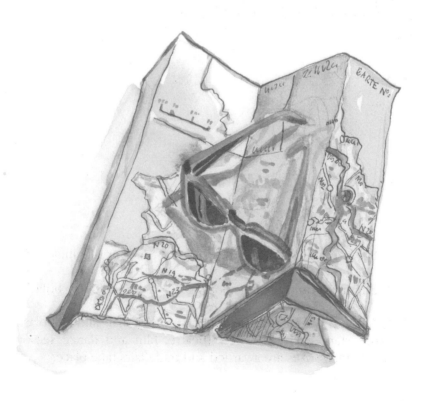

*F*ree time

The French relish their *temps libre* (free time) as an escape from work and the obligations of daily life. Some look forward to having a rest, while others enjoy useful, creative activities, or sports. For parents and children, alone or together, leisure activities represent a significant part of the family budget.

In the evenings, the French may go to the cinema or the restaurant; on holiday, they may look for a change of pace having eagerly awaited this escape all year long. Weekends are the time to do all the things for which there is no time during the week, and to relax.

*T*hroughout the year

- Springtime heralds the beginning of outdoor activities.

- Summer brings the big sporting events and the long holidays.

- Autumn is *la rentrée* when professional and scholastic activities start again. The new theatre, film and dance seasons begin, literary prizes are awarded and trade fairs take place.

● Winter is a time for cosy self-indulgence, for cinema, hobbies and collections, and pottering about the house. The major activity in December is preparing for Christmas and end-of-year festivities.

Whether you are sporty or intellectual, whether you like gardening or antique-hunting, you will certainly find what you are looking for in France. You may even discover new passions.

■■■■ *Calendar*

'A *calendar, that is to say, the future divided into compartments, where I can distribute my projects and my hopes.'*

'Un calendrier, c'est-à-dire un avenir divisé en cases, où je vais pouvoir distribuer mes projets and mes espérances.'

Alain

The public holidays in France are national (Bastille Day), religious (Easter), commemorative (Armistice Day), or cultural (New Year's Day). Most have a set date, but some do move according to the calendar. There are 11 *jours fériés*.

In the Western world, and in France in particular, many feast days are of Christian origin. They are part of our heritage. Other religions have their own calendar.

■■■■ *Happy holidays*

● 6 January is *Epiphanie*, or Twelfth Night, when the Three Kings are remembered with a *galette des rois*. This cake varies depending on the baker and the region, but always contains a *fève* (a little bean). If you are lucky enough to find the *fève* in your part of the cake, you are crowned King, or Queen, for the day with a golden paper crown. All through January, at home, at the office, at school, the French enjoy this tradition. Beware, the 'lucky bean' is made of ceramic!

A VOS CALENDRIERS

January

1: New Year's Day*
6: Twelfth Night
Fêtes des Rois (Epiphany)

February

2: Candlemas
14: St Valentine's Day
Carnival

March

Shrove Tuesday
Mid-Lent
Springtime

April

April Fool's Day
Easter Sunday and
Whit Monday*

May

May Day*
8: *Fête de la Victoire**
9: *Europe Day*
Ascension Day*
Mother's Day

June

6: Normandy Day
*Whitsuntide**
21: *Fête de la Musique*
Summer
24: St Jean
Father's Day

July

14: *Fête nationale**

August

15: Assumption Day*

September

School starts
Autumn

October

Harvest time

November

1: All Saints' Day*
11: Armistice Day*

December

6: St Nicolas
Winter
25: Christmas*
31: New Year's Eve

* Public holiday

- 2 February is *Chandeleur*, or Candlemas. Legend has it that, to be rich all year, you must flip a pancake while holding a gold coin in the other hand.

- 14 February is *St Valentin*. Flowers, love letters and tenderness are exchanged on this day, the busiest of any florist's year. It is also the start of the mating season for the birds!

- *Mardi Gras*, or Shrove Tuesday, is carnival time when children parade in costume and eat pancakes and fritters.

- On *Dimanche de Pâques*, or Easter Sunday, bells ring out in all the churches. Chocolate Easter eggs are hidden in the garden or the woods to be found by children, and eaten with glee.

- *1 Avril,* or April Fool's Day, is the time for friendly jokes and pranks; journalists try to outdo each other by creating false news to trick their readers. On this day, the French buy chocolate fish at the bakery.

- 1 May is the *Fête du Travail.* May Day in France is celebrated as a workers' holiday when everyone has the day off. On the street corner, anyone who wishes to do so may sell *muguet* (lily of the valley), which is reputed to bring good luck. In May, do as you wish (*en Mai fais ce qu'il te plait*).

- In May and June, children prepare for the *Fête des Mères* and the *Fête des Pères* (Mother's Day and Father's Day) by making little presents for their parents at school.

- 9 May is *Journée de l'Europe*, commemorating 9 May 1950.

- 6 June is Normandy Day, commemorating the day when a page of world history was written in the Normandy sand with the dawn landing of British, American and Canadian forces, who would be the 'tide of liberty'.

- *Le quatorze Juillet* is a significant French national holiday, commemorating the 1789 Revolution and the fall of the Bastille. Parades, speeches, celebrations, fireworks, concerts and village dances are all part of the festivities.

- 8 May and 11 November are the days that mark the end of World War One and World War Two when those who died are remembered.

- *Noël*, 25 December, is Christmas Day; for many a religious holiday, for almost everyone an occasion to exchange gifts. The traditional family dinner is served – *foie gras*, oysters, stuffed turkey or duck, followed by a Yule log.

● 31 December is the *Fête de la Saint-Sylvestre* when the French prepare their midnight *réveillon* to welcome in the New Year. Celebrated at home, or with friends at a restaurant, best wishes are exchanged under a bunch of mistletoe, which is supposed to bring good luck throughout the year.

Another national tradition in France is to celebrate anniversaries of 10 years, 20 years, 50 years, to honour a person or a historical event. In 2008, the French celebrated the 60th anniversary of the Déclaration Universelle des Droits de l'Homme, adopted in Paris on 10 December 1948, inspired by the Declaration of the Rights of Man of 1789.

*P*astimes and passions

'Tinkering around and gardening is working for pleasure.'

The French indulge in many manual, technical or intellectual pastimes, ranging from making scale models to calligraphy, from interior design to pottering around the garden. Games such as cards, puzzles and Scrabble are family favourites and some are fond of video games.

▬ *1,000,000 associations in France*

In France, every person may, at least once in their life, be a president. A project and two friends (one to be president and one to be treasurer) are all that is required to start an *association loi 1901 sans but lucratif* (a non-profit association) to work on cultural, sports, humanitarian or civic projects. Associations are not new; famous groups and brotherhoods that unite people with similar tastes or convictions have long existed in France. Today one person in two is a member of an association.

ARE YOU A COLLECTOR?

The French have a tendency to be conservative; they love to collect and hoard things, from the most banal to the extraordinary. There is a name for each type of collecting habit, the earliest of which is *philatélie* (the collection of postage stamps).

Well-informed collectors religiously attend specialized fairs and auctions, and visit junk shops in the hope of finding their treasures at bargain prices.

Profit from your stay in France to enlarge your collection, and perhaps discover the rare piece that you have been hoping to find.

A copy of the statutes of the association must be taken to the local Préfecture, as soon as the association is officially declared by the president. Foreigners may create associations of their own in the same way as the French do.

Today, associations on the fringe of business activity help meet a growing need for assistance among the poor. Some associations have become very professional and even have salaried employees, but most count on the altruism of volunteers to fulfil their mission and aims. If it is considered to be in the public interest, the association receives a special label, *'reconnue d'intéret public'*.

*E*ntertainment

▬ *Cinema*

'Life is a film in which everyone is a star. Find him a happy ending.'
Joan Rivers

Invented by the Frères Lumière in 1895, the cinema maintains a loyal following in France in spite of the growth of home video and

> ## A PASSION THAT BECAME AN ASSOCIATION
>
> The association *Pariroller* gathers every Friday night when more than 20,000 people on Rollerblades travel around Paris, escorted by the police, who stop the traffic and escort the procession for about 30 kilometres.
>
> If you are not so game, you could always join the *Association des Collectionneurs de Plaque de Muselet* (the Association of Champagne Cap Collectors).

cable television. New films are released on Wednesdays, the day when all tickets are reduced in price. The French cinema produces a variety of films and is constantly discovering new talent.

Foreign films are shown in both VO (original version) with French subtitles, or dubbed into French.

Less commercial, *art et essai* cinemas are favoured by connoisseurs, and frequently act as a meeting place for debates on original film productions. *Cinémathèques* and *videothèques* (film and video libraries) have excellent documentaries and classic films in their archives. The *ciné-clubs* are generally run by a university or association, and a subscription allows members to benefit from their programmes.

The cinema is the *septième art* (the seventh art), while television is the eighth, and comic strips are the ninth... not forgetting the *art de vivre*! Maybe this is why foreign film-makers love to set their scenes in France. It may also be because of the romantic French and the beauty of the natural surroundings.

The theatre

The world is a living theatre, and the theatre reproduces the world every evening on stage. There are thousands of people, amateur or professional, in the cities, towns and villages of France, who go on stage to present the great plays of yesterday and today. When the curtain rises, the public are right there for the moment of truth. Classics, variety shows and modern theatre offer something for every taste.

Theatres are also used for dance and musical concerts, especially in the provinces.

In recent years, numerous sites around France have become the scene for *son et lumière* events (sound and light shows). These beautiful shows bring to life an epoch or a historical event, using sound and lighting effects and music.

AWARDS

Film festivals:

- Cannes Film Festival. Every May since 1946, Cannes (Alpes Maritimes) is in the spotlight with its coveted Palme d'Or (Golden Palm Award).
- American Film Festival at Deauville (Calvados).
- Science-Fiction Film Festival at Avoriaz (Haute-Savoie).
- Comedy Film Festival at Chamrousse (Isère).

Every year in Paris, those who work in the world of cinema choose the best actors and the best films and award them the *César*, a statuette created by the sculptor César.

Theatre:

Seventeenth-century French playwright and actor Molière left a remarkable repertoire. Today, his name is used for the *Molière* award made to those who have contributed most to the theatre, whether actors, playwrights or directors.

Music

Music in all its variety is constantly present in the daily life of the French, thanks to radio, television and CDs. The *chanson française* (the French song) boasts several poets, including Brassens, Brel, Barbara, Montand and Piaf, who have all left unforgettable melodies. More recently, numerous songwriters and singers of every kind share the stage.

Most towns have their own *conservatoire municipal*, which trains artists in all schools of music, dance and theatre. The choirs, orchestras and jazz groups bring together those who share a passion for singing or playing an instrument, regardless of age.

TOUS À L'OPÉRA

Once a year French opera houses welcome visitors to enjoy the lyric arts. This is a wonderful free invitation to discover the various artistic work that takes place behind the scenes.

Kiosques de la Belle Epoque *and musical monuments*

In the 19th century, public squares and gardens in French towns had their own *kiosque à musique* (bandstand), where people would meet to gossip and listen to music in the open air. Today these *kiosques* are part of the architectural and cultural heritage of the country. In around 40 towns, during a weekend in May, public concerts bring to life the days of the *Belle Epoque*. The delightful drawings of French artist Peynet often depict young lovers flirting in the shelter of a charming *kiosque*.

The springtime of museums

In May, and throughout the summer, well-known sites and monuments are used for musical concerts of classical or contemporary music, played by young artists from the conservatories of music. On the first weekend in May, most French museums welcome visitors for free, and all night long.

▰▰▰ *Museums for everyone*

France has many treasures. Over 7,000 museums, famous or eclectic collections, and a never-ending number of new souvenir collectors are ready to share their memories and to bring history to life. The *carte pass* gives a discount on admission to museums.

The Louvre Museum in Paris is one of the biggest and best-known museums in the world. In her 0.407 m² picture frame, the *Mona Lisa* has had the same enigmatic smile since 1507. A Louvre Museum is currently being built in Adu Dhabi (UAE) for opening in 2012. Less well-known is France's tiniest museum – Le Placard d'Erik Satie – a cupboard-sized collection dedicated to French composer Satie. Visiting 'the cupboard' only takes five minutes. Satie (1866–1925), whose classical compositions have the charm and appeal of dance music, was known for giving unusual names to his piano pieces. According to him, 'We know that Art has no homeland... the poor thing... its fortune does not allow it.'

Other museums are designed for children, and many lively original visits, or theme workshops organized according to age, are offered at various sites in France. One example is the Musée d'Orsay in Paris, which, on Sundays and during the summer, organizes *halte-jeux* for visitors of all cultures and languages; your children will be welcomed for two hours to participate in discovery workshops. They will sculpt, paint or play, inspired by the museum collections, while you visit the museum at your own pace.

At other sites throughout France, activities involving stories and legends, or nature study, are frequently organized around cultural events, or an exhibition.

The Musée Mondial du Sable (world museum of sand) is a work of art in progress. Since 1989, students from the Collège Jean

LA PAIX

- At Caen, in Normandy, peace has its own museum. Le Mémorial recalls the history of World War Two, and especially D-Day – 6 June 1944 – when US, British and Canadian soldiers came in a much longed-for wave of freedom. The operation *Overlord* was the largest seaborne invasion ever, involving 130,000 men. Scenography recreates the emotion and the history, reinforcing the message to be shared with all generations: *'Se battre pour la paix'* ('Fight for peace'). The gallery of Nobel Prize winners salutes the men and women who have worked to reconcile and liberate people of all countries. Many schools bring their classes to visit this memorial, so that they may better understand the price of peace.

The memorial was dedicated by the American Congress and the Battle of Normandy Foundation.

'We should recount the events of the Normandy Beaches to the youth of today and all that the soldiers did with courage to liberate France and Europe. In turn, they will be witness, since those who lived through this page in history are disappearing like leaves.'

Philip Jutras, Veteran of Utah Beach, 1944

In this spirit 'Les Fleurs de la Mémoire' brings together children, families and friends to place flowers on tombs in the cemeteries of Normandy to honour its heroes. At least once a year, it is a moral commitment: each person comes to place a bouquet on the tomb of 'their' soldier. (www.fleursdelamemoire.free.fr)

MUR DE LA PAIX

- In Paris, the word *paix* (peace) is written in 32 languages and 13 different alphabets on the peace wall, created by Clara Halter and Jean-Michel Wilmote close to the Eiffel Tower. Thousands of messages are left in the cracks of the glass wall. '"La Paix, svP" ["Peace please"], Eve, 2000.'

Monnet, at Château d'Olonne, in the Vendée, with their professors and financial partners, have dedicated themselves to the creation of a sand museum. These budding geologists collect samples of sand from all over the world to complete their construction, and it already includes sand from thousands of sources – enough to make a nice big sand dune.

Art exhibitions

Connoisseurs and amateurs alike crowd into exhibitions showing the work of famous artists, which are regularly held by the great museums and prestigious sites throughout France. Elsewhere, galleries, or other, more unexpected places, such as banks, restaurants or tearooms, lend their walls to the paintings, sculptures and photographs of young artists. The artist will be there at the opening of the exhibition – the *vernissage* – to drink a toast with friends and relations.

Do you like to read?

Reading is the second most popular leisure activity after watching television (25 minutes per day compared to 3 hours 30 minutes per day).

If you are able to read in French, you will obviously have no difficulty finding books in France. French literature has some special treasures, even if it is sometimes, according to Koukla Maclehose, *'un peu considérée comme de l'épicerie fine, pas toujours abordable'* ('considered to be a little like a delicatessen, not always affordable').

Public libraries, open to all, offer all types of books (novels, non-fiction, dictionaries, comic books, practical books, art books and so on) as well as French magazines. The French have the luxury of reading authors from all over the world (one-third of the novels available in France are translated). The conditions for membership at French public libraries vary, but they are almost all free, or very inexpensive. In the countryside, the library bus (*bibliobus*) delivers books to isolated villages. In the big towns, you will find a few English language book-shops and libraries (or places with an English language section).

JUNIOR GALLERY

'Art à la page' is an exhibition of the work of children's book illustrators in Paris. Children are delighted, and surprised, to discover the life-size drawings from their favourite story-books. Visitors may buy postcards, pictures or even litho-graphs. Above all, no one will want to miss the *vernissage-goûter* (the opening tea) and the chance to see the face of the artist who produced the illustrations.

The children's section allows them to look, read at the library, or borrow books for a few days to read at home. Some libraries have a story hour when the children can come and listen to stories read aloud.

There are also university and specialized libraries which you may want to use if you have special research to conduct.

PRIX LITTÉRAIRE

Every autumn, literature lovers avidly follow the book awards (1,500 per year), when new authors are discovered, or estab-lished authors rewarded for their work.

The most famous French prize is the Prix Goncourt, created in 1903. It awards a symbolic cheque of €10 to the best fic-tion published in the preceding year. Although the cheque is usually framed as a souvenir, fame and fortune often follow for the author with the subsequent boost in book sales.

▬▬ *Cultural centres*

Each town or neighbourhood has its own cultural activities. The cultural centre will organize all sorts of classes – for example, arts, crafts, technology and languages – for adults and children. The cost of the various classes differs from place to place. The *mairie* will have all the information.

▬▬ *Sports*

Fencing, golf, American football, squash, boxing, baseball, hockey, roller-skating – whatever your sport, you will certainly find a club to join in France. If you want to play badminton, for example, there are some 600 clubs in France from which to choose – you will find the best club for you by asking colleagues, or at the *mairie*. Some organizations (companies, universities and other groups) have their own sports clubs, with very active teams.

According to their schedule, most people practise their sport in the evening, at weekends or during the holidays. In France, as elsewhere, some actually play sports, while others prefer to watch from an armchair in front of the television.

Soccer and rugby are the most popular team sports in France. Once again *les Bleus* hope to be able to sing 'We are the champions' (by Queen) as in 1998, when the French team won the Football World Cup at the Stade de France.

▬▬ *Games and places to play*

The 'queen' and her 'fool' meet often in France – in fine weather, chess is played in the open air in the Luxembourg gardens in Paris, with silent onlookers following the games. If you prefer reading Tarot cards, or playing bridge, or any other card game, each town has its clubs and groups; you should have no trouble finding them.

Lovers of *billard* (French, US or British billiards) will find a table in quite a few cafés, or in special establishments. These are known as *Académies de Billard* and you will be asked to pay an entry fee.

Pétanque (known to the British as '*boules*') is the national sport of the South of France. In every French town and village, in the square or in the park, you will see little groups, generally men, carefully aiming metal balls at the *cochonnet* (a tiny wooden ball). The rules depend on whether the Marseille or Lyons variant of the game is being played.

Weekends

Even though France's population is increasingly urban, the French are still attached to their roots and to the land of their childhood and family. Many have a country house, or a family home somewhere in the country, where they regularly spend weekends. Fervent lovers of outdoor activities, Parisians are always ready to travel for miles to go biking, jogging or horse-riding, or just to potter about the house, or enjoy the harvest from their own garden.

'The French are millions of individualists, who read the same award-winning authors, visit the same exhibitions, leave at the same time at the weekend and sit in the same traffic jams.'

Perhaps you will be lucky enough to be invited to the country for the weekend. If not, organize your own break, for example, by renting a house for a couple of days, or staying in a bed and breakfast in a region that you have not yet visited.

French gardens

'In formal French gardens, the flower beds are organized in geometric designs... at times emitting a noble melancholy.'

'Dans le jardin à la française, les parterres s'accommodent d'être géométriquement dessinés... une noble mélancolie s'en dégage parfois.'
Charles de Gaulle

The French love flowers. For some, cultivating a garden is a way of life, others prefer to cultivate their secret, inner garden... but all are delighted to mark some special dates on their calendars:

On one weekend in June, the general public are invited to discover some exceptional gardens; under the 'visit a French garden' scheme, many private gardens open their doors to the public. The other major gardening event in France is the international festival of gardening at Chaumont-sur-Loire from July to October, organized by the international school of parks, gardens and landscapes. Some of the most prestigious landscape gardeners in the world design an extraordinary garden on a given theme, within a fixed budget.

Everywhere in France, through the seasons, parks and walkways burst into colour, with fragrant floral exhibitions. In towns, public gardens, parks and squares are precious *espaces verts* (green spaces). Many are equipped with children's play areas, and are pleasant places for walkers and joggers.

It is said that the French have *'une main verte'* ('a green hand') – more than a green thumb or green fingers! Most people will have at least a bunch of flowers, or a plant to water at home; with the coming of spring, garden shops and centres are emptied of plants for window-sills, balconies or gardens.

319

FRANCE IN BLOOM

French towns and villages use lots of imagination to improve their surroundings and to catch the visitor's eye – flowers are planted along the streets, around monuments, at the railway station and in shop windows. Some towns write their name in flowers to welcome visitors, while others prefer less formal, less organized *jardins à la française*. A national competition takes place annually to find the best *villes fleuries* or *villages fleuris*; the winners display a sign showing one or more flowers at the entrance to the town.

Harvest your vitamins (farms and harvesting)

Strawberries in June, green beans in July, tomatoes in August – there are almost as many different kinds of produce as there are gardens. At some farms in France, you can bring your basket and pick the fruits, vegetables and flowers yourself; you then pay according to the weight of your basket. In autumn, there is an abundance of mushrooms in the woods and fields, which people come to pick in the early morning.

NB: Take care before cooking what you pick from nature. If you are not sure that your mushrooms are of the edible variety, check with the *pharmacien*.

Open-air leisure centres

Many regions have open-air nature centres for family walks, weekend picnics, and individual and group sports. You will find water sports (canoeing, rafting, sailing), rock climbing, archery, horse-riding or golf.

▬ *Hunting and fishing*

France is a land of game, big and small; the numerous rivers, lakes and ponds teem with fish. You may, if you wish, hunt or fish, but you must acquire the necessary permit and make sure that you have understood the regulations.

▬ *Theme parks*

FRANCE MINIATURE

This is a five-hectare hexagonal park in which 160 historical monuments are reproduced in miniature. It is located at Elancourt (25 kilometres from Paris). Architects, model makers and landscape gardeners created this 'little France', which will inspire you to discover the originals. (www.franceminiature.fr)

Theme parks, which used to be called *'jardins de plaisance'* in the 17th century, now compete with each other to offer 'an escape into a magic universe'. Some parks have nature, technology or scientific themes, such as *Vulcania* and *Futuroscope*. Special prices are available for individuals or families. These make all the attractions yours to enjoy, whether for the day or for an extended stay.

Parc Astérix, in Ile-de-France, is the home of the little Gaulois Astérix and his friend Obélix. Astérix and his companions, the characters created by Goscinny and Uderzo in 1960, are the heroes of numerous comic strips that are known and loved by millions of readers throughout the world.

Center-Parcs in Normandy, Picardy and Sologne offer a water wonderland in a tropical environment. A glass dome covers the park, and the temperature is always around 30 degrees centigrade (over 80 degrees Fahrenheit), all year long, even if it is raining outside. Lots of sports or nature activities are offered and, if you wish, you may rent a cottage with a fireplace.

Live from the United States, *Disneyland Paris* is the wonderland in Ile-de-France, at Marne-la-Vallée. A magical world, Disneyland Paris is both an attraction park and a convention centre. Children can meet Mickey Mouse, as well as all the Disney characters based on European fairy tales, including *Sleeping Beauty, Snow White and the Seven Dwarfs, Cinderella* and *Pinocchio*.

*H*oliday time

French employees have five weeks' paid holiday a year. Generally, they prefer, if professional or family obligations allow, to divide their holidays, taking three weeks in summer, a week in winter and a week in the spring. The other legal holidays, especially in May and November, are used to make long weekends.

WHERE TO FIND LOCAL INFORMATION

Local newspapers publish listings for cultural and sports events in their Friday or weekend editions. Specialized weeklies announce the town or regional events. In Paris, the best known are *Officiel des spectacles* and the Pariscope (which has an English language supplement, published in conjunction with the London-based company *Time Out*). Local town halls offer programmes of all the events scheduled in their town, and sometimes throughout their region.

For all activities, do not hesitate to ask about the different kinds of membership available for children and adults. The membership pass is called a *laisser-passer*.

If you can, it is best not to take your break during the French school holidays; try to go before or after the July or August crowds. There will be fewer people, and the prices will be lower.

Summer

Everyone longs for their holidays, and plans begin with the first rays of March sunshine, when, suddenly, summer is everywhere – in the shops, in magazines and in everyone's thoughts. The car is still the favourite form of transport. According to statistics, 60 per cent of the French population goes on holiday (the Franciliens, particularly the Parisians, travel the most), with 20 per cent going abroad, others preferring to discover, or rediscover, the natural, cultural, gastronomic or even industrial treasures of France. Each person has his or her own form of escape, from climbing Mont Blanc and visiting the *châteaux* of the Loire by bicycle, to sailing off the coast of Brittany.

The seaside attracts the most visitors. The Hexagon has six sides: three land borders and three sea coasts. Each stretch of coast has its own geographical or poetic name: *Côte d'Azur, Côte d'Opale, Côte d'Argent, Côte fleurie*, etc. The exception is the *Côte d'Or* as it is not washed by the sea but by *le Bourgogne* (Burgundy). It is said that a former Préfet from the *Côte d'Or* was so dazzled by the azure blue of the Mediterranean that he gave it the name *Côte d'Azur*. The mountains are a second choice. Next in popularity are country holidays and foreign travel, or, for some, city breaks. When the destination has been chosen, there is quite a choice of accommodation: clubs, holiday villages, hotels, a rented cottage or apartment, camping or staying with friends.

Winter

The Alps, the Pyrénées, the mountains of Auvergne and the Jura, have snowy winters and all offer slopes and amenities for winter sports and pastimes: skiing, snowboarding and so on.

▰▰ *In search of nature*

Forty-six undeveloped regional parks in France are protected in order to improve and conserve the land; commercial development is permitted only on the outskirts where houses may also be built. In the same vein, nine national parks are classified and protected, so that the site, and its flora and fauna, may be shown off to their best advantage. Many of the parks also have nature study centres, which welcome, entertain and inform visitors.

▰▰ *On the history trail*

Visitors wishing to explore a region's architecture and history will enjoy following a *route historique*; these routes have been mapped out by the Caisse National des Monuments Historiques et des Sites (the French equivalent of the National Trust). The itineraries may go from a *château* to a garden, wander around hillside vineyards, follow in the footsteps of a particular author, take an equestrian or rambler's path or trace a famous pilgrimage. Curious or exceptional landmarks are indicated along the route, and some of the itineraries are themed, such as the 'wine route', and the 'cheese route'.

A DREAM TRIP

Magical in winter and mysterious in summer *Mont Saint-Michel* is an unusual nocturnal excursion among the medieval architecture of Mont Saint-Michel, accompanied by music and visuals showing shadow and light. It transports the visitor back to the beginning of time. Mont Saint-Michel, the Rock of Normandy, is listed by UNESCO as a world-class monument, 'Wonder of the Occident'.

Factory visits

Many companies today, including aircraft factories, nuclear power plants or dams, chocolate factories, and wine and cheese cellars, open their doors to visitors to show off their company. 'Industrial tourism' is in fashion. It is often a source of inspiration for the staff of the company who are given the chance to share their knowledge and their craft.

Visit the tourist office – office de tourisme

All towns have a tourist office, or a *syndicat d'initiatives*, which is always in a prominent spot and easy to find. There, you will find useful maps of the town, and brochures showing local attractions, as well as advice and hotel information. If you wish, you can also make reservations for accommodation. Opening hours vary with the seasons.

Maison de la France

The *Maison de la France* is the French tourist embassy abroad (located in the capital), offering all the necessary information for organizing a holiday in France. Recommend it to your friends before they come to visit you in your new French home.

Maisons de Région

Nine French regions and departments have shown off their dynamic image by opening up shops in Paris. These offices are open all year, and offer useful information on cultural and tourist attractions. Some also have a reservation service to help you organize your holiday in a particular area. See www.maisonsregionales.com.

Package holidays

There are many package holidays available, which vary according to price and comfort. Hotels are classified from 1 to 5 stars and offer *pension complète* (room plus three meals a day), or *demi-pension* (room plus breakfast and dinner). Rentals are available from the tourist offices, rental agencies and individuals, the internet or on request. If you would like to rent a chalet in the mountains, a studio or a house by the sea, start your search in February or March. Your reservation will be confirmed as soon as your deposit (10–25 per cent) has been received.

Holiday clubs offer packages to individuals and families, which include sport or tourist activities, as well as full board and lodging.

Off the beaten track

A *Gîte de France* is another possibility for holiday lodgings. Rooms and set menus are selected and classified by department throughout France: 1–4 *épis* (ears of corn) indicate the level of comfort. Authentic old homes are labelled *'prestige'*.

It is even possible to enjoy *La vie de château*. A number of castle owners, who love old buildings, have maintained or restored these magnificent properties, and business sense and conviviality have led them to open some of their rooms to privileged guests. There, it is possible to learn the history of the house over a drink or a home-cooked meal. *Relais et Châteaux* gives its approval when the standards of comfort and welcome are first class.

Other organizations give their stamp of approval to accommodation they offer in their publications.

Children's holidays

Numerous organizations, recognized by the Ministry of Youth and Sports, offer active holidays for children and adolescents. They can choose from such activities as sports, tourism, language learning, even working on building sites. The *comité d'entreprise* (work council) may organize, or subsidize, inexpensive children's holiday centres for the employees at your company; you only have to ask.

*O*nce a year

Over the years, a number of annual events have become important days on France's national calendar (leisure goes with pleasure for all generations):

- festivals of cinema and music, and Heritage Days *(Journées du patrimoine)*;
- festivals of theatre and dance;
- spring festival of museums, when there is free admission all weekend;
- exhibitions and trade fairs;
- national board game day; and
- sporting events.

AT THE HEART OF EUROPE

France is one of the travel hubs of Europe. Your stay in France will give you the opportunity to visit neighbouring countries by car, train or air. London is 2.15 hours from Paris by Eurostar. There are direct services to the French Alps and Disneyland Paris. By Thalys, Bruxelles, Amsterdam, the Hague or Cologne are easy destinations for a weekend away.

Environment days

World Environment Day, proclaimed by UNO in 1972, is celebrated every June in France. Local government, companies, schools, and the French people in general, have an active interest in the natural heritage of their region. Exhibitions, competitions, workshops, visits and conferences bring together children, adults and professionals.

Festival of science

Every year in France, science leaves the laboratory and its jargon behind for the weekend of *la Fête de la Science*. The scientific museums, laboratories and research centres open their doors to the public, to entertain and inform them about the mysteries of science and technology that transform their daily lives.

The festival of music

The *Fête de la Musique* is celebrated every 21 June in many countries, including France. On the first day of summer, the streets of all the towns and villages are filled with music of all kinds – classical, jazz, rock, blues – until dawn on the 22nd. Many people pass a *nuit blanche* (a sleepless night)!

Heritage days – journées du patrimoine

Since 1984, a number of private and public places of historical interest have been opened to the public on the third weekend in September.

French people of all ages, who are interested in their roots and their heritage, share the treasures of France, and enjoy discovering the well-guarded secrets of private homes, *châteaux*, gardens, churches, mills and even factories and luxury boutiques. The openings offer a splendid history lesson. Other European countries now celebrate their own heritage days.

▬▬*Book time* – lire en fête

October in France is dedicated to books and reading with the *Lire en fête*. Libraries and bookshops use all their imagination to promote reading and writing. Some museums honour their favourite writers, including historians, scientists and seafarers. The Ministry of Culture and the SNCF joined forces to present authors to the public in railway stations, in the *Voyage au Cœur des Livres* promotion. In spring, poetry is in vogue.

UNESCO has declared 23 April World Book Day. This follows on from the Catalonian tradition of exchanging books and roses on Saint George's day.

RENTING A LEGEND

Many famous monuments, including the Château de Chambord and the Orangerie du Château de Versailles, may be rented for receptions, concerts, a film set or an unusual event.

A number of legendary trains, classified as historical monuments, are also for rent. The year 1884 saw the birth of the prestigious *Orient Express*. The legend and the public's continuing enthusiasm for it have led the international company, Wagon-Lits, to reinstate the original trains of the *Belle Epoque*. Many lucky travellers have recreated the sense of adventure of the 1920s in one of the elegant blue and beige carriages, sometimes finding romance. The trains – the *Orient Express, the Train Bleu* or the *Etoile du Nord* – can take you anywhere in France or Europe. They still have a sense of Coco Chanel's perfume, Hitchcock and Hercule Poirot, and a touch of mystery about them. Alternatively, up to 150 passengers can jump aboard just for a short dinner-time trip. (Visit www.wagons.lits.Paris.com.)

Festivals

Theatre rules at Avignon in July; popular and contemporary music at Bourges in April; comic strips at Angoulême in January. The French regions have a calendar of festivals, cultural or popular, national or international, which are all eagerly awaited throughout the year. The festivals attract many visitors and performers, and new works and new talents are often discovered. See www.culture.fr.

TRADE FAIRS IN FRANCE

Each region has its own fairs and exhibitions; some national and international ones bring crowds to Paris. For example:

- the horse show;
- the student salon;
- the international automobile show;
- the book fair;
- the international antique show;
- the international airplane show.

Palais des Expositions de la Porte de Versailles

The Foire de Paris has, since 1904, brought exhibitors from all over France to fairs on different themes, including interiors, gardening and the environment, arts and crafts, and wines and gastronomy. During the inventors' show, the famous Lépine competition is held to encourage creativity.

The international agriculture show is held in March when the exhibition hall is transformed into an immense farm with all sorts of animals; it is very popular with both rural and urban visitors. All areas of France are represented. See www.salon-agriculture.com.

Winter window-shopping

Like cherries in spring and mushrooms in autumn, the fir trees come back each Christmas. From the first days of December, the towns and their shops dress up in the traditional Christmas colours of gold and silver, red and green. Many visitors from around France, and from abroad, choose Christmas time to come to Paris to look at the fabulous window displays of the big department stores, and share in the seasonal cheer. The most famous Christmas markets are in Alsace.

Good sports

Roland-Garros

One of the four *'Grand Chelem'* (Grand Slam) international tennis tournaments is held at the Roland-Garros Stadium in Paris (the others take place in the United States, Australia and Great Britain). Since 1928, Roland-Garros has attracted the best players in the world. A popular and sophisticated event at the end of May or in early June, it is eagerly awaited by tennis fans, some of whom take a few days off work to go to the matches, or to watch them on television. The women's finals are played on a Saturday, and the men's on a Sunday. See www.frenchopen.org.

Tour de France

Cycling is very popular in France and, since 1903, the Tour de France (*La grande boucle*) has enjoyed great success. Each year, the race takes a different route to make it accessible to as many supporters as possible. The finish is always in Paris on a Sunday afternoon in the Champs Elysées. Since 1919, the winner wears the *maillot jaune* (yellow jersey), the colour of *l'Auto,* organizer of the event. See www.letour.fr.

■ *The Paris Marathon*

More than 30,000 people wearing shorts in the Place de la Concorde on a spring Sunday morning? They are neither tourists, nor revolutionaries, but runners who have come from all over the world to take part in the Paris Marathon. The runners, amateurs and professionals, cross the capital via the quays of the Seine, from Boulogne to Vincennes, on a 42.195-kilometres course.

For those who prefer to run in the countryside instead of on tarmac, the Médoc Marathon in October is a trot through vineyards, with a little wine-tasting on the side. This is guaranteed an interesting show – the participants are in fancy dress as for the carnival.

> *'The grape harvest season in the region surrounding Bordeaux is exceedingly romantic. It's also the only time that most Château gates swing closed to concentrate on the harvest, leaving many visitors to wonder what's going on in the fields.'*
>
> Joe Ray

GARÇON!

There is even an annual race for café waiters and waitresses. The contestants run almost five miles in street shoes and their regular uniforms (including black skirts for the women and bow-ties for the men). They carry a normal café tray with three full glasses and a bottle, which must arrive intact. The first three to arrive win a gold, silver or bronze tray.

■ *24 Heures du Mans*

Since 1923, this 24-hour race has tested the endurance of both drivers and cars. The race takes place at Le Mans, in the department of Sarthe (72). See www.lemans.org.

■ *A day at the races*

Horse racing is quite popular in France, especially on Sundays. For the Grand Prix, the *hippodromes* of Paris attract regular race-goers, as well as the 'beautiful people' of business and entertainment; even the President of the Republic comes for the Grand Prix that bears his name. The most famous races are:

- Prix de l'Arc de Triomphe (Longchamp);
- Prix du President de la République; Diane Hermes (Chantilly)
- Prix d'Amérique (Vincennes).

French law prohibits gambling for money, but the administration makes an exception for horse racing, casinos and the National Lottery.

AU CASINO

In the 19th century, the French discovered (after the English) the benefits of sea-bathing and the first seaside resorts appeared along the Normandy coast, attracting many rich Parisians. Since 1850, the Paris–Dieppe train, also called the 'pleasure train', has enjoyed considerable success.

In France, the right to open a casino is given only to spa and seaside resorts. In 1988, this authorization was broadened to include tourist resorts of more than 500,000 inhabitants that have a theatre, an opera company and a national orchestra. Lyons and Bordeaux opened their casinos in 2000. There are more than 170 casinos in France, and if you are over 18 years old and wearing smart clothes you are allowed to enter.

For further information

France – Eyewitness Travel Guide (Dorling Kindersley, 2004)
Paris – Eyewitness, Alan Tillier (Dorling Kindersley, 2004)
Paris Secret et Insolite, Rodolphe Trouilleux (Parigramme)
Guide du Paris Savant, Anna Alter and Philippe Testard-Vaillant (Belin, 2003)
Guide des Hôtels et des Auberges de Charme en France, Tatiana de Beaumont (Rivages, 2003)
Fodor's Bed and Breakfast, Character and Charm
Time Out Paris guide: www.timeout.com
An Hour from Paris, Annabel Simms (Pallas Athene, 2003)
Romantic Paris, Thirza Vallois (Travel Gift Books, 2002)
Speak the Culture France, Andrew Whittaker (Thorogood Publishing, 2008)

French museums and exhibitions:
www.monum.fr
www.franceguide.com
www.european-heritage.net
www.parisbalades.com
www.frenchweek.com
www.culture.fr – cultural gateway
www.tourisme.fr, www.tourisme.fr/carte/carte-region-ile-de-france
www.ficep.info – semaine des cultures étrangères en France
www.gites-de-france.fr
www.fuaj.org – youth hostels
www.cite-sciences.fr
www.jours-feries.com
www.jeunesse-sports.gouv.fr
www.en.parisinfo.com/

10 Comme chez vous... en France

'We are born, one might say temporarily, somewhere; it is little by little that we create our native land.'

'Nous naissons, pour ainsi dire provisoirement, quelque part; c'est peu à peu que nous composons en nous le lieu de notre origine.'
Rainer Maria Rilke

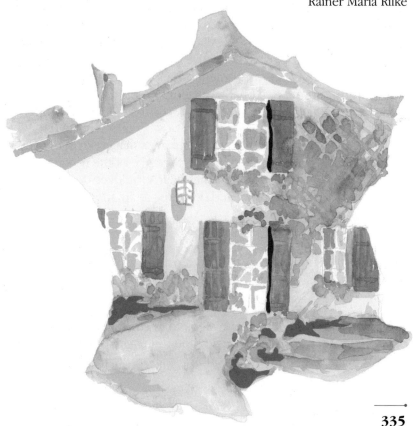

*A*t home... in France

'It was like a candy to me, like a parenthesis in my life, too short yet so full of experiences.'
Edith, Quebec

This final chapter has been written with the help of people from different cultures and nationalities, who have lived in France for various periods, from 2 months to 20 years. All have a clear recollection of their arrival and their settling in, and of their growing understanding of France. All of them remember that the defining moments were sometimes difficult, but that the experience was always a rich one. All were willing to recount their own adventures, smiling, or showing some other emotion, and most managed to temper their criticism with wit.

For each person, expatriation, even if it is desired, planned and expected, is always an exceptional experience; the destination is a *terra incognita*, a distant place, and the expatriate also has to cope with professional change and, perhaps, cultural and linguistic difficulties. The relocation inevitably involves some sort of upheaval and is always stressful. A new environment brings up many questions, about work, health, home, personal life, family, spouse and children. It is therefore essential to anticipate and prepare for a major change.

International organizations and companies that are experienced in expatriation increasingly stress the importance of the accompanying family. The productivity and efficiency of an employee depend a great deal on a successful personal and domestic adaptation.

*A*n enriching experience?

Moving to another country sweeps away existing routines, and an open, practical mind is essential if you are to adapt to places, people and events. An unfamiliar country is another world.

▬▬*Planning your departure*

'There is one thing that people do not realize, starting an entirely new life in another country takes all a man's energy, you hear, all his energy.'
Milan Kundera

- Objectively weigh the pros and cons in relation to your professional and personal life.

- Find out about daily life in France, and its social and cultural customs. Share this information with your family and friends who will undoubtedly have a few preconceived ideas that need to be discussed.

- Watch good French films and videos; this will give you a chance to capture the atmosphere and to see and hear French spoken. Discover French magazines.

- Discuss it with friends who know France and ask them to share their knowledge.

- Organize your departure and plan the practical details well in advance. Take special books or possessions that you treasure with you in order to ease the transition.

As in mathematics, the unknown is a variable to be discovered; relocating is certainly complex, but it is also exciting.

You are right to worry about frustrations and homesickness. All expatriates say that there are days when life far from home is not rosy, but, knowing this in advance will help you keep things in perspective. Of course, you can always invite your family and friends to come and visit you in France; they will bring a little bit of home with them. You might be surprised to find out just how many friends you have when you are living in this much talked-about country!

'In order to maintain a peaceful atmosphere, you explain the misunderstandings between you and your family by the "culture shock", the difficulty you find in defining one culture using the vocabulary of another.'
Nancy, Houston

Four phases of adaptation

Life away from home entails a period of adaptation for everyone concerned. This process of transition has its ups and downs, affecting different people in different ways. Everyone will need to be philosophical about the complications, in order to benefit from the satisfactions. When you are not able to speak the language you are more receptive to everything: gestures, voices – you try to understand.

'Humour is my second language. For some it is a foreign language.'
Guy Bedos

The French like humour and laughing, but for most of them smiling is not a conditioned reflex. This does not mean that they are not happy. A smile above all is an exchange between two people.

'These days shopkeepers will smilingly volunteer information in la langue de Shakespeare *and most Parisians under 30 can make a convincing stab at a complete sentence.'*
Jon Henley

Disorientation

'Who is the stranger? The one who is different, or the one who is still unknown to us?'
Nidra Poller

In the first phase of adaptation, you will probably already have a certain idea about France, and during the first few weeks, your own impressions will be many and varied, and perhaps contradictory. You will:

● discover the advantages; the novelty will not yet have worn off, and pleasant surprises will be fun and easy to deal with;

- tend to the practical side, sorting out the formalities, including your daily life, and your French lessons (at least enough to get by); and

- probably have accomplished most of the paperwork, but you might still be asking yourself, 'What am I doing here?'

> *'Each person's map of the world is as unique as his thumbprint.'*
> Erickson

Reality

> *'We don't see things as they are... We see things as we are.'*
> Anais Nin

In the second phase of adaptation, you will be aware that the days are going by; the unexpected becomes part of daily reality – a leak in the apartment, or losing your child's vaccination record, for example. Being pragmatic and efficient will help you to work things out – actually, most things work out in the end anyway, even if you are neither pragmatic nor efficient.

You will have developed new habits, and have fathomed out when the shops are open, what to eat and how to cook French products. You will have adapted to the rhythm of the days, and to the climate, even if it is very different from your own. 'It is much warmer in winter than in Quebec, but then again the sky is far less blue.' (Michel)

You will be more accustomed to the cultural differences. Disillusionment, disappointment and other upsets will be behind you, and you will be recognizing the many opportunities you now have to use your imagination, your initiative and your ideas.

This is an important phase when you acquire the wise determination and sufficient energy to cope. Do not hesitate to discuss your impressions and worries with sympathetic people. There are many English-speaking groups in France, and joining one of these is likely to make your settling in much easier.

Onwards to adaptation

> 'It is not because things are difficult that we do not dare, it is because we do not dare that the things are difficult.'
> Nietzsche

You have a new life. Your address book is filling up, and you are meeting new friends for a drink, to go to the cinema, or to attend a French class. You plan weekends with your family or others.

If things are not going well at this stage, or you are really anxious, you might consider professional counselling. A doctor or psychotherapist may be able to help you understand your problems and find the appropriate solutions.

Blessed with two cultures

'America is my country and Paris is my home.'

'L'Amerique est mon pays Paris est mon chez moi.'
Gertrude Stein

'Every man has two countries, his own and France.'

'Chaque homme a deux pays, le sien et la France.'
Thomas Jefferson

SOME THOUGHTS

'Will I get used to it? I am sure that everyone asked himself that question.' (Jennifer, US)

'I was so lonely in the beginning that I thought it would be impossible to stay, but after three years I am happy here.' (Johanne, Canada)

'To adapt, you must notice the differences, but avoid constantly comparing the two countries.' (Mary, GB)

'I wanted to do what I never had the time to do before: to play the piano. It is possible to do that in any language.' (Ann, Germany)

Now that you have discovered France, and its language and culture, you are able to take advantage of all the opportunities that the country has to offer you. Your constructive and critical sense allows you to emphasize the positive and to surpass the negative. You have understood the strategy for *réussite* (success) – that is, according to the dictionary definition, a positive result. It is a game played according to rules, and by now you know how to play to win. The synonym is patience.

T*he spontaneity of children*

'Where am I from? I am from my childhood. I am from my childhood
as from a country.'
Saint-Exupéry

Up to seven or eight years old, children spontaneously adapt to new surroundings, not having any preconceived ideas. They are less dependent on habit than adults, and willingly settle down wherever their parents and their belongings happen to be. Very quickly, they are 'at home' and ready to play with others. They quickly find friends and make themselves understood in a foreign language. They may be a little shy, but their natural curiosity will lead them to explore the unknown. Their approach will probably make their parents' adaptation easier.

Teenagers who do not speak French at first may be apprehensive and withdrawn. They will need reassurance until they feel comfortable with their new life.

Children should be encouraged not to forget their family and friends back home. Letters or e-mails will help them keep in contact; those not yet able to write can send drawings, cut-outs, little presents or pretty stamps.

'When I went to school, I entered France; at home I found Russia again with her language and her memories. . . It is possible to melt into France without giving up the poetry of one's roots and family.'
Henri Troyat

THOUGHTS ON CHILDREN

'Here, children play together in the public gardens and make friends at once. This is an opportunity for mothers to meet other parents.' (Jane, Canada)

'Family relations have changed, our children are closer and at the same time more independent. They manage very well outside and love to go and buy the bread.' (George, Ireland)

'One realizes what a genuine privilege it is for children to be bilingual. It will be an advantage in later years.' (Yohji, Japan)

'The children have started a photo album to keep their first memories, and they like to send the same photos to their cousins.' (Peter, UK)

'We love to have parties in France, all the time: carnival, Europe feast, music festival.' (Jean Alexandre and Maxence, 12 and 10 years old)

*H*omesickness and nostalgia

'When you live abroad, you are thrown back upon yourself.'
Paul Auster

Homesickness gives you the blues. The autumn in France can often bring on nostalgia, even if it is sometimes quite warm, but after the holidays everything happens at once – back to work after the summer, the school routine, the shortening days. The rain and cold may make you huddle under your umbrella, or turn in upon yourself. Nostalgia may catch up with you, just at a time when you think you are getting along well. Do not allow yourself to brood on grey days. There is always something interesting going on to cheer you up, so go out and find it!

'Don't listen to advice from anyone except the wind which passes and tells us stories about the world.'
Claude Debussy

FRIENDLY ADVICE

- Live in a busy neighbourhood, near to shops, schools and public transportation, especially if you don't like birds.
- Get to know your children's schools, the shopkeepers and the people in the area.
- Keep up with what is going on in your own country by subscribing to the newspaper you used to read at home.
- Write regularly to your friends and family, and encourage them to do the same. Receiving letters and e-mails is such a pleasure, and comfort parcels are a real surprise.
- Earmark part of your budget for calling home to hear familar voices (compare tariffs).

*F*riendly places

There are many associations in France and English- or Spanish-speaking groups that will welcome you, and help you to create or enlarge your social circle. They are places to exchange information and become acquainted with new people. Some of them publish newsletters and membership directories to make contacts between members easier.

France is a predominantly Catholic country, but most other religious groups have places of worship in the big cities; they often run an active association, which brings together people of the same religion, nationality or language. Other international associations open their doors to all cultures, and you will come across plenty of foreign experiences and offers of help. Even if it is reassuring to be among your fellow countrymen and women or other foreigners in France, do not forget to try some French groups to broaden your horizons. It will be well worth the effort and perhaps make you forget any difficult moments you may have suffered.

WELCOME TO FRENCH TOWNS

AVFs (Accueils des villes françaises, French cities' welcoming centres) will be found wherever you live in France, offering practical information on adapting to your new life, and the chance to get to know the region and its inhabitants:

' "You never know" is often heard in France. In my country in Lettonia, we say, "never say never".' (Inga, Slovenia)

'I would never have thought I'd be welcomed so well in France.' (Tineke, Roswitha, Irène and Kachan)

'For me, finding the AVF was like coming upon an oasis in the middle of the desert.' (Mami, Japan)

'I was taken care of, listened to and I had so much to laugh about during the last 30 months.' (Jasmine, South Africa)

'With my lousy faltering French, and their very well-articulated French, we had a few words of presentation and I realized that I had found many answers to my "whys and hows" about Orleans life. I remember that I was smiling all the way back to my place.' (Cecilia, Canada)

'A country like France cannot be understood immediately. It is a step by step process. After each episode one begins to feel more at home.' (Jane)

'There are at least three ways of replying to a question in French: yes but, no but, baf!' Don't take 'no' for an answer. Try again to discuss with someone. You will be surprised how sometimes 'no' can change to 'yes'. (Ilina)

'Life is made up of encounters; encounters with people, encounters with places! Everything leaves its mark… That mark is made up of all that surprised us, upset or instructed us.'
Jacqueline de Romilly

WHO WAS GUSTAVE BOENICKHAUSEN?

On Sunday 31 March 1889 at 1.30 pm, Gustave Boenickhausen climbed 1,710 steps to raise the French flag on the top of the Eiffel Tower. His family, the Boenickhausens, were foreign immigrants who changed their surname because it was too difficult for the French to pronounce. They chose, instead, to be called 'Eiffel' after the German region near Cologne where they came from.

Gustave Eiffel built the famous tower to mark the centenary of the French Revolution and for the Universal Exhibition of 1889. While detractors protested against this 'tragic lamp-post', it was nonetheless an amazing popular success, and indeed the star attraction of the exhibition. Initially intended to be taken down after 20 years, Eiffel defended his work, proving to authorities that the tower had scientific and communications uses. Almost one hundred years later, on the night of 31 December 2000, the Eiffel Tower celebrated the dawn of the new millennium with a magical lightshow: a glittering spectacle of 20,000 lights sparkling for the first 10 minutes of every hour, all night, which still continues today.

The *'Dame de Fer'* ('iron lady') is the best-known French monument, featuring in songs, paintings and sculptures all over the world. It has helped to establish France as the most visited country in the world, with 80 million foreign tourists in 2007!

*F*or further information

Culture Shock France, Sally Adamson (Graphic Arts Center, 1993)
Bloom Where You're Planted, welcome book from the Women of the American Church, 65 Quai d'Orsay, 75007 Paris
A Moveable Feast, Ernest Hemingway (Touchstone, 1998)
French Toast, Harriet Walty-Rochefort (St Martin's Press)
Almost French: A new life in Paris, Sarah Turnbull (Bantam, 2002)
Eccentric France, Piers Letcher (Bradt Travel Guides, 2003)
Third Culture Kids, David C Pollock, Ruth E Van Reken (Nicholas Brealey Publishing and Intercultural Press Inc, 2002)
www.netexpat.com
www.aaweparis.org – Association of American Wives of Europeans (AAWE)
www.wice.com – The Women's Institute for Education
www.messageparis.org – organization that aims to facilitate parent-to-parent support in family issues
www.soshelpline.org, www.les-parisiens-associés.com
www.french-american.org
My life in France, Julia Child (Knopf Publishing Group, 2006)
Petite Anglaise, in Paris, in Love, in Trouble, Catherine Sanderson (Penguin, 2007)

Useful information

Key dates in the history of France

72–46	Vercingetorix, Gallic chief
50 BC	Caesar conquers Gaul

Moyen Age – *medieval times*

480 AD	Clovis, King of the Francs
800	Charlemagne, Emperor of the Holy Roman Empire
842	First text written in French (*Serment de Strasbourg*)
1066	William the Conqueror, Duke of Normandy, conquers England
1163–1270	Construction of the Cathedral Notre Dame de Paris
1257	Foundation of La Sorbonne by Robert de Sorbon
1226–1270	St Louis, King of France
1337–1453	100 Years War between England and France
1412–1431	Joan of Arc
1494–1553	Rabelais, writer

Renaissance

1539	François I issues the Ordannance de Villers-Cotterêt: French must henceforth be used in legal documents instead of Latin

1553–1610	Henri IV, King of France
1572	Religious Wars (Catholics versus Protestants: Edict of Nantes)
1596–1650	René Descartes, scientist and philosopher
1606	Publication of the first dictionary in French language

▀▀▀ *Classic period*

1612–1715	*Siècle des Lumières* (The Century of Light)
1606–1684	Pierre Corneille, Molière (1622–1673), Jean Racine (1639–1699), famous writers
1638–1715	Dom Pérignon, the monk who refined the process of champagne
1661–1715	Louis XIV, the Sun King (Château de Versailles 1672)
1694–1776	Voltaire, writer
1714	French language becomes the diplomatic language (see your passport!)

▀▀▀ Républiques et empires *(republics and empires)*

1757–1885	Général Lafayette, (Benjamin Franklin's friend) contributes to the US War of Independence (1784)
1769–1821	Napoleon – 1804: Emperor, code civil; 1815: defeat of Waterloo
1789	French Revolution – Declaration of the Rights of Man; fall of the Bastille 14 July
1792	The fall of the monarchy
1802–1885	Victor Hugo, writer, poet and politician
1809–1852	Louis Braille, founder of the alphabet of raised dots on paper for blind people
1822–1895	Louis Pasteur, scientist (discovered rabies vaccine and how to 'pasteurize')

1852–1870	Paris is divided into 20 *arrondissements* following the great renovation by Baron Haussmann, Préfet of Paris
1852	Opening in Paris of the first *grand magasin*: Le Bon Marché by Aristide Boucicaut
1870	Franco-German War: Alsace and Lorraine are annexed by Germany until 1919
1881	Jules Ferry: obligatory, secular and free schooling (1833 *Loi Guizot*: a school in each commune)
1884	4 July, the Statue of Liberty is the gift from France for the centenary of US independence
1889	Inauguration of the Eiffel Tower for the Exposition Universelle
1895	The Lumière brothers invent cinema (first picture show in Lyons on 28 December)
1903	Pierre and Marie Curie discover radiation (Nobel Prize for Physics)
1904	The agreement 'Entente cordiale' between Great Britain and France
1905	Separation of church and state: the French Republic is a secular state
1909	Louis Blériot, aviator and engineer, the first to fly across the Channel on 25 July
1914–1918	First World War (11 November 1918, Armistice)
1919	28 June, Treaty of Versailles (Peace treaty between the Allies and Germany)
1936	Popular Front: Léon Blum (congés payés, paid holidays)
1939	Second World War starts
1940–1944	Regime of Vichy (Maréchal Pétain)
1940	18 June in London, Général de Gaulle makes his appeal for resistance
1944	6 June: D Day, the Allied Landing
1945	8 May, Allied Victory
1945	4 February: Yalta Conference. Roosevelt, Churchill and Stalin divide the world until the reunification of Germany in 1990

1945	Creation of the social security system
1947	Dress designer Christian Dior creates 'the new look'
1950	9 May: Robert Schuman, the founding of the Europe of Six
1953	The founding of *L'Express*, *le Livre de poche*, Who's who … and the *Cocotte minute*

Fourth Republic

1954	Algerian War (*Accords d'Evian* 1962)
1954–1959	René Coty, President of France
1957	Treaty of Rome founded the European Economic Community (EEC)

Fifth Republic

1958	New Constitution
1959–1969	Général de Gaulle is first President of the Fifth Republic
1968	May 1968: students and workers revolt (revolutionary exchange of ideas and the principles of education)
1969–1974	Georges Pompidou, President
1974–1981	Valéry Giscard d'Estaing, President
1974	5 July: the age of majority becomes 18 (instead of 21)
1974	Roland Moreno created the microchip smart card (*carte à puce*)
1975	Legalization of abortion (*loi Veil*)
1975	The first flight of the Franco-British Concorde (Paris–Rio de Janeiro) (2003: the last flight)
1979–82	Simone Veil, the first President of the European Parliament elected by universal suffrage
1981–1995	François Mitterrand, twice elected President

1981	Abolition of capital punishment (*peine de mort*)
1981	27 September: the first TGV on the Paris–Lyon line
1983	Luc Montagnier and his team at the Pasteur Institute discover the AIDS virus
1989	A year of celebration: bicentenary of the Revolution, hundredth birthday of the Eiffel Tower, inauguration of the Grande Arche de la Défense and the Pyramide du Louvre
1994	The Channel Tunnel and the first Eurostar on the London–Paris line
1995	Claudie Haigneré, the first French woman in space aboard the Mir Space Station
1995	The Pont de Normandie
1995	Jacques Chirac, fifth President of the Fifth Republic
1998	World Cup held in France

▬ *New Millennium*

2001	Abolition of compulsory national military service
2002	1 January: the euro, the European single currency (introduced for business in January 1999)
2002	5 May: Jacques Chirac is re-elected President
2004	European Parliamentary elections in the 25 countries
2006	Immigration law strengthening the rules on work and residence permits
2007	6 May: Nicolas Sarkozy is elected president of the Fifth Republic
2008	1 July: France becomes President of the EU for six months

Political and economic organizations

CONSEIL de l'EUROPE (Council of Europe)
(47 states)

OCDE
(OECD)
30 states

Albania
Andorra
Armenia
Azerbaïdjan
Bosnia Herzegovia
Croatia
Georgia
Moldavia
Monaco
Montenegro
Russia
San Marino
Serbia
Ukraine
Ex Yugoslavian Rep.
  of Macédonia

ESPACE ECONOMIQUE EUROPEEN
(European Economic Community)
(E.E.A.: 30 states)

ASSOCIATION EUROPENNE
de LIBRE ECHANGE

(A.E.L.E.: 4 states)

Liechtenstein

Iceland
Norway

Switzerland

UNION EUROPEENNE
(European Union)
27 states
Austria
Belgium
Bulgaria
Cyprus
Czech Republic
Denmark
Estonia
Finland
France
Germany
Greece
Hungary
Ireland
Italy
Latvia
Lithuania
Luxembourg
Malta
Netherlands
Poland
Portugal
Rumania
Slovakia
Slovenia
Spain
Sweden
United Kingdom

Turkey

Australia
Austria
Belgium
Canada
Czech Republic
Denmark
Finland
France
Germany
Greece
Hungary
Iceland
Ireland
Italy
Japan
Luxembourg
Mexico
Netherlands
New Zealand
Norway
Poland
Portugal
Slovenia
South Korea
Spain
Sweden
Switzerland
Turkey
United Kingdom
United States

*F*orming a company in France

	SNC	SARL	SA	SAS	GIE	Association
Legal structure	Société en nom collectif	Société & responsibilité limitée	Société anonyme	Société par actions simplifiées	Groupement d'intérêt economique	loi-1901 à but non lucratif (non-profit)
Purpose	All legal professional activity					
Members	2 or more associates (business)	2 or more associates (up to 50)	7 or more stockholders	1 or more	2 (at least) members (collaboration between businesses)	2 founding members
Capital	–	€7,500	€37,000	€37,000	–	–
Formation	Drafting the Articles of Association Registration at the Registre de Commerce et des Sociétés (Trade Register)					Registration at the Préfecture
Controlling authority			CA or Board of Directors and Supervisory Board		CA General Meeting	CA General Meeting
Directors	Joint Managers	Manager (EURL if only person)	PDG DG		Director (depending on the statutes)	DG General Secretary

Results must be made public at the Trade Register

CA: conseil d'administration (Board of Directors)
DG: directeur général (General Manager)
EURL: enterprise unipersonelle à responsabilité limitée (private company under sole ownership)
GIE: economic interest group
PDG: président directeur général (Chairman & Managing Director)
SA: public limited company
SARL: private limited company
SNC: partnership
SAS: simplified shareholding firms
RCS: Registre du Commerce et des Sociétés

Each company is registered by special numbers:
SIREN (9 numbers)
+ NIC (numéro interne de classement = 5 numbers)
= SIRET (14 numbers)

CONVERSION TABLE

WEIGHTS AND MEASURES

1 kilometre (km)	0.6 mile
1 metre (m)	39.37 inches = 1.09 yards
1 centimetre (cm)	0.39 inches
1 hectare (ha)	2.47 acres
1 are (a)	0.02 acres
1 kilogramme (kg)	2.2 pounds
100 grammes (g)	3.5 oz
1 litre (l)	2.1 pint
15 centilitre (cl)	0.5 fl oz

1 mile	1.6 km
1 yard	0.9 m
1 inch	2.5 cm
1 foot	30.5 cm
1 acre	4046.9 m²
1 sq. yard = 9 sq. feet	0.83 m²
1 ounce	28.3 g
1 pound	453.5 g
1 pint	0.47 l
1 gallon = 8 pints	4.54 l

Deka: 10, hecto: 100 and kilo: 1,000 (from Greek)
Deci : 10, centi: 100 and mili: 1,000 (from Latin)

1 l = 10 dl = 100 cl = 1,000 ml
1 bottle of wine (Champagne, Bordeaux ...) = 0.75 l = 75 cl
1 Magnum = 1.5 l (2 bottles)
1 Jeroboam = 3 l (4 bottles)
1 Nabuchodonosor = 15 l (20 bottles)

TEMPERATURE

Celsius (C)	Fahrenheit (F)
–15 °	5° Mont Blanc in winter
–10°	14°
–5°	23°
0°	32° Freezing point of water
5°	41°
10°	50°
15°	59°
20°	68°
25°	77° Ideal for a dip in the sea
30°	86°
35°	95° Heat wave
36°	96.8°
37°	**98.6°** Normal body temperature
37.5°	**99.5°**
38°	**100°**
38.5	**101.3°**
39°	**102°** Time to see a doctor
39.5°	**103.1°**
40°	**104°**
40.5°	**104.9**
100°	212° Boiling point of water

Celsius : x 1.8 + 32 = ° F
Fahrenheit : –32 x 0.56 = ° C

1 m = 10 dm = 100 cm = 1,000 mm
1,000 m = 1 km

*T*he metric system

Before the French revolution measurements were pretty basic. People either used their bodies (thumb, foot, etc) to measure the length of objects, and baskets and the like to weigh their goods, but there were no standard sizes.

Post-revolutionary France meant trading between regions and countries, so experts created a universal metric system that became compulsory throughout France from 1 January 1840.

Since then almost all other countries have adopted the same metric system. However, in the French market-place you will still see written :*'une livre de beurre',* '1 lb of cherries', the equivalent of approximately 500 grammes. Weight in pounds is an old measure that still lives on.

However, the expression 'il y a deux poids, deux mesures' means there are two ways of judging a situation. The final decision may be biased and not necessarily fair.

Index